The
Columbia
River

· A Historical Travel Guide ·

The
Columbia
River

· A Historical Travel Guide ·

JoAnn Roe

To Steve — Glad to share the river love! JoAnn Roe 1993

Fulcrum Publishing
Golden, Colorado

Library of Congress Cataloging-in-Publication Data

Roe, JoAnn, 1926–
    The Columbia River : a historical travel guide / JoAnn Roe.
        p.   cm.
    Includes bibliographical references and index.
    ISBN 1-55591-102-1 (pbk.)
    1. Columbia River—History. 2. Columbia River—Description and travel—Guide-
books. 3. Columbia River Region—History. 4. Columbia River Region—Description
and travel—Guide-books.
I. Title.
F853.R64   1992   91-58486
917.95'470443—dc20   CIP

Printed in the United States of America
0   9   8   7   6   5   4   3   2   1

Fulcrum Publishing
350 Indiana Street, Suite 350
Golden, Colorado 80401

Contents

Acknowledgments

Essential to this book was access to libraries and museums throughout the Northwest. A big thanks to the reference librarians at Bellingham Public Library: Gayle Helgoe, Jane Lowrey, Margaret Ziegler, Bruce Radtke and Linda Hodge. The Wilson Library at Western Washington University has an astonishing collection of historical books and manuscripts, some very old and obscure. I appreciate the collections and services of: Selkirk College Library, Castlegar; David Thompson Library, Nelson; Columbia Basin College Library, Pasco; Mid-Columbia Regional Library, Kennewick; and Astor Public Library, Astoria.

Historical societies and museums along the length of the Columbia River were most helpful, several double-checking my first drafts. My gratitude to Windermere Valley Museum, Invermere; Golden District Museum, Golden; Revelstoke Museum, Revelstoke; Arrow Lakes Historical Society, Nakusp; Doukhobor Historical Village; Rossland Museum; Stevens County Historical Museum, Colville; the Grand Coulee Pioneers; North Central Washington Regional Museum, Wenatchee; archives and historians of Colville Federated Tribes at Nespelem and Coulee Dam and of Yakima Indian Nation, Toppenish; Skamania County Museum, Stevenson; Cascade Locks Historical Museum; Oregon Historical Society, Portland; U.S. Army Corps of Engineers, Portland; Clark County Historical Museum, Vancouver; Cowlitz County Museum, Kelso; Ilwaco Heritage Museum, Ilwaco; Heritage Center Museum, Astoria; Columbia River Maritime Museum, Astoria; Fort Stevens Museum on Clatsop Spit.

I am grateful to the more than 250 people I interviewed but cannot list here, but particularly thank: Derryll White, Carol Seable, Don Yanko, Winifred Weir, Ian Weir, Ian Jack of Kootenay National Park, Peter Schlunneger, Philip Hein, John Buffery, Marg and Jim Sproat,

Ruby Nobbs, Gordon Bell, Margaret McMahon, Al McAskill, Jack Harris, Joe Biagoni, John Charters, Adelin Fredin, Andy Joseph, Wyn Self, Jim Black, Edith Lael, Craig Sprankle, Chic Phillips, Bill Brauner, Keith Murray, Brycene Neaman, Hu Blonk (who checked the Grand Coulee Dam info), Wilfred Woods, Irene Van Doren, Debby Hall, Virginia Wyena, Robert Ruby for consultations about Indian history, Tom Moak, Marilyn Druby of Westinghouse Hanford, Rich Steele, Captain Keith Rodenbough, Christof Cook, Walt Smith, Gus Norwood, Jim Barbouletos, Cliff Crawford, Dick Montgomery, Fay Nelson, Carl Floten, Gladys Seufert, Irene Sidwell, Henry and Jean Reents, Sam McKinney, Irene Martin, Stanley Everman, Noreen Robinson, Captain John Roe, Jim Suomela, Don Marshall, Darrell Murray, Lt. Bill Harper, Steve Felkins, Bob Peterson, Jerry Ostermiller, Bruce Berney. Thank you to visitors centers all along the river who double-checked information for the travel segment. A special thanks to my husband, Ernie Burkhart, who endured my frequent absences on research. Above all, thanks to editor Mae Reid-Bills who kept me straight on everything.

JoAnn Roe
Bellingham, Washington

Preface

During my extensive travels in the Northwest researching other books and articles, I often drove along the Columbia River or crossed its broad waters. Its variable moods and the diverse terrain through which it flows caused me to speculate on its effect on historical events and people. When a celebration was planned to commemorate Robert Gray's discovery of the Columbia River, the first known entry by a nonnative person, I wanted to write the river's story. I wanted to discover and share with travelers to the river and armchair historians, too, "what happened around here, anyway."

Upon a skeletal framework of the political and scholarly history of the Columbia River's immediate environs I have told about the people who used the river, fought it, narrowly escaped death on it, some of them ordinary, others renowned. The *river* is the star of the saga. During 1990 and 1991, I spent one-third of my time on or along the river; the other two-thirds of the time I delved into scholarly histories, accounts by individuals who have had direct experiences on the river, historical society accounts by people who lived or worked on the Columbia, and talked with hundreds of people about the river and its influence on their lives and works. As a result, I have fallen in love with the river more than ever. I am filled with awe at the sheer force of so much water in motion. In one book on a vast river, I confined my text to the river itself and its immediate environs. Remember, however, that the Columbia River watershed takes in a vast area from east central British Columbia to Nevada, the Rocky Mountains to the Pacific Ocean, except for certain portions west of the coastal Cascades Mountains.

To help the stranger visiting the Columbia River, I also share information about places along the river. The listings are not intended as a complete directory, only some of my own choices.

PREDEVELOPMENT COLUMBIA RIVER

LEGEND

– – – International Border

⊗ Elevation (in feet)

1991   David Jungkuntz

Scale
in
Miles

50 40 30 20 10 0   50   100   150

N

Features labeled on map

PACIFIC OCEAN

Olympic Mountains

Mount Olympus 7954

GRAY'S HARBOR

WILLAPA BAY

Baker Bay

Gray's Bay

Columbia Bar

COLUMBIA RIVER

COWLITZ RIVER

WILLAMETTE RIVER

Sauvie Island

Mount Rainier ⊗ 14408

Mount Saint Helens ⊗ 9677

Mount Adams ⊗ 12307

Mount Hood ⊗ 11245

Cascade Mountains

Cascades Gorge

Columbia Gorge

The Dalles / Celilo Falls

DESCHUTES R.

JOHN DAY R.

YAKIMA RIVER

COLUMBIA RIVER

Priest Rapids

Cabinet Rapids

Rock Island Rapids

Gorge Below Gingko

Lincoln Rock

Umatilla Rapids

Walla Walla Gap

WALLA WALLA RIVER

Blue Mountains

SNAKE RIVER

CHELAN RIVER

WENATCHEE RIVER

Earthslide

Methow Rapids

LAKE CHELAN

Grand Coulee (Canyon)

Box Canyon

Hell Gate

Earthslide

COLUMBIA

SPOKANE RIVER

PRESENT DAY COLUMBIA RIVER

LEGEND

- - - - - International Border
- · - · - State/Province Border
· · · · · · Reservation

● Community   ⟍ Dam
⊗ Elevation (in feet)

Scale in Miles

50 40 30 20 10 0   50   100   150

1991 David Jungkuntz

Discovery

On May 11, 1792, Captain Robert Gray on the American ship *Columbia Rediviva* courageously tackled the formidable entrance to the Columbia River from the north Pacific Ocean and came into a quiet inner bay. It seemed to be an anchoring of little consequence, but it changed North American history.

For three hundred years after Columbus' voyage of 1492, Europeans intruded into Mexico and the eastern and southern coasts of today's United States. The Pacific Northwest coast and the lands west of the Mississippi River were known only to the native people and a handful of wandering trappers—most of them Hudson's Bay Company people who worked from scattered posts across the northerly forests (Canada now). In the lands that became Alaska, the Russians established colonies at Kodiak (1784) and Sitka (1799). Before Gray's discovery of the Columbia River, both Britain and Russia had better claims to the Northwest lands than the United States.

In addition to plying a profitable fur trade, British captains sought a northwest passage, hoping for a benign strait that would make it unnecessary to challenge the hoary sea gods of Cape Horn, with their towering waves and gales.

Other European explorers searched, too. In 1775, Don Bruno de Heceta of Spain came ashore at 47 degrees 30 minutes north latitude on the Washington coast to get fresh water and take possession of the area for Spain; but his landing party was killed by local Indians. Returning southward, Heceta was intrigued by muddy stains far at sea. He guessed there was a mighty river, perhaps even the fabled passage, north of 46 degrees latitude and duly noted it in his logs and charts as "Bahía de Asuncion Entry." Captain James Cook of the British navy passed by the Columbia and Strait of Juan de Fuca in 1778, and found

Nootka Sound on the west coast of Vancouver Island. But the tantalizing possibility of a passage remained in the back of mariners' minds. In 1787, an enterprising New England merchant, Charles Bulfinch, put together a combine of six investors under a general manager, Joseph Barrell, to launch a trading voyage to the fabled Northwest. The *Columbia Rediviva*, 83 feet 6 inches long, was placed under the command of John Kendrick, a well-experienced but aging officer; her companion, *Lady Washington*, a 90-ton sloop probably 64 feet long, was given to a younger man, Captain Robert Gray. The plan was to obtain furs from Northwest Indians in exchange for gewgaws, then sail for China and barter or sell them for teas and silks sought after in New England. The two ships left Boston on October 1, 1787.

Captain Kendrick proved to be a strange fellow, procrastinating in every port as if reluctant to face the dangers ahead. He antagonized members of his crew, causing First Mate Simeon Woodruff to request discharge in the Cape Verde Islands, where ships bound for the Pacific stocked up with food and water. Another capable officer, Robert Haswell, requested transfer to Gray's ship. (Haswell wrote a valuable log of the two voyages of the *Columbia*.)

In the ocean wilderness of the South Pacific, the two ships became separated, Gray continuing to the rendezvous at Nootka Sound. En route he landed for supplies, since his men had scurvy, at Tillamook Bay, just south of the Columbia River bar. After several days of friendly trading, local Indians turned aggressive, and Gray's ship barely escaped the bay,

The Snake Indians watching white men float down the Columbia River in makeshift rafts. From an original oil painting by Frederick L. Hubbard entitled "White Men on the Columbia." Used by permission.

which he called Murderer's Harbour (Tillamook Bay). He sped northward to Clayoquot Sound and then Nootka Sound.

After arriving at Nootka, over a month behind the *Lady Washington*, Kendrick assigned Gray to gather furs along the southeast Alaska coast. When a full load of furs was ready for transport to the Orient, Kendrick inexplicably wanted to trade commands with Gray. Thus, Gray sailed off for Macao and Whampoa (port for Canton) as commander of the *Columbia*, returning to Boston via the Cape of Good Hope in August 1790.

The financiers of the voyage were disturbed at Kendrick's meanderings, and neither he nor the *Lady Washington* figured again in history significantly. Kendrick was shot dead in 1794.

In Boston, however, general manager Barrell determined to send the *Columbia* back to the Northwest under Gray. Two of the shareholders sold their shares, some to Captain Gray.

On September 28, 1790, Gray sailed off into history, making the trip to Clayoquot Sound near Nootka in eight months, rather than the eleven spent on the first voyage. Ever since learning of Heceta's report, Gray had hoped to explore Heceta's "Bahía de Asuncion Entry," perhaps on this voyage. First, though, he had to discharge his trading duties for Barrell's investors.

Gray's crew built the sloop *Adventure* to ply local waters for fur-trading, the first American vessel built on the west coast. Under command of Robert Haswell, she headed northward.

The *Columbia* turned south on April 12, 1792, as much to explore as to gather furs. At 46 degrees 10 minutes north latitude, the water was as muddy as observed on an earlier passage, but turbulent waters raised by gale-force winds kept Gray from entering, even though he cruised offshore for nearly two weeks. On April 28, anchored off the entrance to the Quillayute River (La Push), he met Captain George Vancouver, H.M.S. *Discovery*, and Lieutenant William R. Broughton, tender *Chatham*, on an exploring mission. The two parties compared notes, and Vancouver was said to scoff at the existence of a big river. Broughton, however, was listening hard to Gray.

After a foray into the Strait of Juan de Fuca, Gray again stood southward on May 5, in calmer weather. This time he spied an opening in the coast, sent a pinnace ahead, and entered Gray's Harbor (which he called Bulfinch's Harbor). On May 10, 1792, he sailed past Willapa Bay in the dark, possibly considering it a large cove, and at 46 degrees 7 minutes saw an opening in the line of breakers, quieter than before. Under short sail he slowly entered the Columbia, partially blocked by two large sand bars. Following the calls of a competent leadsman, he moved smartly up the river to find anchorage on the north side about six miles from the bar (Gray's Bay). Gray estimated the river to be about four miles wide and named it "Columbia's River." Later historians speculated whether it was to honor Gray's ship or the United States, affectionately referred to as "Columbia."

Astounded to see a white-winged ship within their river, the Chinook Indians led by one-eyed Chief Comcomly met one-eyed Captain Gray. The friendly people brought otter skins to trade for copper, iron spikes and other articles.

For nine days, until May 20, the ship's crew enjoyed a respite from the stormy Pacific. They explored upriver seven or eight miles, patched up their ship, explored ashore, and traded.

After leaving the river, Gray in the *Columbia* returned to fur-trading, both in company and separately with the sloop *Adventure*, among the island-studded waters of today's British Columbia and Southeast Alaska, coping with natives friendly one moment, hostile the next. When he had a full load of furs, Gray sold the *Adventure* to the Spaniards at Neah Bay and returned home to Boston via the Orient.

Thereafter the ship *Columbia* was sold; later, she succumbed to shipworms and was sold for scrap in 1801. Given command of the brig *Alert*, Gray and his crew sailed for the Pacific once more in 1798, the time of an undeclared naval war between France and the United States. Off South America the French frigate *Republican* seized the *Alert*, retained the chief mate and a boy, and sent her to the Spanish port of Montevideo, Uruguay, under a prize crew. Gray and the remaining crewmen were confined on the *Republican*. Several months later they were released at Montevideo when the French ship put in for supplies and managed to escape in the American schooner *James* that had been seized and moored at Montevideo. The Americans sailed home to Boston in the leaky vessel, and Gray received command of a different ship. His activities thereafter were unremarkable, and in 1806, the good captain died of yellow fever contracted at Charleston, South Carolina.

Meanwhile, with the door opened to Columbia's River, the next craft to enter was the small British fur-trading schooner *Jenny*, anchoring in the bay named for her master, James Baker, in the autumn of 1792. Discovering her at anchor was the Englishman, Lieutenant W. R. Broughton, who in October successfully made it over the turbulent entrance in the *Chatham* (leaving Vancouver standing out to sea in a gale). In a small boat, Broughton proceeded to explore upstream with a cutter and launch to the mouth of the Sandy River above Portland, crossing to the Washougal River. This excursion formed a partial basis for British claims that they had discovered the river and had a right to adjacent lands.

The Columbia River did not prove to be the Northwest Passage, but it did form an avenue for exploration and settlement of Oregon,

Washington and British Columbia. Later a portion of the river became the boundary between Oregon and Washington states.

Let's return to that discovery year of 1792. What might a Pegasus explorer have reported, silently galloping through space above the wildly romantic Columbia's River? (Modern place names are used to provide orientation.)

Between the Purcell and Rocky Mountains of British Columbia in a mountain valley as lovely as a new mother, the Columbia River is born with a murmur. It flows northward purposefully from Columbia Lake to Lake Windermere, then spreads its arms to embrace lazily the entire upper Columbia Valley, often a mile wide with shallow channels between reeds and marsh grass.

North of Golden it narrows and, with little warning, plunges through Surprise Rapids to emerge, once more tranquil, in Kinbasket Lake. The broad river sweeps northwesterly, then sharply veers southwesterly, descending swiftly now in a series of wicked rapids that extend over a hundred miles. It flows tranquilly as the incomparably beautiful Arrow Lakes for 134 miles, only to become a brute again.

The river speeds through the narrow canyons by Castlegar, amplified by the cacophony of rushing water as the giant Kootenay River comes in. Through the steep-walled bluffs it tears, caroming off boulders and foaming around obstructions to form eddies or giant whirlpools many feet in diameter, whirlpools that have claimed countless lives over the centuries.

Churning between high sand bluffs, topped by ragged, boulder-strewn hills, it is joined by the Pend Oreille River with a rush that sends three-foot waves across its width. The Columbia surges into the United States past Northport into the Little Dalles, where the eroded walls of the river bounce the waters back and forth, building frightening waves in the center. It plunges over 20-foot Kettle Falls, where Indians caught fish, and moves on through rock-strewn Rickey Rapids and terrible Box Canyon with their dangerous eddies.

The Columbia passes the primeval Grand Coulee, once the river's bed, an awesome, desolate side canyon. Joined by the Okanogan River in a serene marriage, the Columbia slows to reflect the dry, high benchlands through which its monster ancestor river tore its way.

Blocked by the North Cascades Mountains, the river is shunted southward for over a hundred miles, rippling through rapids less terrible than those above. It loops southeasterly, punctuated by a midstream pinnacle standing starkly like a sentinel, through valleys and canyons parched and deserted. Beyond the Tri-Cities the mighty Columbia turns westward toward its rendezvous with the Pacific, widened by the swift waters of the Snake River.

The river runs straight now, intent on reaching its goal. Over roaring Celilo Falls and the eight-mile rapids of the Dalles it charges, and rushes swiftly through the grand cascades of the Columbia gorge. It becomes a broad flow that will carry singing Hudson's Bay voyageurs by canoe to Fort Vancouver, and anxious settlers by makeshift flatboat to the Willamette of Oregon.

The ever-broadening river seeks myriad channels around islands as it makes a double curve north and west past Longview. Still the hypnotic eddies swirl as the swift current separates and reforms.

Finally the goal is in sight. Occasionally more than six miles wide, the mighty Columbia River carrying the drainage from 259,000 square miles of Northwest lands forces its way into the north Pacific Ocean. The seething clash between fresh and salt water, between opposing currents, throws up plumes of foam and creates huge breakers. Vicious patternless waves bounce off each other to form peaks of water like the mountains of the Columbia's birth. Into its maw will go feeble boats and ships crossing the Columbia Bar, a shifting strand of sand and rock.

Staining the water with silt for miles into the Pacific Ocean, the 1,214-mile Columbia River rests at last, relinquishing its flow to the mightier ocean.

The
River in Canada

CANOE R.

WOOD R.

MICA DAM

Columbia Icefield

THE COLUMBIA IN CANADA

LEGEND

International Border

State/Province Border

0 5 10 25
Scale in Statute Miles

Community

Dam

1991 David Jungkuntz

N

Monashee

COLUMBIA

LAKE KINBASKET

Selkirk

British

Rocky

RIVER

REVELSTOKE DAM

Donald

KICKING HORSE R.

Alberta

Mountains

JORDAN R.

Hwy.

Trans-Canada

Rogers Pass

Golden

KICKING HORSE

Banff

Revelstoke

COLUMBIA

Mountains

UPPER

Shelter Bay

Galena Bay

RIVER

KOOTENAY

Mountains

ARROW

Mountains

Invermere

LAKE WINDERMERE

LAKE

Nakusp

Bugaboo Range

COLUMBIA LAKE

LOWER

Kaslo

KOOTENAY

Purcell

Canal Flats

ARROW

KEENLEYSIDE DAM

LAKE

Nelson

Mountains

RIVER

LAKE

Fort Steele

Castlegar

KOOTENAY

C A N A D A

Trail

KOOTENAY RIVER

British

PEND

Columbia

Washington

COLUMBIA R.

OREILLE R.

Idaho

Montana

U N I T E D   S T A T E S

CHAPTER 2

The Headwaters

In a mountain valley of spellbinding beauty 2,601 feet high, hemmed in by the Purcell Range to the west and the Rocky Mountains to the east, the Columbia River—only a few feet across—flows northward from Columbia Lake. The lake is fed by springs and Dutch Creek, and no one can be truly sure which is the exact birth site. A scant mile and a half across a gravelly barrier 11 feet high, the Kootenay River flows southward from its birthplace west of Banff. The two will meet again thirty miles north of the international border after distant meanderings.

The Columbia River follows the deep Rocky Mountain Trench, mirroring the towering crags of the mountain ranges. Interesting to geologists is that, on the west, the largely granite Purcell and Selkirk ranges were raised perhaps 160 million years before the Rocky Mountains of limestone/sandstone base on the east. On September 4, 1845, Father Pierre J. deSmet contemplated with admiration "those rugged and gigantic mountains where the Great River escapes—majestic, but impetuous ... and in its vagrant course it is undoubtedly the most dangerous river on the western side of the American hemisphere." (J. Monroe Thorington, "The Historical Geography of the Columbia-Kootenay Valley," p. 18, pamphlet, 1933, at David Thompson Library, Canadian International College, Nelson, British Columbia.)

During the Pleistocene Age, glaciers formed and receded, scouring the valleys deeper and leaving gravel behind. As the earth warmed, stubborn ice-filled depressions resisted melting to form Lake Windermere and Columbia Lake. North of Windermere still another large ice block finally melted through to carve out the Big Bend channel. In this young Rocky Mountain/Selkirk region, little erosion has yet taken place to form tillable areas. South of Columbia Lake, the Kootenay River, however, overflowed to create vast, fertile deltas.

In ancient times Kootenay Indians from the south and Shuswap Indians from the north periodically traveled into the Columbia Valley to hunt and fish. Around 1800, a band of fifty or sixty Shuswap Indians, mostly the extended family of Chief Kenpe'sket (or Kinbasket), settled permanently in the upper Columbia's valleys. Another band, of uncertain ethnographic origin, settled near the Arrow Lakes. Indian camps, probably seasonal, were found on the Slocan River, at Arrowhead, and north of the Columbia-Kootenay junction. Early settlers reported Indian sweathouses around Arrow Lakes, and told of meeting American Indians coming north to fish. Sir George Simpson called the people "Sinachicks," a version of their own word, "sngaytskstx." In 1909 writings, ethnographer James Teit estimated that the Arrow Lakes band included twenty-six members.

Early explorers commented that the local Indians were honest and handsome. They used underground homes in winter (except for the Arrow Lakes bands), building circular underground cellars to preserve fish and other perishables. ("Dimples" from these are visible near Columbia Lake.) They were superb canoeists, using a curious shovel-nosed or sturgeon-nosed canoe unlike others in North America and thought to be directly related to Siberian-style canoes.

In summer the Indians used transportable Plains-style tepees. The men wore decorated skin shirts fastened with thongs at the shoulder, and breechcloths with leggings. Women's garments were loose and fastened with a fancy belt. Shuswaps were more lively than their Kootenay cousins, who were reported as serious and steadfast.

Both were excellent fishermen, using dip nets, fish spears, lines with bone hooks or large nets similar to today's gill nets. They built fish weirs or traps near outlets of streams and lakes, the remains of one visible in the early 1900s near the mouth of the Kootenay River at Robson. To capture deer they used unusual corrals built into the water with only one escape gate, closed by a watchful attendant when the deer were inside drinking.

Heavy snows and bitter cold discouraged settlement around the Big Bend and Revelstoke. These areas usually were shared (somewhat uneasily at times) for hunting and fishing by the Shuswap and Kootenay, as well as Stony and Piegan parties.

In those years salmon migrated all the way from the Pacific Ocean to Columbia Lake, especially favoring gravel beds at Athalmer in the Columbia River channel where it left Lake Windermere. At spawning time, so far from the ocean, the fish began to deteriorate in the upper reaches and were usable only after being smoked or dried. The hunting was good. The marshy river formed one of the best wetlands cradles for wildlife and birds that exists in North America. Intense populations of osprey, eagles, brants, mallards and geese still thrive there, building nests in the dense brush of the marshy islets, heavy with the sweet smell of clover. Between Fairmont and Invermere is a sanctuary for the rare blue heron. Transient species rest in the valley, part of the Pacific Flyway. Profuse numbers of humming birds winter in the valley, and locals have a persistent theory that when summer comes, these tiny birds migrate southward by clinging to the underfeathers of the stronger Canadian geese. A charming story, but wildlife experts are skeptical.

In winter thousands of Townsend's solitaire feed on juniper berries. Western tanager and slate-colored junko dart about, as well as one of the highest populations of blackcap, boreal and mountain chickadees in the Pacific Northwest. Year-round residents include robins, ravens and Canada jays or whiskeyjacks.

The spongy channels are a natural home for Columbia ground squirrels, muskrats and beaver, early attracting trappers. Higher on the pleasant terraces formed by past glacial melts, elk and whitetail deer winter; in summer they gravitate farther to the upland fastnesses to join bighorn sheep, mountain goats, black and grizzly bears. Curiously, bighorn sheep are almost unknown in the Purcells, preferring the warmer, grassier, westerly facing slopes of the Rockies. As late as 1922, numerous wolves as large as one hundred pounds prowled the Selkirks around Slocan Lake, killing deer but not bothering humans.

In the shadow of the Purcells and Selkirks, rainfall is moderate. Prevailing southwest winds are blunted. High above the valley, those same winds rage wildly as they confront the Rocky Mountain barrier, often creating exciting flight conditions for light aircraft.

Signaling turbulent conditions aloft, lightning storms play over the sky-piercing peaks. Thor's legendary thunderbolts reverberate through the valley. Curious phenomena occur among the peaks. In the fall of 1946, among the icy pinnacles of Mount Trident, a family saw the replica of the three sharp peaks of the mountain, suspended in the sky like a phantom. The phenomenon is known as "The Spectre of the Brocken" and is formed when the sun, low in the sky, shines on a bank of clouds, mainly ice crystals, in high mountain areas.

A Swiss guide, Herr Carl Sulzer, had an odd experience at a height west of Mount Tupper. He was sketching the scenery when a thundercloud enveloped him. Suddenly, two stone slabs facing each other nearby began to make a humming noise, and the metal holder of his sketching pencil buzzed. When a mist set in, his dampened fingers buzzed. He related that he realized the potential danger but convinced himself it was not lethal.

During an expedition ordered by the North West Company, explorer David Thompson told of watching a storm form over the steep sides of the

Rockies above the Columbia River. He said: "Its first direction was from the Pacific Ocean, eastward up the valley of the lower Columbia River, and McGillivray's River [Kootenay]. ... the Sun was shining on these steep Rocks when the clouds of the Storm entered about 2,000 feet above ... in large revolving circles, ... circle within circle for nearly twenty miles along these high Hills until the clouds closed on me, and all was obscurity: it was a grand sight, and deeply riveted my attention." (J.B. Tyrrell, editor, *David Thompson's Narrative*. [Toronto: The Champlain Society, 1916], 404.)

After Gray's discovery of the mouth of the Columbia River, searchers eagerly sought for its headwaters. Lacking in geographical knowledge, some people thought the river flowed from Lake Superior to the Pacific. Between 1783 and 1793, Alexander Mackenzie searched too far north and found not the Columbia, but the grand Mackenzie, the Peace and the Fraser rivers. The mysterious Columbia had been called the River of the West, the Thegayo and the Rio de los Reyes.

Trying to outflank its rival Hudson's Bay Company, the North West Company sent David Thompson in 1807 to locate the source of the Columbia and establish posts in today's British Columbia and Washington.

A well-educated, moral and intensely energetic man, David Thompson was a surveyor formerly employed by Hudson's Bay Company. He had switched allegiance to the North West Company in 1797. On June 30, 1807, he crossed the Rocky Mountains and came down the Blaeberry River to the Columbia River about twenty miles north of today's Golden. (He referred to today's Columbia as the *Kootanie*, using various spellings.) Tracing the river upstream to Columbia Lake, he discovered the second river, McGillivray's River (Kootenay), a south-flowing stream. Although he felt intuitively that the "Kootanie" River might be the Columbia River, he had no time then to explore. First he established a trading post, the *Kootenae* House, on Lake Windermere, then worked from there to establish other posts along McGillivray's River in what is now Idaho and Montana.

In early September 1810, he was running late on his return trip from Rainy Lake to the Columbia Valley. Winter threatened as his party approached the Rockies and the Blaeberry trail. Wisely he left his family at Fort Augustus (Edmonton). Twenty miles from the Rockies with an advance hunting party Thompson learned that his four trading canoes had been stopped by Piegan Indians, angered that the North West Company was selling guns to the Flatheads, traditional enemies. After a brief skirmish the canoe brigade retreated with injuries. Thompson's hunting party circled around the Indian camp and rejoined the canoeists; luckily a snowstorm obliterated their tracks.

Determined to return to Kootenae House, Thompson obtained horses to follow an old Assiniboine footpath toward Athabasca Pass.

By December 29, in the dead of winter, he began the formidable crossing with dogs and sleds.

On January 10, 1811, the party was in Athabasca Pass (elevation 5,735 feet). To the right lay a huge glacier perhaps 2,000 feet high "of a clean fine green color." But the men "were not at their ease," drily remarked Thompson. No wonder. They were enduring temperatures to -32° F., slogging along on snowshoes—hard work on sternly rationed food. Thompson moved down the western slope, steep and ragged, where storms lashed the men and melted the snow, crusting to ice. Dogs and sleds often came to rest on opposite sides of trees.

Lacking three men, who had deserted in the heights of Athabasca Pass, Thompson's party came down the Wood River to its junction with the Columbia and the Canoe River. On the delta there, a point he called Boat Encampment, he wisely chose to stop. In a cedar cabin twelve feet by twelve feet the men spent a cramped winter.

Thompson mentioned the immense trees—white cedars of 15 to 36 feet girth, pines from 18 to 42 feet in girth with no branches for the first 200 feet of trunk. He also noted that the different species did not intermix, growing in plots adjacent to one another.

Boat Encampment later became the regular transfer point from canoe to horse for fur traders traveling east to their company's headquarters. This does not mean that the trail became improved. In 1817, Ross Cox said that, to cross the Wood River at a point called the "grande traverse," owing to its great depth and breadth, the men had to hold hands and, even then, slightly built men were often swept off their feet by the force of the current.

In 1989 a young mountaineer, Phil Hein, who has a business in the Waputik Range adjacent to Yoho National Park, was asked by the Ministry of Forests to trace Thompson's Athabasca trail on the western slopes. (The pass portion lies within Jasper National Park and is maintained.) The trail was listed as a Heritage Trail in 1973, protecting the path itself plus a short distance to each side, but little of it had been found. The Ministry feared the trail might be obliterated if subjected to heavy logging machinery. This had happened earlier to the Blaeberry Trail.

Hein and his friend, Jim Oseychuk, set out into the wilderness. Since explorer Walter Moberly brought 250 horses over the trail in 1873, no record existed of its use.

"It was a thrilling project, as I love the history of the Columbia River," said Hein. "We read everything we could find about Thompson's travels to give us clues, and in 1980, the Ministry of Forests had located a few bits of trail."

The men climbed the Grand Côte, the steeply ascending ridge dividing the Wood River from Pacific Creek. They found two faint, discolored blazes in a regrowth forest, some on dead trees, and signs of a horse trail across a rocky section. In a luxuriant, overgrown forest near what appeared to be an old campsite, Phil excitedly yelled to his partner, "Look!"

Several feet above ground there were odd circles with blister-like protrusions, as if an old wound had been repaired. There, inside each bared circle lay ancient blazes on the trees.

Able now to follow the trail, though with difficulty, Hein and Oseychuk found other items, animal traps placed by twentieth century trappers, and best of all, the carved name of "F. Moberly," who must have been with his brother Walter when he came west.

With a strong sense of history Phil Hein, Jim Oseychuk and three young helpers cleared 12 to 15 kilometers of trail, finishing at the Committee Punchbowl promontory one evening. There they watched the setting sun send shafts of orange and pink over the Columbia River Valley. The ghost of David Thompson was strong.

Returning to Thompson's story, in the spring of 1811, as soon as winter's grip eased, Thompson and his men started for Kootenae House, dragging their canoe over ice in Kinbasket Lake. South of that, the river was open, and they reached their post. On May 14, Thompson went by canoe and horse to Spokane House, where Finan McDonald was stationed. Hardly pausing, Thompson moved swiftly to a point below Kettle Falls and ran down the Columbia River to its mouth, arriving on July 15. He found Americans in firm possession of newly built Fort Astoria.

Old and friendly competitors (as individuals), the Americans outfitted Thompson for his return trip, but both parties realized their nations had conflicting claims to this territory. Subsequently, during the War of 1812, the Americans sold Fort Astoria to the North West Company, which merged into Hudson's Bay Company in 1821.

Thompson shortly returned upriver and, entering the Snake River, obtained horses to travel to Spokane. Soon he came back to the Columbia, built another canoe above the falls, and made his way up river to Boat Encampment. He had proven to himself and the world that this was, indeed, the Columbia River, the great river of the West.

The Upper Columbia Valley

The Upper Columbia Valley remained pristine for a decade after Thompson's discovery, except for the transient visits of George Simpson, James Sinclair, Father deSmet and other explorers. François Morigeau from St. Martin's, Quebec, came with his family in 1819 to become the valley's first permanent settler. He moved near Fort Colville, Washington, in 1845, but his son Baptiste returned as an adult to farm, to scout for Major A. B. Rogers of the Canadian Pacific Railway and to operate a store at Golden from 1883 to 1885.

This remote alpine valley burst into the news when gold was discovered in 1864 on Wild Horse Creek, about sixty miles south of Windermere. Prospectors swarmed through the area—many struggling through the bewildering northern Moyie River swamps, others coming over old Rocky Mountain trails to the Columbia or Kootenay river, then south to Wild Horse. That year John Galbraith started a ferry service across the Kootenay, around which arose a small permanent settlement, Galbraith's Ferry. The rush subsided as quickly as it began, many prospectors moving on to the Big Bend of the Columbia above Revelstoke—the next promised land. By 1882, only eleven white settlers remained in the headwaters region.

Then came THE RAILROAD. As early as 1857, the British Crown sent explorers to assess the wisdom of building a railway to the Pacific. When British Columbia Colony was promised a railroad as an inducement to join the Confederation of Canada, the surveys became more urgent. Back east many schemes for railways were mere promotions that lined the pockets of real estate developers or amplified the importance of politicians. Yet surveyors sent out West did return with valuable information, especially the expeditions of Captain John Palliser in 1857 to 1859 and Walter Moberly from 1865 to 1874.

Palliser was accompanied by the eminent geologist, Sir James Hector. Near the crest of the Rocky Mountains, Palliser led one group of men into the Columbia Valley by the Kananaskis River, arriving near Canal Flats. Hector led another to travel the Bow River to the Vermillion, then the Beaverfoot to the Kicking Horse River—named thus because a packhorse gave Hector a good smack there.

Palliser met with Walter Moberly, who was then working in Victoria, British Columbia, to express his pessimism over the wisdom of an east-west railroad. A road surveyor during the Barkerville gold rush, Moberly was intrigued, not daunted, by Palliser's report. After his own inspections, Moberly recommended building the railroad directly along the Columbia's Big Bend from Golden to Revelstoke, then westerly through Eagle Pass, a narrow opening twelve miles west (Three Valley Gap).

As it turned out, Major A. B. Rogers, Engineer in Charge of the Mountain Division for Canadian Pacific Railway (CPR), located and surveyed the present route between 1881 and 1884, crossing the Selkirk Range. Crews working from east and west joined the rails at Craigellachie in 1885.

A supply center, Golden got its name when surveyor F. W. Aylmer was told by the mail carrier that Carlin's Camp east in the Rockies had named itself "Silver City," whereupon Aylmer, not to be outdone, said, "Well, then, we'll call our camp Golden City," later shortened to Golden. By 1888, Golden was still a railroad and mining town, a tough place to let off steam at a couple of taverns. In 1890, a tourist found there only a dozen wood and canvas shacks plus the Queen's Hotel built of logs. Golden's chief importance was as an exchange point from rail to Columbia River steamboat or stagecoach.

A member of the Aylmer surveying party, Frank P. Armstrong, quit the CPR in 1884 to preempt 320 acres of land east of Columbia Lake and raise potatoes. He rowed all the way to Golden to sell them to the railroad. With boundless energy but minimal carpentry skills, Armstrong then fashioned a stern-wheeler in 1886 to transport passengers and freight from Golden to Columbia Lake. The *Duchess*, a laughably ugly craft of lumber varying in thickness and sizes, drew only fourteen inches fully loaded, making her admirably suited for the Columbia's shallow channels. Low-hanging trees, fallen trees, shifting channels and occasional rapids made travel a challenge. Frequently, passengers were pressed into cutting wood for the insatiable boiler.

Armstrong's inept maritime efforts were visionary, however. With easier access by rail, prospectors again thronged to new finds at Wild Horse Creek, many going to Golden and then south on his boat.

There was also a stage of sorts from Golden to Galbraith's Ferry, uncomfortable and hazardous. Stage stops like the one at the Hog Ranch south of Golden, named because patrons lay around drunk as hogs, or at Brisco operated by Harry "Shorty" Achison, a man addicted to spitting tobacco juice anywhere in the house—well, they did not constitute gracious overnight traveling. In one incident, a stage fell through a bridge into the cold waters of the river. Yes, the best path to the diggings was on Armstrong's crude craft.

Trouble started brewing in 1884, when two men were murdered near Golden (Deadman's Creek today)—prospectors Mathew Hilton and William Kemp. More than two years later, the Kootenay constable arrested and jailed two Kootenay Indians because they had Hilton's saddle. Outraged, the Kootenay band's Chief Isadore stormed into town, broke open the jail and freed his men, saying they had merely found the saddle and the men dead. A land developer, James Baker, expropriated favorite pasture lands of the Indians at St. Joseph's Prairie (Cranbrook). The Indians argued strenuously with Baker.

In came the Mounties to Golden. They engaged the *Duchess* to carry the officers' baggage, oats and supplies, instructing Armstrong to rendezvous each night with the mounted troops. After striking a snag, the overloaded craft sank in fourteen feet of water. The Mounties then hired the *Cline*, a miserable scow powered by the engine off a Manitoba steam plow and just as slow. It took three months to move the 60 tons of supplies stranded in Golden and intermediate points.

With swift Canadian justice the Mounties found the Indians could not be guilty, and they mediated the land dispute, mostly in Baker's favor. After patrolling the valley and "showing the flag," they left in August 1888, via Crow's Nest Pass. The community was so impressed with Commander Sam Steele and D Division that it renamed the community "Fort Steele."

Fort Steele remained a major commercial center until 1898, when an ungrateful Joseph Baker persuaded the CPR to build the B. C. Southern through his property (today's Cranbrook), instead of through Fort Steele, by donating part of his land to the railroad. Fort Steele's population sharply declined.

But Fort Steele lives again, restored as a living historic town in 1961. Now its rotting buildings are repaired and painted. Employees walk the streets in period costumes. Clydesdale teams clump through the dirt streets pulling wagonloads of delighted tourists. A steam train chuffs around a circular track.

Frank Armstrong (of the ill-fated *Duchess*) proved to be the lord of the rivers. Although he had competitors at times, Armstrong monopolized the steamer trade on both the Columbia and Kootenay until 1898 and continued on the Columbia until the railroad forced him out. One of his last boats sank in the river, just south of Columbia Lake, and is still distinctly visible.

Traveling from Golden to Jennings, Montana, was an adventure. From Golden to Columbia Lake (depending on high or low water), steamboats ran on the Columbia River ... maybe. Low water near the lake was a problem. In 1891 Frank Armstrong, his brother, J. F. Armstrong, and Thomas B. H. Cochrane organized the Upper Columbia Navigation and Tramway Company to construct a short tram from Golden town site to the Columbia River docks, and a longer one with a passenger and freight car from Adela or Mud Lake, south of Windermere, to the Kootenay River, where waiting steamboats churned downstream to Jennings.

In 1889, English big game hunter, mountaineer and entrepreneur William A. Baillie-Grohman conceived the idea of building a canal between the two rivers. He proposed to divert water from the Kootenay to allay flooding of fertile plains near the international border, to solve periodic low water problems in the upper Columbia River, and to provide a direct steamer route between the two rivers. The distant provincial government in Victoria gave him a permit for this rather ill-thought-out scheme, which could have raised havoc with salmon runs, river shores and towns from British Columbia to Oregon.

Fortunately, there was an outcry from Canadian Pacific Railway officials, who feared inundation of newly built rail lines. As a condition, therefore, the provincial permit required Baillie-Grohman to build a lock. He came to Golden with materials to open a sawmill and a supply

The Columbia Lake, birthplace of the Columbia River.

store for the canal project. At Golden station, he had to unload his own freight within twenty-four hours and leave it in the open, since the station consisted only of a small office building. Baillie-Grohman grumbled that the lack of competition made the railroad company high-handed.

He completed his canal in 1889: 6,700 feet long, 45 feet wide and a small and flimsy log lock 100 feet long and 30 feet wide. The lock was to be opened only to allow the passage of a steamboat or to divert water from the Kootenay to the Columbia during flood periods. (Without canal or locks, the Kootenay River did overflow into the Columbia River in the 1950s.)

Only one known boat went through the locks north to south, Armstrong's *Gwendoline*. In 1893, Captain Armstrong laid the steamer's hull and basic structure on the Kootenay River, then dragged her on skids and rollers over Canal Flats to Columbia Lake and towed her to Golden for completion. In 1894, the *Gwendoline* went south through the canal without serious incident. Not so with a 1902 attempt to take the larger *North Star* from south to north. Since the boat was too wide for the decaying locks, Armstrong sawed off its guard rails. The boat entered the locks but was too long; so Armstrong destroyed the rear lock and rebuilt a log and sandbag dam behind the craft. When all was ready, he dynamited out the northerly section and in a wild ride careened into Columbia Lake (destroying any hope of restoring the locks in the process).

With all this activity on the land barrier between the rivers, a small settlement had developed called first Grohman, then Canal Flats. The flats themselves enjoyed a brief gold rush. Today the handful of homes, a small logging operation and a few stores sleep peacefully in the summer sun, surrounded by fragrant sweet clover and pine. At the venerable, historic Columbia Inn, oldtimers like Stan Johnnie and Logan Atwood (a regular with his name carved on a pub chair) swap stories of the days when the Atwoods, McCurchies, Coys and Tegarts fattened cattle in the valley to feed the miners.

The hopefuls who came on Armstrong's boats to prospect in the Upper Columbia Valley seldom made expenses. Among the better-known early mines were the Findlay Creek Mining Company, the Adela Mining Company and the Ptarmigan Mine near the Lake of the Hanging Glaciers in the Bugaboo Range. A gypsum mine still operates on Mount Swansea, east of Lake Windermere.

Three other mines did produce commercial quantities of ore: the Mineral King on Toby Creek, the Sheep Creek Mine and the famous Paradise Mine, originally spelled "Parradice." On August 29, 1897, the Paradise was staked as several claims. They were rich in silver contained in sand carbonates, the easiest form for processing—so easy in fact that, when a brush fire burned sacks of ore at a mine dump, the resulting lump was silver bullion. The original prospectors sold their claims to Randolph Bruce, a developer of many Upper Columbia Valley properties and later the Lieutenant Governor of British Columbia. Bruce built a good wagon road from the mine to Wilmer, where ore was loaded aboard Columbia River steamboats for Golden, thence to Trail for smeltering. In winter the ore came down by rawhiding: the ore was bound into a large steer hide hooked behind a docile horse. Hide flapping at his heels over the slippery snow, the horse pulled the material to the river.

Bruce was involved around 1911 in a land scheme, partly to attract investors who had quit South Africa during the Boer War. The Columbia Valley Irrigated Farm Lands Ltd. (CVI) acquired a whopping 49,000 acres, extending north from Columbia Lake for thirty miles and advertised 10- to 40-acre parcels of land for fruit orchards. They built irrigation systems, wooden flumes, siphons and ditches, but not one ever contained water. This and two other similar schemes failed, disappointed immigrants left when World War I broke out, and CVI was left holding bankrupt lands.

A small portion of the CVI land included the site of David Thompson's Kootenae House. Basil Hamilton, accountant for CVI, Colonel Dennis of the CPR, and Randolph Bruce—with the cooperation of Hudson's Bay Company—jointly bore costs of construction of a conception of Kootenae House. A splendid building of logs with a vaulted roof, it was completed July 4, 1922, and was used for twenty-six years as a community center. Residents enjoyed glittering social events and musicals in the building— although it had its drawbacks. Pioneer Ian Weir told me, "Every time the wind blew, the building drifted full of sand. Howard Cleland, a partner of Bruce, literally shoveled it out. There were bats living in that high ceiling, too. I was a saxophone player with a band there, and sometimes bat droppings became new quarter notes on the score."

No one would assume responsibility for upkeep of the David Thompson Memorial Fort, several historical associations refusing on the grounds that it was not authentic; so it was burned to the ground to make way for residential development.

The demise of CVI gave rise to a new industry: land was sold dirt-cheap to Christmas tree producers. Among buyers was the Kirk Forest Products Company, a Washington firm, which bought 35,000 acres of land near Cranbrook and Golden. During the Depression the demand for trees was a lifesaver, for a cutter could earn perhaps thirteen hundred dollars in the fall.

Retired employee Walter Verge of Golden said the trees were cut as they grew at first. Later, crews pruned and shaped them. Independent horse operators brought trees into an assembly yard for sorting, bailing and shipment by train to distant points. In experiments plantation trees planted in rows did not thrive as well as those seeded by "mother trees" left scattered in a semi-cleared plot.

Land clearing had a secondary market—to provide ties for the railroad. Not only railroad ties but lumber for homes and stores was in demand as soon as settlement began. The enterprising Captain Armstrong operated one of the earliest sawmills in 1887 near Brisco, while McKenzie and McDonald opened another larger mill at Donald. Where proper roads did not exist, lumber companies often used portable mills hauled by horses along narrow tote roads clinging to the sides of mountains and along boiling rivers.

In 1902, Columbia River Lumber Company Ltd. of Golden was the largest holder of standing timber in British Columbia. Loggers stacked logs beside the Columbia during winter to be rolled into the river after spring thaw. The storage booms might be half as wide as the river and five miles long. The log drives were exciting and dangerous with men nimbly skipping over the rolling logs to "corral" them. Men lived in tents on shore, but the cookhouse on a raft moved along the river as needed. One became known as "the Ark."

Popular road cook Pete Faber came from a Luxembourg brewing family. He filled an oak hogshead with scrubbed potatoes, added black molasses and buried the closed barrel in horse manure for six months to produce excellent one hundred proof dark rum.

The enemy of the loggers was fire, set by lightning or by sparks spewing from locomotives. In 1912 a fire burned for three months near Cabin Creek. Valley residents could not see the sun, bears fled the fire to roam through the streets of towns and the air was full of cinders. Fierce fire storms blazed through forests so fast that only the branches were burned, the timber left intact. Loggers cut the "blackwood harvest," looking like coal miners each night.

In 1985, such a fire burned for six months on both sides of the upper valley, despite water bombing and the efforts of smokejumper crews. Smoke was so thick that Canal Flats was evacuated for a time. Again timber crews salvaged the singed tree trunks. An odd bonus appeared. In burned-over clearings, thousands of morel mushrooms popped up, where fire had sterilized the ground against parasites that otherwise destroy them. Locals earned good wages picking them for drying and export to Japan and Europe.

Still another giant fire destroyed the Columbia River Lumber Company in 1926, when it burned much of the firm's logging equipment. In 1931 a successor—Evans Forest Products Company Limited—began its British Columbia operations, using yellow cedar to produce battery separators. In 1969 Evans acquired Kicking Horse Forest Products Ltd., precious timber licenses, a veneer plant, sawmill and powerhouse, adding Selkirk Spruce Mills Ltd. of Donald. There, a major Evans plant operates today, employing eight hundred people.

The watershed of the Columbia produces a climate that, according to Brett Salmon, Evans' forestry manager at Golden, is "almost coastal, giving us the advantage in growing cedar as a crop. Much is second growth from fires of the 1880s, now 120 to 130 feet tall."

Fast growth is important because responsible loggers replant and "farm" every cut area, researching new ways to speed growth. Today's methods produce a tree three to four feet tall within five years, and in eighty years, harvestable at 125 to 130 feet tall.

Logging camps are a far cry from the tents of old. Men are housed two to a private room and have facilities ranging from laundry equipment to pool tables and television. Furthermore, with tough trucks and road systems, most loggers are able to sleep at home each night.

CHAPTER 4

The Railroads
and the Tourists

With the coming of the Canadian Pacific Railway to Golden on the Columbia River in 1885, railroaders told their Eastern acquaintances about the beautiful Rockies, Selkirks and Purcells. First a trickle and then a flood of visitors came.

One of the first adventurers was William Baillie-Grohman, who came before 1883 to climb the peaks of the Purcells and Selkirks. In 1887 came two Englishmen, Lees and Clutterbuck, who wrote a whimsical book about their extraordinary experiences.

Tourists usually arrived at Golden. In about 1890 an English tourist, Edward Roper, unable to get rooms in the decent Queen's Hotel, stayed in a log shanty where small individual roomettes were walled and roofed with calico. He wrote cheerfully: "In many places the tacks with which the cloth was fastened had come out .... We would lie in bed and converse with comfort, and there was an airiness about the place that was charming." (John Marsh, "Early Tourist Impression of Golden," in *Golden Memories*, [Golden and District Historical Society, 1982], 3.)

One might call Sir Sandford Fleming a tourist. Chief engineer while CPR was government-owned prior to 1881, Fleming was asked by the new private company, Canadian Pacific Railway, to assess the proposed railway route in 1883, including the formidable pass selected by Major A. B. Rogers. That summer Fleming, the Reverend Principal Grant and S. Hall Fleming, sitting at the summit of Rogers Pass in a field of flowers, organized the Canadian Alpine Club. The meeting was supervised by blue-white glaciers, the sentries of mounts Macdonald and Tupper and the pyramid-shaped peak Cheops.

One of the earliest ramblers was the Reverend William Spotswood Green, an Englishman and experienced "Swiss mountaineer," who mounted an exploration in 1888 with the cooperation of the Royal

—— 23

Geographical Society. Green is considered the top pioneer climber and topographer to enter the Selkirks, and he named many points in use today. Emil Huber of the Swiss Alpine Club visited the Selkirks in 1890, also Harold W. Topham of the English Alpine Club. Huber was scornful of comparing them with the Alps, but Green suggested that in purity, sheer numbers of peaks and attractive glaciers, the Selkirks could "hold their own" with the Swiss and Italian Alps. Members of the prestigious Swiss Alpine Club, and the Appalachian Mountain Club of Boston, explored the Selkirks more thoroughly in the 1890s.

In 1888, CPR built a charming hotel, Glacier House, elevation 4,093 feet, in the trees at the base of Mt. Abbott, facing a lovely 1,200-foot waterfall. Like several other lodges, it was intended to house and feed passengers and crews, so that locomotives did not have to pull dining cars over steep passes. However, mountaineers soon made it their base. With a huge dining room but only a half-dozen bedrooms, Glacier House needed more space for overnighters and a sleeping car was parked on a nearby siding. Later there were ninety rooms and a sightseeing tower. A high fountain graced the lawn. For some years a tame bear, chained to a post by a collar, entertained visitors. D. W. Wilcox, author of a century-old book, said of his visit to Glacier House in 1893: "There is something pre-eminently comfortable and homelike about the Glacier House. ... One ... scarcely realizes that civilization is so far distant ... writing his diary, or enjoying the pleasure of music or literature, while the rain is falling constantly. ... The manner in which the clouds come sweeping up the Illecillewaet valley at the base of Mount Cheops and turn toward the flank of Eagle peak or Mount Sir Donald is very impressive. ..." (A. O. Wheeler, *The Selkirk Range* [Ottawa: Government Printing Bureau, 1905], p. 298-99.)

Responding to the influx of tourists, the Canadian Pacific Railway constructed lodges and tourist hotels along the railway from Banff in Alberta to Victoria, British Columbia. The company hired Swiss mountain guides to work for them in the Rocky Mountains and Selkirk Range. A "Swiss mountain guide" was the epitome of skill and reliability.

The first two Swiss guides, Edouard Feuz and Christian Hasler of Interlaken, came West in 1899. In 1900 Hasler went to Mt. Stephen House in the Rockies, and Jacob Muller, Karl Schlunegger and Friedrich Michel joined Feuz at Glacier House. They made several ascents of Mount Sir Donald and other peaks. Their climbing parties often went out for weeks at a time, using pack trains for supply.

From 1899 to 1911, guides came in the summer and went home to Switzerland in the winter. (Climbing was impractical in heavy snow.) Near the banks of the Columbia River in 1911, the CPR built a Swiss village for the guides and their families, urging them to stay all year and assist with tourists. The elite group remained small; among them were Edouard Feuz, Sr. and Jr., and later Ernest, Gottfried and Walter Feuz; Chris Jorimann, Christian Hasler, Rudolph Aemmer, Charles Clark (an interpreter), F. Michel and Karl Schlunegger. Edward Feuz, Jr. died at Golden in 1981, after working as a guide for seventy-three years; he climbed difficult mountains until he was over ninety-five years old.

Glacier House closed in 1922 and was torn down in 1929. The descendants in spirit and in blood of the Swiss guides today work from Revelstoke, Golden and Invermere. Peter Schlunneger, Karl's grandson, works out of Golden. He guides mountaineers and also owns Alpine Rafting, the oldest company offering white water raft trips on the Kicking Horse River. Rafting is the latest "mountaineering" adventure of this area.

Quickening the Columbia's pulse as it flows northerly are the Spillamacheen, Kicking Horse, Blaeberry, Wood and the huge Canoe rivers. Beyond the Big Bend on the southerly flow are the Goldstream, Illicillawaet, Jordan and others. These tributaries frequently rush to the Columbia over impressive rapids. On a world-rated scale of 1 to 6 (a 6 gives one a 50/50 chance of survival!), many are rated 4.

Young mountaineers like Peter Schlunneger, and John Buffery and Ralph Koerber of Glacier Rafting, are guide rafters in summer, alpine enthusiasts in winter. Buffery talks of the rewards, such as his appreciation of the rapids, of wildlife and interpreting the experience for a blind rafter. He rhapsodizes about the purity of winter snow and the awful beauty of the Selkirks.

Hans Gmoser is the pioneer of heliskiing in the Selkirks and Monashee Mountains. His company, Canadian Mountain Holidays, operates trips from several locations. "Rabid" skiers often save for years just to have one exultant week of heliskiing, for it is not an inexpensive sport. Lodges are luxurious; some have Europeans chefs, saunas and whirlpool baths at mile-high locations.

Phil Hein, who opened the David Thompson trail on the Wood River, is one of few native Canadians who is a licensed Senior Guide of the Canadian Association of Mountain Guides, a member of the International Union of Mountain Guides. Like the old Swiss Guides, Hein put in years of apprenticeship before taking an examination. He operates an alpine lodge at 6,700-feet elevation, north of the Wapta Ice Fields (northeast of Golden).

Newest of the wilderness ski sports is snowcat skiing, a bit tamer than heliskiing but still done along ungroomed slopes. For nonskiers the Invermere, Golden and Revelstoke areas have wilderness tour guides in four-wheel drive vehicles to show such sights as the Lake of the Hanging Glaciers in the Bugaboo Mountains, the Columbia River at sunset from Mount Swansea or old mine diggings. Don Yanko of Incredible Mountain Tours told me of a surprise one trip: "I shined my light on a mossy looking thing on a ledge, and it began to pulsate like an alien being. Spooky! I was about to take off, when I looked closer. It was a big hibernating glob of daddy longlegs, all huddled together."

Mountain adventures are part of the offerings at historic Fairmont Hot Springs Resort, one of the valley's oldest spas north of Columbia Lake. Succeeding John Galbraith and George Geary, Sam and Helen Brewer owned the property in 1890, when an English sightseer, Adela St. Maur, wrote about visiting the spa. She tramped over a steep trail and found two large basins, the first of which was 8 or 9 feet long, about 2 feet deep and 4 feet wide, and quiet. The second bubbled up boiling hot like champagne, while an adjacent mountain stream was icy cold.

Owner William Heap Holland improved the property in 1923 by building a flume from the springs to a pool 40 by 60 feet, a restaurant, tent camp and cabins to accommodate seventy guests. The place even had electricity generated by overflow from the pool. Over the years visitors waded the Columbia River, rode horseback, played tennis on gravel courts, camped, fished or soaked in the therapeutic waters.

Columbia valley entrepreneurs Lloyd Wilder and family acquired the springs in 1957, and today the resort sprawls over four thousand acres—a four-star lodge, golf courses, recreation center, indoor and outdoor pools, public lands and five-star time-share villas. Wilder family members form the executive corps, with Carol Seable the general manager.

To supplement cross-country skiing the resort developed downhill ski runs catering to beginners and families. During the planning stage, a pilot was flying Lloyd Wilder over the hill to reconnoiter, when a sudden downdraft forced the plane to the ground, killing the pilot and, quite literally, scalping Wilder. Half-conscious he stumbled down the mountainside and was tracked by rescuers from the trail of blood. He jokes today that although doctors sewed his scalp, he has been picking pine needles out of it ever since.

The Wilders preserve almost half the historic Fairmont property for environmental concerns—the beginnings of the Columbia River, the Pacific Flyway, an elk herd that considers the golf course its private grazing ground, a cabin used by Baillie-Grohman, the Golden-Columbia Lake stage stop (now home of a Fairmont owner) and Captain Armstrong's last sternwheeler lying surprisingly well-preserved beneath the cold Columbia.

Between Fairmont and Columbia Lake are traces of the Spirit Trail of Kootenay Indians. The narrow, steep path through heavy forest was an ideal place for ambushes by traditional enemies, the Blackfeet or

Piegans. At the beginning, end and hazardous midpoint of the trail, the Indians broke off a branch and laid it on an altar-like heap, an entreaty for safety or gratitude for a successful trip. Ancient pictographs were painted on the cliff face using vermilion (ground iron oxide mixed with bear grease and fish oil, sealed to the rock with chewed fish eggs and saliva), of braves with arrows in hand, animals, a papoose board and other items. Most of the pictographs have disappeared through natural erosion.

Something about the Upper Columbia Valley evokes a sense of mystery and spirit. In 1912, local resident Charles D. Ellis captured the feeling as he walked the historic headwaters trail: "Smoke from the funeral fires of many a mighty forest, hung like a pall across the valley. Distant trees, wrapped in the purple mist, lost themselves as the enfolding clouds grew thicker, reappearing at intervals like the wrath of their departed kindred; ... a fitter place to be peopled by fairies and elves never was ... ." (From Charles D. Ellis diary, Windermere Valley Historical Museum.)

Spiritual feeling touched many races as they entered or traveled this overwhelmingly beautiful birth valley of the Columbia River and its adjacent canyons. In times misty with age, at Radium Hot Springs, Indians soaked in the springs to ease their pains. Dale Zieroth tells the story of Kootenay Indian Amelu, who came to the springs searching for his guardian spirit "nipika." He had gone without food for three days and had drunk sparsely in his pilgrimage, waiting for a vision. On the fourth day near the pool he heard the spirit of the trees singing in the wind: "He followed the song until he stood at the edge of the pool. The mist rose up in one great swirl ... he knew his guardian nipika was there. ... With one step, he was in the water, the hot mist wrapping around him like smoke ... and he felt the spirit go deep in his chest. ... He heard the nipika tell him that now he was a man and that he would be protected all his life." (Dale Zieroth, *nipika*, [pamphlet, Parks Canada, 1978], 7.)

The springs lie a scant two miles from the Columbia River in Sinclair Canyon, which is entered through a narrow cleft between cliffs towering 120 feet high; the sun's rays hardly penetrate to the canyon floor. In 1841 Sir George Simpson passed through this valley and called it a "horrid gorge, an angry stream, a dreary vale," and was glad to escape it. He apparently did not discover the springs. Later in 1841, leading a group of fractious settlers from Red River (Winnipeg), James Sinclair detoured to search for the springs—having heard of them from his guide Mackipictoon. Disgruntled and weary, Sinclair eased into the pool and found himself relaxing and dreaming dreams that soared beyond logical bounds and reached into the past.

Modern man tends to dismiss such mysteries, but a marvellous cure was responsible for raising money to develop the springs. Financier Roland Stuart purchased the springs and 160 acres of land from the crown for $160 on May 27, 1890. He planned to develop the springs as a spa and to sell bottled water. However, he needed a road to bring tourists—tourists that were beginning to swarm into Banff on the CPR or to come north from the United States to Golden. He created Radium Natural Springs Syndicate Ltd. in 1913 and published a prospectus for development.

The scheme came to the attention of a wealthy man associated with the Perrier waters company, St. John Harmsworth, who was paralyzed from the hips down following an accident. Eager for a financial backer, Stuart made sure Harmsworth got to Radium. The crippled man was lowered into the springs in a hammock, and each day for four months he soaked in the springs. Whether his "nipika" or spirit came or whatever, Harmsworth was able to move his feet for the first time since the accident. He financed Stuart.

Despite the financing, Stuart did little except build a concrete pool and a bathhouse, until the Banff-Windermere Road backers took matters out of his hands. Among them was developer Robert Randolph Bruce of Invermere. The group looked to the federal government for finishing the western slope of road. The government agreed, on condition that the province of British Columbia give them five miles of land on each side of the road as a national park. On April 21, 1920, the Kootenay Dominion Park was declared. Then the government pressured Stuart and others to sell private holdings along the proposed road. In 1922 the Park expropriated Stuart's property for $24,692 (plus a later sum of $15,000), and the springs became park property.

In 1923, the Banff-Windermere Road was completed, a one-lane gravel road in places, but a road. Travelers came to the springs and the Columbia Valley. In 1929 five hundred cars a month traveled the road. Fine lodges were built, still serving visitors today, including Radium Lodge, Radium Hot Springs Resort (not at the springs itself) and the more modest Blakley Bungalows. The springs were encased below a concrete pool, which could be chlorinated, and a handsome Aquacourt with food and change facilities constructed.

The Big Bend
and Revelstoke

West of the Selkirks, Revelstoke was settled by CPR workers in the mid-1880s. Before any white settlement, the site was popular with Shuswap Indians, who caught fish near the dangerous whirlpool called the Big Eddy, formed by the rush of the Jordan River into the curving Columbia River.

Continuing to enter the valley at Boat Encampment over the route David Thompson pioneered, fur traders, missionaries and a few settlers had a hazardous introduction to the West. Among the famous traveling this way were Sir George Simpson of Hudson's Bay Company and frontier artist Paul Kane, whose inscription on a tree "Paul Kane 1847" was found by a twentieth century traveler. The wood has been cut out and is in the Provincial Archives, Victoria.

Boat Encampment at the Big Bend of the Columbia possessed a lonely, harsh beauty that made gnats of humans. Some of North America's heaviest snowfalls occur there. In the nineteenth century the exquisite Kinbasket Lake, a relatively quiet widening of the Columbia, usually froze over. Eminent author Stewart Holbrook suggested that, if one saw Kinbasket, he needn't bother with the alpine lakes of Switzerland. In places one could see the glittering Columbia Ice Fields.

If a traveler were going downriver, however, tranquility ended at Boat Encampment. As the Columbia turned southward, its roar was heard miles away. Intermittent, violent rapids awaited the hapless canoeist—all the way to Revelstoke's site.

It is a tribute to the skills of Hudson's Bay brigades that they could use this stretch as a thoroughfare. Not far below the Big Bend, Les Dalles des Morts or Death Rapids was a chain of killer whirlpools. Ross Cox told of his passage upstream in April 1817, where between Les Dalles and Boat Encampment, the river was so swollen with spring melt that—even by lining canoes and portaging supplies—it took an entire day to make it three miles upstream.

In 1838 the infamous Dalles claimed twelve lives of an expedition that included almost forty men, women and children. With them were Father Francis N. Blanchet and Father Modeste Demers. Hudson's Bay Company officials had sanctioned the sending of priests to establish missions on the Cowlitz and Willamette rivers, and the only way to get there was in Hudson's Bay Company canoes bound for Fort Vancouver. The party arrived at Boat Encampment on October 13. This day, a Sunday, Father Blanchet offered the Holy Sacrifice of Mass, the first time in Oregon (Blanchet's designation). It was a good thing he did.

After looking at Les Dalles des Morts, the leaders decided to run the hundred miles of river to House of the Lakes near Arrowhead, in relays. The two boats set out with about one-third of the party, including Blanchet and Demers, and arrived safely. One boat returned to transport those left behind. Unwilling to wait for another round trip, the passengers all crowded into the boat. At the next rapids (thereafter called Priest Rapids) the overloaded boat wallowed and took on water. Crying to passengers to sit still, the pilot headed toward shore. Before he touched the bank, English botanist Robert Wallace grabbed his wife Maria (unacknowledged daughter of Sir George Simpson), stood on the gunwale and jumped over, capsizing the boat. Not only they but ten others drowned from this impetuous departure.

In 1865 Walter Moberly almost drowned in the Little Dalles just north of today's Revelstoke, as he returned downriver after discovering Eagle Pass for the railroad route by watching the flight of two eagles. He was taking bearings when the canoe's bowman shouted, "Bad water—all will be killed!" As they swept into the Little Dalles, Moberly leaped to the paddles. The two men managed to escape being sucked into the whirlpools, but Moberly said, "Sometimes one end of the canoe became the bow, and at other times the opposite end."

Significant gold was discovered in 1865 near the Big Bend, along Goldstream, Carnes, French, Downie creeks and other tributaries. Prospectors thronged in from Wild Horse Creek, from eastern Canada and the United States. The early rushes were no more successful than those of Wild Horse, but men swarmed down the Columbia, which claimed more lives as unsuspecting miners swept around the Big Bend in makeshift boats.

More came from the south. Captain Leonard White brought a supply boat, the *Forty-Nine*, upriver from Washington to the foot of Death Rapids in 1866—quite a feat. He continued to serve the prospectors for the brief time it took for enthusiasm to run out. After three trips, paying passengers northbound were few, free passengers southbound, many.

Poor prospectors sometimes lived on flour alone and developed scurvy. They spent grimly cold winters, isolated in a typical cabin of chinked logs heated by a sheetrock stove. An egg case nailed to the wall made a shelf. Other furnishings were a small bench with a wash basin and soap, a crude bed and a miner's candlestick stuck in the wall. Most of the prospectors went on to new Eldorados, leaving the mosquitoes to feed on a handful of stubborn or better-funded miners who persisted into the twentieth century.

With the arrival of the railroad around 1885, surveyor Arthur Stanhope Farwell laid out the settlement of Farwell at Big Eddy. Only twenty-eight miles of railroad west of Farwell remained unfinished, and prospectors could reach Golden and Revelstoke easily. This led to renewed prospecting along the Big Bend. The Columbia River was still the north-south avenue.

Harbinger of late twentieth century catamarans, the *Despatch* was launched in 1888, running from Revelstoke to Sproat's Landing (Castlegar). The futuristic craft had two 54-foot pontoons with the paddlewheels between. Although designed for two engines, her owners could afford only one; so she was slow and difficult to manage in a blow. The design permitted minimal freight. Partners in the venture were J. F. Hume, W. Cowan and Captain Robert Sanderson.

Watching the freight enterprise from the wings were men known on British Columbia lakes: J. A. Mara, a steamboat operator from the Shuswap Lakes waterways; Captain J. Irving of Fraser River experience; and Frank S. Barnard, whose father had organized the Barnard Express to Barkerville's gold fields. The three bought in, naming their new company the Columbia and Kootenay Steam Navigation Company (CKSN), capitalized for $100,000, a solidly managed firm and eventual thorn in the corporate flesh of the CPR.

CKSN launched the *Lytton*, on July 2, 1890, and bought Captain Frank Armstrong's *Marion*, transported from Golden to Revelstoke by rail and re-launched at Revelstoke.

In 1897, the *Lytton* came from Arrow Lakes to Revelstoke, but she had to have her stack shortened to pass under the CPR bridge. With fairly powerful engines she managed to travel through the vicious Little Dalles to carry heavy mining machinery to La Porte, two miles south of Les Dalles des Morts. It is said that she took six hours to ascend the Little Dalles but only six minutes and fifty-one seconds to descend. Five years later Revelstoke residents combined to build a powerful vessel, the *Revelstoke,* that could manage the rapids. Instead of braving the Little Dalles every trip, it started upriver above them and went to La Porte. She was almost wrecked on February 18, 1903, in Arrow Lakes when a massive wave caused by a thundering rock slide slammed into her.

Packers jumped into the supply business, too. George LaForme trekked north from Revelstoke with as many as thirty-five animals. He was wiped out on a return trip from French Creek in November, 1896, when rain crusted the snow and horses broke through and cut their legs. There was no forage, and no help to be had. LaForme wound up shooting all the horses.

Andrew Rupert Westerberg was a legendary mailman to the Big Bend for thirty-five years, mostly trudging the hundred-mile route. Another colorful local man was "Ole the Bear," a miner who had won a hand-to-hand fight with a grizzly. He had a tame, trained black bear that would obey his commands. One day he left home, telling the bear to stay. A mile or so away he noticed that a bear was following him. Thinking it was his disobedient pet, he yelled at it, threw a rope around the startled animal's neck and dragged it home—a very unwilling captive. Only when he approached his home did he discover his tame bear was still there.

Farwell's townsite thrived, but very few decent women helped to civilize the place. A visitor, Colonel Edward Mallandaine, said of Farwell: "The town consisted of one street on either side of which were wooden and log shacks; chief among them was the Columbia Hotel ... the life was exciting, especially on paydays. There were brawls continually and gambling night and day with men of all nationalities throwing away their hard-earned pay at faro, stud poker and other games of chance. What the gamblers and saloon men did not get the women of the town did." (From *Revelstoke Review*, June 29, 1940.) To avoid being cheated by card sharps, players threw the decks out the window between card games, to the point that the street was "paved" with playing cards.

The Canadian Pacific Railway refused to pay Farwell's prices for land to build a roundhouse, marshaling yard and station, and built it on land uphill from Farwell. In 1899 the new town of Revelstoke was incorporated around the railway center, named for a lord who had bailed out the CPR during a financial crisis. It absorbed Farwell to become both a rail and river port. Local sports founded a racetrack along Big Eddy, patronized by riverboat passengers. The Turf Club building is the clubhouse today of Revelstoke Golf Club; faint outlines of the racetrack are visible.

Four smelters were established to process the miners' ore—at Revelstoke, Nelson, Golden and Trail. In 1889 at Revelstoke, the Kootenay Smelting & Trading Syndicate constructed a smelter, boarding house, store, brickyard and railroad spur on the east side of the Columbia River. The smelter itself probably was a rectangular water-jacketed furnace perhaps 6 feet long and 3 feet wide. On July 23, 1891, it produced the first lead bullion drawn from any Canadian smelter. But that was its entire claim to fame. The Columbia River began to undercut the smelter's land, and because land titles were a subject of contention between British Columbia and the Dominion of Canada, neither would assist in allaying the erosion. The entire installation fell into the river in 1898.

The Revelstoke smelter was inefficient, anyway. About 1920, a war veteran purchased the smelter's ore dump for $5, hauled some of it to the Trail smelter and made his fortune.

The CPR consolidated its offices in 1899 by moving the Donald operations to Revelstoke, dismantling and moving most of the Donald buildings. The tiny wooden church was scheduled to be transported by railroad flatcar, when Lake Windermere stagecoach operator, Rufus Kimpton, and others spirited it away on a riverboat and reassembled it at Lake Windermere. Kimpton and his wife Celina had become fond of this first Anglican church in the Rockies. They and their friends weathered the outraged protests and threats of Revelstoke residents, and there in Windermere the church remains today. The "stolen church" was rededicated for Christian use in 1905.

Pleased with the profits from tourism that resulted from bringing Swiss Guides into the region, the CPR was happy to see the establishment of national parks in the region. Glacier National Park was established in 1886 and Mount Revelstoke National Park in 1914.

With the emphasis on tourism and snow sports, competitive ski jumping began at Revelstoke in 1915, with Norwegian-born Nels Nelsen

The "stolen church" at Windermere.

jumping 240 feet in the 1925 Mount Revelstoke tournament—a record until 1932. Bob Lymburne also broke a world record at Revelstoke, and much later Johnny McInnes, hometown boy, was a many time Canadian ski jump champion. The Tournament of Jumps was held annually from 1950 to 1972; among the local champions was Larry Nelles, later coach of the Canadian National Ski Team and now a resort rancher.

The lore of the railway workmen who operated over Rogers Pass has been touted in numerous books—the avalanches, loneliness of station attendants, the storms. Problems included the invasion of caterpillars in 1923, making the rails so slippery that train service stopped. Colossal snowfalls of nine feet a week were not uncommon. Often the crews had to stay in the mountains for days, clearing tracks with snowplows. On March 4, 1910, sixty-two men died in an avalanche while clearing a slide from the tracks at the 4,300-foot level. The railway finally built the five-mile long descending Connaught Tunnel *inside* Mount McDonald.

Railroad operations changed. In 1940, Revelstoke Division of CPR stretched from Field to Kamloops. The eighteen-stall roundhouse and outdoor freight car repair operations bustled. Between 1950 and 1960, the trains were being converted to diesel, reducing the need for a roundhouse (although it was used for repairs until 1990). Making Revelstoke the busiest terminal in Canada are the 108-car coal trains from Natal (near Alberta) to Roberts Bank, a seaport near Vancouver. An average of six trains each twenty-four hours roll through Revelstoke. The car repair division moved to Golden in 1989.

Until 1962 the only way to cross the Selkirks from Golden to Revelstoke was by train. Retired CPR employee Al McAskill told me, "Almost everything was transported by rail—food, fuel, heavy machinery. There also was a special train from Revelstoke toward Golden each Sunday night called the Hobo. It took men from town to their various camps (railroad, logging, forest) and stopped anywhere." As autos became more practical, drivers ventured cross-country. In response to the need for this link of the Trans-Canada Highway, work began on the Big Bend Highway adjacent to the Columbia River in 1929. The scenery was inspiring—one worker remembers the sun setting "into" the Columbia during midsummer—but conditions were not comfortable for workers.

Construction began around May 1 each year and ended with the first heavy snowfalls (October or November). Workers lived in camps of about fifty men in buildings with wooden floors and walls and canvas roofs. Clouds of mosquitoes, devil's club as high as a man's head, insistent skunks in and under the cabins and cookhouses and bears added to the challenges for men and horses.

Boats took supplies up Kinbasket Lake where waves 4 to 5 feet high drove them to shelter at times. Teams pulled Fresno scrapers and plows to break up the earth. So far from any town, workers spent their Sundays off fishing or playing cards. About once a month they got to town, usually Golden.

One can imagine the lively times in the taverns and Helen's Sporting House, when lonely men—hungry for diversion—arrived for a couple of days or, in November, for the winter. Prudent workers bought next year's supplies first before they spent the rest of their money in riotous living. Golden was variously described as "one of the toughest towns anyone could imagine," and "a surprisingly pleasant and orderly community." No doubt it was both; if you were with Scarface Stewart who drank a mickey (about 13 ounces) of overproof rum without stopping and died there on his barstool, you saw one side. If you were a sawmill worker, taking home your pay to a wife and seven kids, sitting on a porch enjoying the scenery of an evening, you saw another.

Crews built a steel bridge to cross the Columbia River at Boat Encampment, and travel was possible by 1937. Rough, graveled, with few facilities, the highway was a stepchild of a road, but it served its purpose, though sometimes flooded by the Columbia or closed by snow. Deep snow made the landscape so featureless that a logging company near Boat Encampment had to send a helicopter out to locate its buried D-8 caterpillar tractor. A man was employed solely to shovel snow off Big Bend Highway bridges in winter, tramping from one cramped shelter to another.

Its travails are not forgotten. Gordon Bell, present owner of Three Valley Gap Resort in Eagle Pass, traveled the highway in the 1960s, hauling building materials from Alberta. Once the road north of Golden was marked "closed" due to flooding, but Bell said, "I just took off the fan belt and drove through water as deep as two and one-half feet for about two miles, following the edge-of-road stakes."

Bell treasures the local history and has gathered original historic buildings and replicas on his resort property. Among the truly precious structures are the original St. Stephen's Church from Donald, built in 1886, rededicated in 1967 (in big demand for weddings); C. B. Hume's general store from Revelstoke built in 1892; the entire Hotel Bellevue from Mara Lake, Sicamous, British Columbia; and Halfway House, a roadhouse from the Big Bend Highway.

The old highway is under water now from Donald to Mica Creek. Death Rapids, the Little Dalles and others between Boat Encampment (which is under 600 feet of water) and Revelstoke have vanished beneath the lakes formed by Mica Dam and Revelstoke Dam. Spurred by the need to control destructive flooding and, in the process, to create more power, Canada and the United States signed the Columbia River Treaty on September 16, 1964. Among its terms, Canada would build three dams to provide 15.5 million acre-feet of water storage. Since British Columbia then did not need the power, the province sold its share of power for the next thirty years to an amalgam of American utilities, the Columbia Storage Power Company.

The original three dams were: Duncan on the Kootenay River completed July 31, 1967; Hugh Keenleyside Dam above Castlegar operational October 10, 1968; and Mica Dam finished March 29, 1973. Revelstoke Dam came along in 1985. Keenleyside impounds runoff from the Arrow Lakes and includes locks for transport of logs to the Castlegar mills. Mica is the more dramatic, looming 800 feet above bedrock in the narrow canyon upriver from Death Rapids.

About two thousand workers lived in three-story bunkhouses below the damsite, scattering after the dam's completion. Only a handful remain to staff the dam, some of them living ninety miles away at Revelstoke.

Marg and Jim Sproat stayed, often isolated in winter storms; yet the couple loved living next to nature. Marg worked at the Interpretive Center, Jim as maintenance foreman. Grizzlies, cougars, caribou and pine martens were among their companions. One day in 1977, Marg wondered why her husband was making so much racket on the porch. She opened the door to come face to face with a huge grizzly that had come over the porch rail and gotten stuck between the rails somehow. She slammed the door and waited for the furious bear to get loose and leave. He went off but returned the next day to do the same thing. Common black bears would open doors and appear in the power-house; now the doors are always locked.

Still operating between Mica and Revelstoke at Downie Creek is a historic roadhouse. It was purchased in 1946 by Margaret Ruth Wallis and her son Edward. Loggers, road builders, and shaken-up motorists rested there at the tearoom and cabins. Mom Wallis' homemade soups, breads and huckleberry pies were legendary, and during construction of Mica Dam, the place was always packed. When Wallis cooked, the sweet smells lured bears to the kitchen. If the door was not closed tightly, a bear would walk in any time. If it was closed, one came in, anyway, after ripping the screen door off.

Mrs. Wallis' grandson, Don Munk, took over the resort in 1986. It offers a step back in time, and Don also demonstrates the art of gold panning to guests.

Curious phenomena accompany the variable river levels since construction of the dams. At Mica the larger lake surface has moderated temperatures somewhat. Revelstoke sustains smothering dust storms. The Columbia River carries immense quantities of silt, depositing it in the riverbed. Now, when Keenleyside Dam "draws down" to allow for spring runoff, the Columbia River channel returns to normal width, uncovering a broad band of powdery silt. It blows easily, causing dust storms so dense one cannot see the surrounding mountains, "like the Sahara," say locals. A potential solution would be a low weir dam to retain enough water to cover the river bottom.

Only thirty miles south of Revelstoke lie the Upper and Lower Arrow Lakes, one hundred thirty-four miles long, really broad portions of the Columbia River. Early Arrow Lakes travelers such as Ross Cox expressed appreciation of their beauty, Cox writing in 1817 that he enjoyed a fine view of the snow-covered Rocky Mountains.

A century or so later the Arrow Lakes Board of Trade described them passionately in a promotional pamphlet: "The sunset glow suffuses the far flung arch of the sky with scarlet and gold, ... the deepening shadows set the sombre masses of the mighty hills into sharp relief against an iridescent sky ... here is a setting, a panorama of scenic beauty and mountain majesty."

Written in the flowery language of the time, the tribute is yet an accurate sketch of the beauties of these remote and appealing lakes, named because Hudson's Bay travelers saw mysterious groups of arrows in a hole in the cliffs of Lower Arrow Lake, their meaning unknown.

The Columbia River and its sister river, the Kootenay, bracketed the gold mining operations, large and small, that sprang up after railroads came. From 1886 on, CPR anchored the north end of the district and the Northern Pacific roughly formed a southern boundary in Montana. The Great Northern and others came along later; indeed, one needed a program to make sense of the cast of characters in the tic-tac-toe pattern of railroads and connecting steamers. The pace of laying rail accelerated as Canadians feared the entire largesse of the upper Columbia would bleed down into American coffers.

Truly promising gold mines opened all over southeastern British Columbia, among them the North Star and Sullivan at Kimberley, the Paradise in Invermere, and legions of others in the central Selkirks.

Sprawling between the two rivers, a bevy of towns sprang up like mushrooms after a fire and boasted "a thousand people" within weeks, but most of them were soon abandoned. These are lovely hills, often carpeted with blue daisies and dotted with serene lakes, but few miners really saw the beauty. The wise built supply stores; the eager dug in the mines. Camborne was a booming town. Cody had two thousand residents and a concentrator mill for the Noble King Mine. New Denver on Slocan Lake and Nakusp on Upper Arrow Lake became important shipping points. Silverton clustered around the Mammoth Mine Mill, the largest at Slocan Lake. Kaslo was an important center at one end of Kootenay Lake,

Nelson at the other; both remain so. In 1893, rails were laid between Sandon and Nakusp to connect with riverboats for shipment of ore to smelters.

A sad chapter of North American history was played out in the ghost towns of the Selkirks—Rosebery, Lemon Creek, Popoff Farm, Sandon, New Denver. When war with Japan came in 1941, the Canadian government transported to that beautiful but hard wilderness thousands of Japanese from coastal towns. Of the 21,439 Japanese removed, more than half lived in abandoned mining towns—old homes converted to apartments, a saloon dance hall housing three families.

At the Popoff farm in Slocan Valley, hundreds of Japanese spent 1942 in tents, waiting for shacks 16 feet by 16 feet to be completed. The Japanese worked at construction, on road crews, did stoop labor, or sewed on piecework, clerked and did office work, usually at low wages. For the first year there were no schools for the 1,811 school children. The resilient Japanese earned the friendship of local residents, and soon compassionate villagers helped as they could. In October 1942, to prove their loyalty to Canada, the Japanese organized a Victory Bond Drive. When the war ended, the Japanese went home, often to find their properties were gone.

Sandon had been repaired, but in 1955 an old flume plugged up during runoff and overflowed to wash out most of the town. Treminco Resources Ltd. today operates the Sandon mine, and a museum remembers the poignant past of those towns in the "Valley of the Ghosts."

Keenleyside Dam flooded out many lakeside peach orchards along Arrow Lakes, plus the buildings at Halcyon Hot Springs (not the springs), shoreside wrecked sternwheelers, the old railroad barge docks at Arrowhead, Renata, Forest Glen, Fosthall, Deer Park, Graham's Landing and the saloons and card rooms of Brooklyn town. There a determined preacher, the Reverend John Munroe of the Presbyterian Church of Trail, played one hour of popular music in a saloon whenever the patrons would agree to listen to an hour's sermon afterwards.

Nakusp, Burton, Fauquier, Needles, Edgewood, Galena Bay—these small towns still enjoy the broadened reaches of Arrow Lakes. Thirty miles below Revelstoke, the Shelter Bay-Galena ferry, part of the highway system, provides a free thirty-minute "scenic cruise." Captain Roy Peterson says there is a 70-foot variation in the lake's level. Storms still blow up suddenly, and the ferry stops running when waves get 5 feet high. On rare occasions the lake freezes. One winter the captain saw two deer stranded on a small ice floe. He edged the ferry up to the floe, the deer calmly walked aboard the car deck and jumped off near the opposite shore like veteran ferry travelers.

Mining
and Tourism

For several decades the most practical and comfortable access to the towns between the lakes was by water. Both the Kootenay and Columbia rivers teemed with sternwheelers, the soft sigh of their passage hardly disturbing the waters.

One of the finest sternwheelers on the Columbia was launched at Nakusp on July 1, 1895. The town's namesake *Nakusp* was 171 feet long, with luxurious appointments, although she could carry 300 tons of freight. From balconies on the "Texas" deck one looked down to white linened tables with bouquets. Artistic chandeliers swung from the white and gold ceiling, 17 feet high in the dining room.

Near Christmas, 1895, the ship was trapped by ice in Lower Arrow Lake. Owners sent the smaller *Arrow* to break up the ice in the narrows and open a path for the *Nakusp,* but the *Arrow* capsized in a killer gale and drowned its captain and engineer. In 1897, the *Nakusp* fell victim to fire at Arrowhead. Despite weather problems, such sternwheelers operated regular routes from Arrowhead (fed by a rail spur from Revelstoke in later years) to Castlegar, Trail and Northport.

Trail was founded by Eugene Sayre Topping when he preempted 343 acres of land on Trail Creek and the Columbia River. He was a deputy mining recorder in Nelson, a modest man on a workman's salary. One day he was confronted by two excited miners who had five claims to stake and were allowed only two each. They offered Topping the fifth if he would pay all five recording fees. Thus Topping acquired a share in the soon fabulously rich LeRoi Mine at Red Mountain above Trail.

In 1890 to 1891 Topping brought samples of ore from his LeRoi Mine to Butte for analysis, then sold his interest to ecstatic purchasers for $30,000. The mine later sold for $3 million, but after all, he had paid only $12.50.

Enter Fritz August Heinze in 1894 on the steamer *Lytton* from Northport, an experienced smelter man and speculator from Butte. He purchased 40 acres at the present site of Cominco and built a smelter in six months. Heinze's company was incorporated in New Jersey as British Columbia Smelting and Refining Company Limited and the furnace fired up in February 1896.

Workers flocking to steady employment found conditions little better than the mines. J. R. Widmer said about Trail, population three hundred: "There were no sanitary conveniences. Water was delivered from house to house by water wagon. Smoky gas lamps lit the eight or ten hotels and the log and rough board cottages that huddled at the foot of smelter hill. Some of the hotels had double-deck bunks filled with loose straw for mattresses." (From article in *Orbit*, Cominco Magazine, September 1988, 8.) A later employee, Frank Verzuh, told me that the bed bugs became so bad in the hotels that he and three other men scrounged lumber and built their own rough cabin.

Heinze was juggling lawsuits in Butte from past dealings, development of the smelter and construction of the narrow gauge Columbia & Western Railway from Trail to Rossland—all the while staving off intense competition. The Northport smelter was ready to open in 1898, and American D. C. Corbin had thrust a rail line from Spokane to The Dalles below Northport in 1890 (then the foot of riverboat traffic), plus a spur to Red Mountain (Rossland) by December 1896.

Both speculators, Corbin and Heinze, sold their holdings to the titans in 1898. Heinze sold his smelter and railway holdings to Canadian Pacific Railway. Corbin sold the Spokane Falls and Northern to the Great Northern. Corbin had bitterly opposed the Great Northern, and some say he was unaware that his line would wind up in their hands during third party sale negotiations.

The CPR was forced to buy the smelter with the rail interests and although not keen about being in that business, they determined to do a good job, putting a capable engineer, Walter H. Aldridge, in charge.

Too late, he discovered that the CPR had paid only for railway and smelter, not for certain rolling stock and supplies to operate the smelter. A grinning Heinze suggested that he and Aldridge play poker for the $300,000 additional purchase price, but the more conservative Aldridge asked for arbitration. Upon resolution of the matter, the outfit was known as Canadian Smelting Works until 1906, when the Consolidated Mining and Smelting Company of Canada, Limited, was formed (Cominco), a subsidiary of Canadian Pacific Railway.

Meanwhile, workers clamored for better conditions at the LeRoi Mines of Rossland, impetus for the whole matter. In 1895, Rossland miners organized Local 38 of the Western Federation of Miners, the first in Western Canada, and built the still-standing Miners Hall. In 1898, they obtained an eight-hour workday credited to the efforts of Jim Martin, Rossland legislator. The miners were on strike for nine months in 1901, a bitter time but with no violence. Miners eventually were represented by United Steelworkers of America.

Among the workers at Rossland were about two hundred Chinese, employed as cooks, houseboys or proprietors of small stores. Laundrymen delivered clothes carried in one big sheet, the corners tied together. From verdant gardens, the Chinese "vegetable man" delivered produce door to door from two enormous baskets slung over his shoulders. He marked the recipient's accounts on the door frame of the house, consternation reigning if a paint job covered the reckoning. Relationships were quite amicable between Europeans and Chinese. White guests were invited to the opening of a Chinese Masonic Lodge with a membership of one hundred men. Guests described the event: "In the lodge room were altars at either end of the room bearing lighted candles ... joss sticks smouldered. ... Chickens well browned and inviting, candles of the Chinese varieties, cakes ... and sam suey galore graced the refreshment stand but the Celestial Masons did not bother with refreshments until noon. ... The concluding feature was a procession about the lodge room, each making obeisance to the master and other officers." (From Alice Martin manuscript, Rossland, British Columbia, Museum.)

When a Chinese person died, he or she was laid to rest with a twenty-five cent piece in his or her mouth to pay the way into the other world. The departed one was buried for three years, then disinterred and the bones returned to China for burial. In later years Canadians attempted to return numerous sets of bones to their Chinese homeland, in accordance with old custom, but the Communist government refused to accept them.

An inventor flared briefly into fame in 1902. Lou Gagnon built and flew the first helicopter ever to get off the ground in North America, a contraption that skeptical Rosslanders called the "Flying Steamshovel." Since it crashed after takeoff, a humiliated Gagnon left town.

Today Rossland is a prime ski destination. It is also the hometown of Olympics and World Cup ski champion Nancy Greene. A prophet, perhaps, was Olaus Jeldness, a Norwegian miner. On a dare from cohorts in 1896, he raced on 9-foot carved wooden skis from the summit of Red Mountain to the streets of town. Urging him on were the cheers of crowds well-oiled from the five local breweries and forty saloons. The feat led to Rossland's first annual winter carnival, still held each year in February.

The transportation war continued. Alarmed by the encroachment into Canada of the Great Northern, which touched the Kootenay in Montana, the Canadian Pacific Railway bought out the entire Columbia and Kootenay Steam Navigation Company. Thus, it could squeeze out competitors by changing ports of call while it built more spur lines in Canada. By World War I the Canadian Pacific Railway won the battle, only to renew rivalry with the Great Northern farther west.

The sternwheelers continued to serve. However tranquil the Arrow Lakes and Kootenay Lake might be *usually*, winds and ice took their toll. On Kootenay Lake on November 29, 1898, nine people lost their lives. Art Downs described the incident:

> The *City of Ainsworth* left Nelson for Bonners Ferry but got caught in a gale. Eight cords of firewood on her bow made her sluggish and she began to ship water. ... Her paddlewheel virtually stopped and she swung broadside to the waves ... each roll worse than the preceding one. Then she heeled over so far that water poured into her smokestack.
>
> When she began to wallow, First Officer Perrier launched a small lifeboat but it swamped. Four of the five aboard vanished into the snow-lashed waves. Then Captain Lean and some crew members launched the other lifeboat ... it capsized. Five more people vanished into the storm. (Art Downs, *Paddlewheels on the Frontier* [Sidney, British Columbia: Gray's Publishing Ltd., 1972] 126–28.)

Despite further rescue efforts, the final toll was two passengers and seven crewmen.

Newer sternwheelers of the 1900s included staterooms with private washbasins, raised dining areas for better passenger visibility, stained and leaded glass windows and other amenities. They were powered by more efficient engines and designed for the rough waters of the Columbia rapids. Many of the vessels were built at Nakusp. The four-decker *Bonnington* went into service April 24, 1911, on the Arrow Lakes. Furnishings were of golden oak and Australian mahogany and, in the ladies' salon, there were plush carpets and soft armchairs. With a steel hull and relatively powerful engines, she was designed to manage shallow water. Her chief problem was her great height; the large amount of freeboard made her tricky to dock in a wind; however, passengers enjoyed her luxurious accommodations until she ceased operations in 1931. Construction of the *Bonnington* was part of a master plan by the Canadian Pacific Railway to extend its tourist lodges to the Arrow/Kootenay scenic areas. The company built a luxury hotel on Kootenay Lake, accessed by a short train ride from Robson (Castlegar). The *Bonnington* brought passengers from Revelstoke, and a sister ship was available for passage or pleasure cruises on Kootenay Lake.

Tourists did come to the Arrow Lakes, especially to the hot springs resorts. On Upper Arrow Lake two locations opened to serve tourists, miners and loggers with aching muscles. In 1901, the Hotel St. Leon on Halfway Creek was open, lavishly decorated by owner Mike Grady with proceeds from sale of the Standard Mine, Slocan Lake. It was open sporadically, but few tourists came because the pipes carrying water from the springs were too small, and the water grew cold before reaching the hotel. Old travelers remember Grady as a lake character, a man with a flowing white beard who always met arriving steamers.

Riverboat Captain Robert Sanderson started the Halcyon Hot Springs Hotel in 1894, merely a dressing room of cedar bark nailed to poles and a sod-roofed log structure over the springs. Eventually the springs were purchased by Governor C. H. Mackintosh, who built Swiss-style guest cottages, seeded a lawn and built a wharf for steamer service.

In March, 1924, Halcyon was sold to retired Brigadier General F. E. Burnham, a World War I hero and Head Surgeon at Sarajevo, Serbia. He established the hotel as a White Cross sanatorium with healthy food and strict rules—no drinking and lights out at nine (although this was partly because of a low-powered generator). His friend Jack Harris remembers him as somewhat eccentric but a dedicated philanthropist and doctor who predicted smoking would cause cancer.

Burnham felt the waters were a gift from God and should be available to everyone who needed them. Burnham's rates remained very low and if one could not pay, he could cut firewood for the aging steam plant. Later he changed to fuel oil, and his parsimonious ways became his death sentence. He refused to hire a repairman to fix a leaky oil stove, catching the drips in a pail instead. One morning in 1955, the hotel exploded in flame, becoming Burnham's funeral pyre.

Not so grand, the Nakusp Hot Springs continuously operated and remains open as a public springs and pool, with camping facilities and overnight chalets. Historic Ainsworth Hot Springs on Kootenay Lake still is an operating spa.

Of the sternwheelers on the lakes, two survived into the 1950s to serve isolated miners and loggers, farmers and retirees. The *Minto* on Arrow Lakes and the *Moyie* on Kootenay Lake were fabricated at Toronto to be reassembled for duty in the Klondike gold rush; when plans changed, they were rerouted to the Kootenays. The *Moyie* was reassembled at Nelson. From a thousand labeled parts the *Minto* was reconstructed into a vessel 162 feet long and launched at Nakusp on November 19, 1898, three weeks after the *Moyie*.

The *Minto* was destined to become a legend on the broad Columbia River lakes. As the twentieth century wore on, the vessel became the only link to the outside world for isolated settlers—the occasional prospector, loggers in remote camps, the brave orchardists growing peaches on meager flatlands along the lakes. The ship carried mail and freight ranging from a spool of thread for a housewife to mining machinery, tractors or horses.

In 1949, a traveler reported the *Minto* had fifty-six berths and a crew of twenty—the berths sharply in demand. Passengers otherwise had to sit up and snooze in chairs for the twenty-six hour trip between Arrowhead and Robson. To see mule deer, caribou, elk or bears cavorting along the shores was a common experience—all the animals accustomed to the throbbing whoosh-whoosh of the *Minto's* paddlewheel. To hail her anywhere, one just waved two white flags or built two small fires; for an emergency it was three of either. The ship ran day and night except for the narrows between lakes, which the captain traversed only in daylight, determined not to add his beloved ship to the hulks rotting there on shallow, shifting gravel bars.

Locals said Captain Otto Estabrooks of that period could "take the *Minto* across a tureen of consommé without disturbing the vermicelli," according to Richard Neuberger writing in 1949 in the *Saturday Evening Post*.

The ship's colorful 134-mile voyages seemed doomed to end before World War II, with only four thousand passengers a year; however, young men who trained for war at camps in the Selkirks returned after the peace to visit or settle the region again. Capacity crowds came once more to the *Minto's* decks.

Paddlewheel from an original riverboat, the Moyie, *being restored at Kaslo.*

Finally, weary from three decades of continuous use, and outrun by cars and railroads, this last sternwheeler quit. On her farewell voyage, April 24, 1954, under Captain Robert Manning, the teary farewells of locals and dignitaries could have floated the vessel. There were flags and songs, a wreath from Burton citizens on the ship's bow, a bagpipe lament and a welcoming crowd when she pulled in to Nakusp, the place of her "birth."

Outraged at the idea of scrapping the historic *Minto*, elderly John Nelson of Upper Arrow Lake purchased the vessel and planned to restore her as a museum, but he was too old and his project too ambitious. After he died in 1967, the stripped *Minto* was towed out into the lake and burned as part of the Dominion Day celebration in 1968.

Her memory lives on, though, in her sister ship, the *Moyie*, which is being reconstructed as a museum at Kaslo on Kootenay Lake. The former luxury of her interior is being restored: a ladies' salon with piano and upholstered chairs where tea and crumpets were served; a forthright men's saloon that had gambling tables, a bar and spittoons. Wood carvings over the cabin doors that provided openwork for ventilation are repolished. As work proceeds, a veritable treasure house of "garbage" is uncovered—candy wrappers, beer labels, newspapers of a century ago, where they were stuffed into apertures in the walls by passengers.

The foundation sponsoring restoration is also searching with modern sonar, diving gear, and cameras for the *City of Ainsworth* that sank in 1898. So far the only item located has been an intact jar of pickles thought to be from the vessel.

Though the paddlewheelers are a memory, tugs still pull huge log booms along the Columbia River/Arrow Lakes. The trees are felled by independent loggers who use continuous track tractors or high lead logging to move them, instead of horse teams. A high lead system involves a logging jammer, a central small A-frame device that winds logs into the center from about a 500-feet radius. Hauled to the shore, the logs are scaled or measured before being rolled into the lake, where they are corraled in bag booms—big round enclosures—to await tugs. The tow may be a quarter-mile-long procession down lake, a week's trip, to the locks of Hugh Keenleyside Dam. There booms are cut loose, lowered to river level and picked up by another tug for transport to Westar's lumber mill.

In 1960, Celanese Corporation of America opened the first pulp mill in interior British Columbia at Castlegar, to make bleached kraft pulp from waste material—chips and small softwood logs. Shipped all over the world, the end product is fine finished, coated papers.

At first Celanese bought and consolidated many small mills up river and managed Celgar Pulp, Celgar Lumber and Celgar Woodlands

Divisions. In 1986, the firm sold the timber operations to Westar Timber Limited and retains the pulp mill.

Westar uses independent truckers and loggers to harvest blocks of trees from crown lands, after which they replant the cleared areas within five years. James Cavaliero of Westar told me that the private companies buy or grow their own seedlings to reforest the areas.

The marine division of Westar manages the river craft, including tugs and boom boats (small, almost circular "tubs"—powerful craft that surge in among logs to sort and bundle them into rafts). One boom boat is fortified as an ice breaker for infrequent use.

Not surprisingly, a pulp mill like Celgar wrestles with emissions of unpleasant odors and materials into the river. Today the company asserts that its recycling plant returns water to the river cleaner than it entered, but totally eliminating odors is an ongoing and costly project.

Area telephone books show many Russian names. By 1912, about five thousand Russian religious dissenters called Doukhobors had settled in British Columbia, perhaps half around Castlegar and the central Selkirks. Their lifestyle involved no physical churches except community homes where the people met for prayer (religion was within the heart, not the Orthodox Church), vegetarianism, rejection of killing anything or anyone, abstinence from alcohol, tobacco and—in rare cases—minimizing sexual intercourse. They recognized only God as their authority.

This independent attitude led to frictions with governments. In Russia it was objection to conscription; in Saskatchewan, their first Canadian home, it was refusal to make an Oath of Allegiance required by the Homestead Act before properties could be deeded. Doctrinal differences developed. While still in Saskatchewan, the Doukhobors became divided into three groups, of which vestiges linger: (1) Independents, who live on individual homesites; (2) Community, who live in communal villages; and (3) Freedomites or *Svobodniki*, the dogmatic arm that seeks return to absolutely nonmaterialistic living.

By 1924, under leader Peter V. Verigin, the sect had acquired 21,648 acres of land. In Castlegar it lay mostly south of the confluence of the Columbia and Kootenay rivers. The Doukhobors set up villages with thirty-five to fifty people per home, each family having a separate room, but sharing meals and property. Industrious and creative, the people cleared and farmed land, planted orchards and eventually had sawmills, oil presses, flour mills and a jam factory—the latter highly praised. The Castlegar Golf Course is the site of old blacksmith shops, barns, kitchens and a pit for distilling oil from birchbark for waterproofing shoes, all gone before the course was built.

Old ways changed. Children were forced by the Canadian government to attend schools, a ruling that caused arson of schools laid chiefly at the door of the Freedomites. Doukhobor extremists also were blamed for the purported assassination of Peter V. Verigin on a Canadian Pacific Railway train between Brilliant and Grand Forks in 1924. Several miles west of Castlegar a massive explosion blew up the railway coach in which Verigin was riding, killing him, a female friend, and nine other passengers. The consensus is that the helpful Doukhobor man who carried Verigin's suitcase aboard had planted a bomb in it. Others say, since miners often illegally carried dynamite on trains, that unstable explosives caused the blast. In recent years a CPR employee said that the explosion was typical of a gas light malfunction. We will never know for sure.

In 1943, extremists burned down the Doukhobor jam factory above the Columbia River at Brilliant, as well as leader Ivan Verigin's home. The main body of Doukhobors shuns turmoil and tried to disassociate themselves from the violence. The Freedomites also were blamed, fairly or not, for using fire and nude parades as protests between 1958 and 1962, when—for nearly the first time—the protests involved burning Canadian governmental properties. Before that, it seemed that the protesters burned out their own.

Peaceful ways prevail today. Most Doukhobors now live in individual homes but retain their gentle ways and faith, including the belief that love is of paramount importance. The Doukhobors have developed wonderful choral groups that perform worldwide. The scores are unusual, possibly deriving from Gregorian polyphony, the original, ancient style of Greek-Orthodox singing, a style so ancient that other Russians may have forgotten it.

A non-Doukhobor Russian, Alexander Zuckerberg, a high-born refugee from the Bolshevik Revolution, came to teach Russian to the Doukhobor and Castlegar children. He discovered a small forested island in the Columbia River, a few yards from shore, and inquired about its purchase. The provincial government was amazed, saying there was no such island, but Zuckerberg finally convinced them that it existed. There he built a Russian-style country home, paths, gardens irrigated from the Columbia through a waterwheel and sculptures— including one commemorating his wife when she died in 1960. It is a park now, compliments of Zuckerberg and funded by the Rotary Club, a haven of peace reached over a suspension foot bridge.

World War I brought an urgent need for zinc used in munitions. Cominco researcher Ralph Diamond discovered new extraction methods that resulted in profitable expansion at Trail, a boon to the community, very dependent on the smelter. In World War II, Cominco developed "heavy water" used in the atomic bomb, a project so secret researchers did not know the reason for the project until very shortly before the bomb was dropped on Hiroshima.

Cominco gets consistently fine marks from local citizens as a good corporate citizen, but its early-day emissions of sulphur dioxide led to complaints from downwind Washington farmers of damage to foliage. Research resulted in new ways of capturing 94 percent of the sulfuric emissions to use in fertilizers. Instead of polluting the atmosphere, the fertilizers marketed as "Elephant Brand" speed growth of crops in the Prairies. Today lead for auto batteries constitutes 70 percent of Cominco's output; zinc for galvanizing steel against rust is next.

Necessarily, emissions continue to be sharply reduced. "We definitely get the heavy metals out of waste water returned to the river," says a spokesman. But the damage of decades ago, when industrialists did not recognize such hazards, is not entirely healed, even though the river is coming back swiftly. Trail "river rat" and avid fisherman Joe Biagoni claims that there are now good stocks of rainbow trout and kokanee. Kokanee are landlocked salmon that have adapted to living their entire lives in fresh water and do reproduce. They tend to be smaller than the wild strain, but for two years there were dramatic increases in numbers and sizes after introduction of fresh water shrimp to the Arrow Lakes as fish food. Fishermen take huge sturgeon from the river, and there are increasing numbers of walleye pike.

In past days fishermen built cedar slab boathouses, mounting them on logs and anchoring them to shore. An elderly resident who still owns one has an ongoing battle with a beaver that insistently tries to dam up the opening to his boathouse. One week he found it half full of branches. A pair of otters calls the boathouse home, a mixed blessing since they eat fish and excrete on the boat. However, the "river rats" delight in such small problems, because it means the river is recovering from pollution. Biagoni has seen bear, wildcat and an extremely rare albino cougar coming to the river in years past.

Below Castlegar the Columbia River runs into Washington State largely unchanged from the old days. Here is the Columbia of the impressive Waterloo Eddy below Castlegar that bounces off a rock promontory to form whirlpools as big as a house (Biagoni has watched large logs upend there, disappear and emerge 300 feet downriver), of the rugged canyons at Murphy Creek, the killer rapids at Deadman's Eddy just below the border—where the remains of anyone who falls into the river and drowns are usually found.

Travel and Trivia
The River in Canada

On a twelve hundred-mile river, I am suggesting only those activities or places of unusual interest or personal enjoyment. Ask infocenters for visitors' guides listing all data in an area.

Captain Robert Gray's ship was the *Columbia Rediviva*. Maritime artist Steve Mayo of Bellingham, Washington, was commissioned to do an official oil painting of the ship, from which posters were made. For prints, contact Kirsten Gallery, 5320 Roosevelt Way Northeast, Seattle, WA 98105. (206) 522-2011.

General tourist information for British Columbia is available at Tourism British Columbia, Parliament Building, Victoria, BC V8V 1X4. Telephone outside British Columbia 1-800-663-6000. In British Columbia (604) 387-1642.

Invermere Area:

Tourist Info Centre, Main Street, Invermere, BC V0A 1K0. (604) 342-6316 (seasonal).

Fort Steele Heritage Town. Connected to earliest Columbia River Valley history. Sixty restored buildings. Storekeepers and historic characters in period clothing operate shops or stroll the streets. Demonstrations of quilting, spinning, churning butter (you do it), rides on wagons behind Clydesdale teams. Two live professional shows presented daily except Mondays. A scenic tour in an East Kootenay Railway Company train behind a venerable steam engine. Grounds open year round. On Highway 93/95 near junction with #3. Special celebrations of Dominion Day (July 1), Harvest Day (horse-drawn farm equipment used) mid-August, Thanksgiving. Fort Steele, BC V0B 1N0. (604) 426-6923.

Recommended reading: Book about Fort Steele by Derryll White,

Fort Steele, available at gift shop or by mail order and in Columbia Valley bookstores.

Cranbrook Railway Museum. Slide shows, guided tours, old engines and cars of Canadian Pacific Railway and rail lore. Dining in dining car. Cranbrook and Railway Historical Archives. Railway Capers September 1+. Downtown Cranbrook on Highway 3/95. (604) 489-3918.

Cranbrook has Sam Steele Days mid-June, Canada Day July 1, pro rodeo at Wycliffe Exhibition Grounds in mid-August.

Write for free road log of natural history between Cranbrook and Golden on Highway 93/95. Larry Halverson, Kootenay National Park, Box 220, Radium Hot Springs, BC V0A 1M0.

Kimberley, site of one of the world's largest lead and zinc mines, Sullivan Mine. The town has converted its downtown area to a charming Bavarian theme. Browse through shops or dine at sidewalk restaurants. Visitor attractions include Cominco Gardens, The Bavarian City Mining Railway (a ride). In winter the Kimberley Ski Hill. Events include old-time accordion competitions in mid-July; the third weekend in July is July Fest with oompah bands, sports; elk bugling (professional elk buglers from Canada and the United States try their calls) some years; Alpine Folk Dance Festival (August 31+). Kimberly Infocentre, 350 Ross Street, Kimberley, BC V1A 2Z9. (604) 427-3666.

Fairmont Hoodoos Mt. Resort, adjacent to weird sandstone formations, near Dutch Creek (a Columbia River source), a simple country resort, housekeeping cabins. One hundred camp sites. Box 67, Fairmont, BC V0B 1L0. (604) 345-6631.

Columbia Lake Resort is a swimming beach south end of lake. Showers, boat launching, provincial park. It's thrilling to stand there and know it is the birthplace of the Columbia.

Columbia Inn, historic old pub where old-timers hang out. A few rooms, bath down the hall, modest but friendly. No food. Canal Flats downtown. Unusual and riotous Canal Flats Wilderness Rendezvous on Canada Day weekend July 1+. Original early day dress, day's horseback ride (your own horse), ride to Palliser River Guides and Outfitters base camp, outdoor barbecue and dance. Sunday there is hatchet and knife throwing competition, black powder shoot (muzzle loaders).

Fairmont Hot Springs Resort straddles the newly born Columbia River. Splendid golfing and recreation resort, first class rooms and food, golf courses, skiing in winter, natural hot springs. Historic—see text of book. Guests pampered in every way. Handsome time-share villas, too. On Highway 93/95, and accessible by air to Fairmont airport. P. O. Box 10, Fairmont Hot Springs, BC V0B 1L0. (604) 345-6311, 1-800-663-4979.

Suggested reading: *The Legacy of Fairmont Hot Springs* by Janet Wilder, one of owning family. Available locally or write Fairmont Hot Springs Resort.

There are many campsites and RV locations—ask Tourism British Columbia.

Invermere on Lake Windermere is a summer resort town with fishing, riding, pack trips, tours by four-wheelers, boating, hiking, mountaineering. The main street of town has sidewalk cafes, small shops and gift shops. Horse and carriage rides through town.

David Thompson's **"Kootenae House"** plaque at the junction of Toby Creek and the Columbia River. Turn off main street toward Wilmer. Just across Toby Creek on the right. (Site of *original* cabin does not have any markings. Ask museum for location, if interested.)

Windermere Valley Museum. Small museum with displays and considerable local lore in archives. 622 3rd Street, Invermere. (604) 342-9769.

Recommended reading: Charming fictionalized facts about early history. *Tales of the Windermere* by Winifred Weir, local historian related to steamboat captain Frank Armstrong. See text. Available locally and at museum.

Invermere Inn, full service hotel right downtown. Hotel dining room has some of best food in town. Early residents Tom Foyston, Hubert Kirsch and others like to swap stories over coffee each morning here. 1310 7th Avenue, Invermere, BC V0A 1K0. (604) 342-9246.

Lakeside Inn, a pub popular with young set. Full menu, casual decor, pool tables, deck overlooking lake. Rentals for windsurfing, water skiing, jet skiing, zodiac boats, canoes. North end of lake, Invermere. (604) 342-6711.

Strand's Old House Restaurant serves a big-time menu, items like peppersteak, chicken Oskar and pavlova in an old home with leaded glass windows, formerly occupied by Dr. Filmer E. Coy, only doctor from Golden to Cranbrook in early 1920s. Three generations of pioneer Weirs grew up there. Strand's imports chefs from Switzerland. 818 12th Street, Invermere. (604) 342-6344.

Smoothie's Restaurant, main street of Invermere. Casual dining good for families. Natural foods. Try grilled tomato, mushroom and cheese sandwich.

Incredible Mountain Tours, operator Don Yanko. Tours by comfortable van to Bugaboo Range, Lake of the Hanging Glaciers, the wildlife refuge, Paradise Ridge or Sunset on Mount Swansea to watch the sun go down over the Columbia River. See the river from Columbia Lake to Golden. Yanko is full of local lore and can tailor a tour to any level of effort. Operates from Invermere Inn lobby. Leave message there or call (604) 342-4433.

Hang gliders like to launch from Mount Swansea's crest, east of Invermere.

Bed and breakfast houses: Canterbury House built in 1926 on Lake Windermere, 422 14th Street, Invermere, BC V0A 1K0. Delphine Lodge Country Inn (the first hotel in Wilmer, built in 1899), Main Street Wilmer, Box 2797, Invermere, BC V0A 1K0.

Fenimore Llamas. Rearvuemere Ranch raises quality llamas for sale. Llamas are increasingly popular to carry your gear when you hike. P. O. Box 595, Invermere, BC V0A 1K0. (604) 342-9021.

St. Peter's Church in Windermere downtown was stolen from the town of Donald by Rufus Kimpton. The CPR had offered to transport stores, hotels, and personal effects to Revelstoke when it moved its headquarters there. Kimpton and J. C. Pitts dismantled the church and moved it to Windermere. Despite loud outcries from Revelstoke, the church stayed reassembled in Windermere and was reconsecrated in August 27, 1905. It's a popular place for wedding ceremonies.

Bavin Glass. Jim Bavin attended the prestigious Pilchuck School in Darrington, Washington, internationally known for glass-blowing art. He is an amateur archaeologist and is doing Kootenay Indian pictograph designs in glass. Unusual colors. His imagery uses wind and water themes. Reasonably priced now, but just wait. Located in old village of Windermere near the "Stolen Church." Box 40, Windermere, BC V0B 2L0. (604) 342-6819.

Patrick Heaps creates unusual mirrors from oak and other woods at **Inner Reflections**, foot of Lake Windermere, Box 1047, Invermere, BC V0A 1K0

Village Arts, an artists' cooperative. Downtown Invermere.

Ian Jack of Kootenay National Park urges that readers think about **canoeing the Columbia River** itself, quiet most of the way in British Columbia, and running through huge scenic lakes. Opportunities to view birds and wildlife, e.g., at Wilder National Wildlife Area about five miles north of Invermere. Very few canoe-rental places, but great for those who bring their own.

According to local people, **reliable horse packers** for trips into the mountains, hunting, camera, scenic: Joe McDonald (604) 342-3125. Dix Anderson (604) 342-6601. Cody Tegart, descended from one of original valley pioneers, Palliser Guide Outfitters (604) 347-9247.

Panorama Ski and Summer Resort is near Invermere in the Purcell Mountains. Not far from old Paradise Mine, one that paid off. Varying accommodations with condos, one- and two-bedroom suites, hotel rooms, fireplaces, hot tubs, bar, children's programs, etc. From there— twenty miles west of the Columbia River—one can go whitewater rafting right from the resort, trail riding, fishing, golfing. There are salmon barbecues, and in July and August the Murder Mystery Dinner Theatre. 1-800-663-2929.

Among festivals are:

Panorama Grand Prix–Canada Cup Cycling Series in mid-May; Alberta Appreciation Day in July; Windermere Annual Squaw Fish Derby; Annual Lakeside Inn Hanggliding Event on Lake Windermere in August.

In winter the **Bugaboo Mountains** in the Purcell Range are prime **heliskiing** territory. At least six major outfits offer skiing trips, usually a week long, furnishing comfortable lodge rooms and foods high in the mountains, helicopters, etc. This sport usually requires at least a good to expert skier, although all runs are guided by qualified people. Expensive but thrilling for ski enthusiasts. Heliskiing starts from Invermere, Golden and Revelstoke airports. Some offer cross-country skiing. Ask infocentres for names and check thoroughly.

Among reliables is **Canadian Mountain Holidays** with Hans Gmoser, "father" of helicopter skiing in several mountain ranges. P. O. Box 1660, Banff AB T0L 0C0. (403) 762-4531.

Golden area:

Golden & District Chamber of Commerce, Golden, BC V0A 1H0. (604) 344-7125.

Golden District Forestry Office, 600 North 9th Street, Golden, for information on Forest Service Recreation sites. (604) 344-7500. Conservation Office in Provincial Courthouse, 606 N. 6th Street, Golden, for fishing and hunting regulations and information. (604) 344-7585.

Taliesin Guest House. A polished log two-story country home on a bluff overlooking the Columbia River south of Golden. A log dump structure used for the sides and roof. Sweeping views toward Purcell Mountains over Columbia River. Often see coyotes, elk, deer, occasionally bears. Natural home-grown foods from garden. Bed and breakfast but, due to isolation, dinners by advance arrangement. Basic rooms. Home has electricity and television. Box 101, Parson BC V0A 1L0. (604) 348-2247 or 348-6055.

Chalet Motel, situated on a steep ridge, has breathtaking views of Columbia River, Purcells and Rocky Mountains from most rooms, many with balconies. Jacuzzi, sauna. Microwave and refrigerator in rooms, no food served. Year-round. Winter skiing at Panorama only about twenty minutes away. P.O. Box 456, Radium Hot Springs, BC V0A 1M0. (604) 347-9305.

Radium Hot Springs Aquacourt is a public springs, the original Sinclair Springs or Radium Hot Springs (see text). The parking lot is just past the springs on the right, across from a massive red rock formation. A public facility, only nominal charges for using the springs, modest food prices and a gift shop. Just east of Highway 95. In the small town there are many motels and restaurants, often with a Bavarian or Swiss accent.

Radium Hot Springs Lodge is directly across from the Aquacourt on such a steep bluff that access is by elevator "up" from the highway. A lounge and dining room take advantage of the precipitous setting with wonderful views. Regular hotel facilities. 1-800-663-4925 or (604) 347-9622.

Best Western Radium Hot Springs Resort lies in the foothills a mile south of the town and is a full golfing resort. There are hotel rooms and condos, an indoor pool, racquetball, tennis and squash courts, golf rentals, etc. Extensive remodeling in 1990 made the restaurant and patio dining even more enjoyable. Springs Golf Tournament in mid-June. Box 310, Radium Hot Springs, BC V0A 1M0. 1-800-528-1234 or (604) 347-9588.

Blakley's Bungalows, only two blocks from the Aquacourt, offers light housekeeping family units in a park-like setting. Original Blakley was a steamboat captain with Armstrong (see text). Box 190, Radium Hot Springs V0A 1M0. (604) 347-9918.

Radium Days Festival, late May each year, includes a dance, beer garden, parade and golf tournament.

Towering Rocky Mountains east of Golden and psuedo-covered wagons of Beaverfoot Lodge.

Beaverfoot Lodge is historic. Hector of the Palliser Expedition passed right through the lodge's grounds. The isolated country log lodge has basic second-floor rooms and top-notch wholesome food, a dude ranch atmosphere, with lots of horseback riding, river fishing, hiking, wildlife. An unusual feature is a circle of pseudo covered-wagons in a secluded nearby meadow, complete with cookhouse and modern bathrooms—great wilderness experience for groups (large or small). Open in the winter for cross-country skiing. Very scenic in the historic heart of the Rockies. East of Golden, partly on graveled road. Box 1560, Golden, BC V0A 1H0. (604) 346-3216 or 346-3205.

Phil Hein, one of fifty licensed senior guides, operates in the Rocky Mountains northwest of Yoho National Park on private land. There he has a comfortable alpine cabin, to which you are lifted by helicopter. Extremely scenic alpine skiing (see text). Box 990, Golden, BC V0A 1H0. (604) 344-2381.

Golden is a **whitewater rafting center**, especially the swift Kicking Horse River with rapids like "Hopi's Hole," "Flying Hot," "Penny's Plunge," "Witch's Rock," "Last Waltz," "Table Saw," rated up to 4 internationally. You can ask for tame float trips, too. Toby Creek at Invermere is one of the other whitewater rivers; outfitters can go anywhere but usually operate locally. Two responsible operators at Golden are: **Alpine Rafting Company**, P.O. Box 1409, Golden, BC V0A 1H0. (604) 344-5016. Peter Schlunneger, owner, is a descendant of an original Swiss guide (see text). **Glacier Raft Company Ltd.**, on Highway 95, Box 428, Golden, BC V0A 1H0. (604) 344-6521 or 943-4249 in winter. On Toby Creek there's **Off the Wall Adventures Ltd.** booked from Panorama Resort Adventure Centre (604) 342-6941, ext. 328.

Amiskwi Air Ltd. offers flights over the glacial country in five surrounding national parks, including the famed Columbia Icefields. Twin-engine planes. Golden Airport. Fly-in fishing trips. Box 1589, Golden BC V0A 1H0. (604) 344-2534.

Golden District Museum has displays and archival material. Open every day in summer. 1302 South 11th Street, Golden. (604) 344-5169.

Horseback riding along David Thompson's first trail, the Blaeberry River. Triple C, RR 1, S8, C8, Golden, BC V0A 1H0. (604) 344-2670.

Golden has a **municipal campground** with fine evening interpretative programs for the public, including a walk to the Columbia River Valley Wetlands, and a review of history at the Golden Museum. (604) 344-5169.

Top of the World Tours offer four-wheeler trips for hiking and scenery. Box 1974, Golden, BC V0A 1H0.

B.C. Wildlife Museum east of Golden on Highway 1. Stuffed wild animals. A world record grizzly bear. Box 1854, Golden, BC V0A 1H0. (604) 344-6330.

Nikki's Restaurant, at the only traffic light in town, has great pasta, steaks and pleasant decor. Box 1680, Golden, BC V0A 1H0.

Kingmik Expeditions offers dog sled tours in winter, an unusual way to see the sights. 644 Highway 95, Nicholson, Golden, BC V0A 1H0. (604) 344-7288.

National and provincial **parks** abound along both sides of the Columbia River. For information: Kootenay National Park, Box 220, Radium Hot Springs, BC V0A 1M0. (604) 347-9615. Although it is about an hour's drive from Golden, the **Yoho National Park** should not be missed with its startling sheer rock faces and broad glaciers. Center of the Yoho area is the town of Field on Highway 1. At Yoho in 1909, the **Burgess Shale** was discovered. Scientists are uncovering the best examples in the world of pre-Cambrian marine life and fossils, 530 million years old, some never before seen. It was named a World Heritage Site in 1981.

Kinbasket Lake Outfitters is the only known service providing boat trips on the vast Kinbasket Lake. Almost two hundred years ago David Thompson, miners and missionaries traveled this lake. Box 4137, Golden BC V0A 1H0. (604) 344-2277.

Golden has **Annual Rodeo** in September, Labor Day Weekend. At tiny Parson, south of Golden, there's a July **Blue Grass & Chili Bash**.

Revelstoke area:

Revelstoke Chamber of Commerce, 300 First Street West, P. O. Box 490, Revelstoke, BC V0E 2S0. (604) 837-5345.

Mica Dam, daily tours, drive north from Revelstoke on Highway 23 to end. No facilities except basic supplies and gas, can eat during limited hours at company cafeteria. Crude boat launching facilities for *small* power boats on lake. (604) 834-7382.

Mica Dam area. A gravel road on the south side of lake takes you to the plaque commemorating David Thompson's discovery of the Columbia at the Wood River/Canoe River/Columbia River junction—which is across the lake.

Revelstoke Dam Visitor Centre north of Revelstoke has self-guided tours, open mid-March to November. (604) 837-6211.

Regent Inn, 112 Victoria Road, P.O. Box 450, Revelstoke, BC V0E 2S0. (604) 837-2107. Downtown location, quality accommodations, restaurant and lounge.

McGregor's Motor Inn, 201 West 3rd Street, Revelstoke, BC V0E 2S0, pool, sauna, whirlpool, restaurant, pub, good food.

During summer live entertainment in bandshell on **Grizzly Plaza** downtown.

Revelstoke Heritage Walking & Driving Tour, see Chamber of Commerce or TravelInfo offices for brochure. See Revelstoke Courthouse, replica of Old Bailey, London. Across street in old house is Courtyard Cafe, excellent food.

Feel like a gnat at the **giant cedars park** about eighteen miles east of Revelstoke on TransCanada 1.

Alpine Rafting Company, Alpine Village Shopping Centre, downtown Revelstoke. (604) 837-5378. Same outfit as in Golden.

Ski and gawk at winter scenery with Cat Powder Skiing Inc., like **heliskiing** only access by tracked snow machine. Box 1479, Revelstoke, BC V0E 2S0. Call collect (604) 837-9489.

Mount Revelstoke National Park. Mostly day sites. Ask for brochure about hiking trails, long and short. Great views of Columbia River north and south. Cross-country and downhill skiing in winter. Wonderful wildflowers in summer. Revelstoke has Alpine Mountain Festival second week of August.

L & R Nelles Ranch is a bed and breakfast house on a working quarter horse ranch. Larry Nelles, formerly a coach for the Canadian National Ski Team, offers daily trail rides on fine horses in area toward Mount Begbie overlooking Columbia River. Nice rooms, sociable evenings. Highway 23 South, Box 430, Revelstoke, BC V0E 2S0. (604) 837-3800.

Black Forest Restaurant just west of Revelstoke on TransCanada Highway. Chef Kurt Amsler offers continental delicacies like Hasen Pfeffer in red wine sauce, Swiss cheese or Provencal fondues, fancy desserts, in a Bavarian-style chalet. (604) 837-3495.

Casual dining in Revelstoke at **Zala's Pizza and Steak House**, family prices, 1601 Victoria Road.

Scenic flights over glaciers and rivers in a safe, twin-engine Cessna Skymaster, Silvertip Aviation (604) 837-4414, from Revelstoke Airport.

Three Valley Gap Motor Inn has excellent rooms and suites, historic **Eagle Pass area**, lake, beach and historic town. Steak barbecue parties with live entertainment at Golden Wheel Saloon for groups of thirty or more. Weddings at historic St. Stephens Church (see text). Box 860, Revelstoke, BC V0E 2S0. (604) 837-2109.

Downie R.V. Resorts Ltd., on the Columbia River 43 miles north of Revelstoke on Highway 23 North, has hookups, a limited store, gas, and boat launch. Canoe rentals, gold panning, cross-country skiing. Historic location since Big Bend Highway days. Two housekeeping cabins.

The many moods of the grizzly bear are a favorite subject for **Revelstoke sculptor**, William Alonzo Cameron, using soapstone and serpentine found near Revelstoke. Ask local store or call (604) 837-4127.

Mount Mackenzie Ski Area three-and-one-half miles outside of Revelstoke has T-bar, two chairlifts, one handle tow, ski school, snacks, etc. (604) 837-5268.

Williamson's Lake Campground. Beach. Three miles south of Revelstoke at 1818 Airport Way. Hookups for RV's and tent sites.

Revelstoke Golf Club above the Big Eddy of the Columbia River is open to the public, has restaurant and lounge. Originally the clubhouse was the 1904 Revelstoke Turf Club. Ask for brochure about it.

Ask TravelInfo or Chamber of Commerce for brochure on **snowmobile trails**.

Revelstoke Historical Association's Museum at 315 West First Street will help you understand the interesting past of this railroad and alpine town.

Canoeing on the Columbia River between Revelstoke Dam and Mica Dam is magnificent with usually smooth water (watch out for sudden squalls, though) and wonderful reflections of glacier-covered crags. Enough flat land periodically for campsites and a few boat launches (Five Mile Provincial Park, Martha Lake Provincial Park, Downie Creek Provincial Park) and **primitive campsites** off Highway 23 north. While camping, remember you are in bear country—black and grizzly—and take precautions with food to avoid attracting them. Watch out for ups and down of water levels due to dams' varying usage.

SnowFest is a week-long celebration of the often impressive snow packs of the area, first week of February, crazy events like outhouse races and cordwood curling.

Boulder Mountain Ride-In the week prior to SnowFest has snowmobilers joining for a trek to the top of Boulder Mountain—locals and visitors. Bring your own or inquire of Chamber of Commerce regarding possible rentals (scarce).

Rogers Pass lies between Revelstoke and Golden on the Trans Canada Highway with an interpretive center at the pass—movies about Canadian Pacific Railway, avalanches, history etc., large lodge with dining facilities.

Outfitter Phil deMaze gets good marks from locals for **horse pack trips** into the wilderness around Revelstoke. (604) 837-2397.

Selkirk Tangiers Helicopter Skiing Ltd. operates in the Monashees and Selkirks west and east of Revelstoke. Box 1409, Golden, BC V0A 1H0. (604) 344-6016.

Arrow Lakes and Kootenay Lake area:

Nakusp Infocentre, Box 387, Nakusp, BC V0G 1R0. (604) 265-4234. Nakusp Heritage Walking Tour brochure.

Suggest obtaining **Kootenay Visitor's Magazine** (604) 489-3455 or **Go & Do** 1-800-663-4619 for activities near Columbia River in Canada.

On the **Arrow Lakes**, R & E Sports, 86 4th Avenue, Nakusp rents small boats for fishing. A reliable reputation. Scottie's Resort north of Castlegar is a marina with facilities, about six miles above the Keenleyside Dam. Hiking trails abound and good swimming, though waters are usually chilly in this area of melting snow. Great lonely scenery; one can imagine the Hudson's Bay traders traversing these long open stretches of water.

Lord Minto Restaurant in Nakusp in an old United Church remembers paddlewheeler steamer days and gold fever with artifacts, including stained glass art of a paddlewheeler. The *Minto* was the last steamer to ply the Arrow Lakes (see text). Selections include perogies (potato and cheddar filling, a meat pie popular with Eastern Europeans), beef stroganoff. 93 5th Avenue, Nakusp. (604) 265-4033.

Among **interesting books** concentrating on paddlewheelers are: *Paddlewheels on the Frontier* by Art Downs (Sidney, BC: Gray's Publishing, 1972), and *Sternwheelers and Steam Tugs* by Robert D. Turner (Victoria: Sono Nis Press, 1984).

Directly on the Arrow Lakes (which is the Columbia River, remember) is **The Goose Downs**, a bed and breakfast house, and an arts and crafts store, about nine miles south of Nakusp on Highway 6. Box 39, Burton, BC V0G 1E0. (604) 265-3139.

In steamer days Nakusp was a lively port and shipbuilding center. The venerable **Leland Hotel** on the lakeshore claims to be the oldest continuously operating hotel in British Columbia, since 1892. When steamers docked in older days, prospectors and travelers ran up the bank to compete for the few available rooms. Owner Klaus Toering is deep into renovation of the hotel, resurrecting old woodwork and grillworks, finding ancient stove-heated water heater and furnaces with pokers and scrapers in the basement. It has a ways to go but for historic overnighting at a very reasonable rate, several rooms have original-style furnishings but with bathrooms. Coffee shop and deck overlook the Columbia. Box 640 Nakusp, BC V0G 1R0. (604) 265-4221 or 3314.

Houseboat holidays on the Arrow Lakes at W-4 Park and Marina in Nakusp. 47-foot vessels, and houseboats are scarce on Arrow Lakes. R.R. #1, Waterfield Road, Nakusp, BC V0G 1R0. (604) 265-3553. In the early 1900s the CPR maintained a houseboat for rent on Kootenay Lake, that could be towed to your choice cove.

Nakusp Hot Springs, eight miles east of town. Cedar Chalets (Box 172, Nakusp), (604) 265-4505. Also thirty campsites along the gurgling Kuskanax River. The hot springs are led into a modern pool with change facilities and are open to the public year-round. Cross-country skiing possible nearby.

There are only two places to cross the Arrow Lakes from Revelstoke to Castlegar (162 miles): Thirty miles south of Revelstoke is the **Shelter Bay-Galena Bay Ferry**. Thirty-four miles south of Nakusp is the **Fauquier–Needles Ferry** (Highway 6 goes toward the Okanagan Valley).

To understand the juxtaposition of Kootenay Lake and Arrow Lakes and their interrelationships for gold mining, shipping, steamers and railroads, it is helpful to visit the remaining towns and ghost towns between the lakes. The few towns along **Kootenay Lake** and its tributaries such as the Lardeau are important links, as well as those in the **Slocan Valley**. Among them are New Denver and Silverton on Slocan Lake. Silverton has a mining museum with excellent displays of mining machinery, big and little. New Denver has the Silvery Slocan Museum, open every day in July and August.

At **New Denver** is **Lucerne Restaurant** at the junction of Highways 6 and 31A, an attractive little coffee shop with fantastic blueberry pancakes.

Ten miles east of New Denver is the half ghost town of **Sandon**, well worth a visit to see the mining museum and old buildings that withstood a major flood of Carpenter Creek. The operating Treminco mine does not have tours, but one can see equipment working on the heights above.

Idaho Peak at 2,280 meters (7,480 feet), is the acknowledged most spectacular view destination. Remember: This is bear country. Leave Sandon on a rather steep natural gravel road; four-wheel drive is recommended. Usually not snow free until July 1—ask first. Noted for matchless display of alpine flowers.

The **Tin Cup Cafe** at Sandon—at far end of town in an old home being restored. Old stove, miner decor. Huckleberry pie, homemade miners' stew.

Kaslo, about 60 miles east of Arrow Lakes on Kootenay Lake, has survived the demise of the mining fever to be a charming small tourist village with an art and summer stock facility housed in the Langham Cultural Centre, a hotel building of 1883. The **Festival of the Arts** takes place in mid-August for two weeks.

Kootenay Lake from **Kaslo to Nelson** is a summer playground of houseboating, fishing, windsurfing, hot springs, pubs and every tourist comfort. Fishing at Trout Lake and the Lardeau is excellent. The gravel bed of the Lardeau River is the spawning ground of giant Gerrard Rainbow Trout, which can reach 25 pounds. Cody Caves. Near Nelson at Balfour a ferry transports autos and passengers to access the east side of the lake.

The **old paddlewheeler** *Moyie* is under reconstruction at 324 Front Street, Kaslo. It is representative of many of the boats plying the Columbia River system. Tours daily.

To see the **gold country** of the Selkirks on horseback, Mistaya Outfitting gets good marks. Box 28, Silverton, BC V0G 2B0. (604) 358-7787 early or late.

Nelson Travel Infocentre, 225 Hall Street, Nelson, BC V1L 5X4. (604) 352-3433.

Nelson has a Summer School of Arts in mid-July and an "Artwalk" June-September. In July it has a Summer Festival and a Kootenay Classic Cycle Race and in February a Sno Fest. Nelson clings to an abruptly rising shore from the Kootenay River, where it swings westward from the lake to keep its date with the Columbia River at Castlegar. The attractive, tree-lined streets of Nelson belie the rough and tough reputation it once had in miners' days. Today it woos tourism. The Canadian International College hosts students from the Orient for intercultural experiences. Its history is irrevocably tied to that of the Columbia River Valley at Castlegar and Trail, so Nelson must be visited to gain a complete picture of this area's history.

Nelson has maintained or regained its ornate Victorian architecture and claims more than 350 turn-of-the-century buildings designated as heritage sites. Ask TravelInfo for a brochure on **Architectural Heritage Tours**.

Heritage Inn is an old hotel with period restaurant, pub and rooms. A slice of Nelson history right downtown, 422 Vernon Street, Nelson, BC (604) 352-5331.

A remarkable French country menu is lovingly turned out at **Le Chatelet Restaurant**, 903 Nelson Avenue, Nelson, almost under the Kootenay River bridge. A Frenchman with the unlikely name of Eric Eriksen, the chef/owner, cooks unusual turnovers, shaped artistically, in a wood-burning brick oven, open at the front so you can watch your dinner bake. Specialties also include DeSevigne, a savory stew, pasta dishes, St. Honorat—a 5-inch sea shell filled with crab, fish, scallops and shrimp. Eric's wife, Essylt, and daughter share in the management. The Eriksens grow most of their own herbs and garden produce, and bake their own breads. Dining here is French experience in largely British Canada. (604) 354-3911.

Willow Point Lodge is a bed and breakfast above Kootenay Lake. Edwardian architecture. Author enjoyed hand-picked huckleberry pancakes on the front porch. Does outdoor tours. R.R. #1, Nelson, BC V1L 5P4. (604) 825-9411.

Ainsworth Hot Springs Resort has first-class rooms and dining, as well as the hot springs. Springs emerge in an eerily lighted, horseshoe-shaped cave. Box 1268, Ainsworth Hot Springs, BC V0G 1A0. (604) 229-4212.

Castlegar area:

Castlegar **Chamber of Commerce**, 1995 6th Avenue, Castlegar, BC V1N 4B7. (604) 365-6313. National Tourism Week, third weekend in May.

Zuckerberg Park, Castlegar. Follow main street and watch for signs. Off Larch Street. Parking area. Walk across suspension bridge to island.

Doukhobor Historical Village (see text), near junction of Highway 3 and 3A. (604) 365-6622.

Brilliant Cultural Centre off Broadwater Road at Brilliant, north of Kootenay River.

West Kootenay National Exhibition Centre hosts traveling art and cultural exhibits, including those from Royal British Columbia Museum, Canadian Craft Museum, and Communications Canada. Has included exhibits on fur trade, quilts, ancient Chinese ceramics. A handsome building near the Doukhobor Village.

Brilliant Dam on the Kootenay River north, Highway 3A.

Hugh Keenleyside Dam upriver from Castlegar.

Verigin's Tomb above Kootenay River contains the remains of Peter V. Verigin (Peter the Lordly); his son, Peter P. Verigin (also called Chistiakov, Peter the Purger, Peter the Cleanser); their wives; and Anna P. Markova, daughter of Peter P. Verigin and mother of today's Doukhobor leader, John J. Verigin. Take Broadwater Road toward Robson, turn to right on indicated road in about a mile. Open days.

Leaded glass and antiques from Scotland and elsewhere make an unusual decor for **Gabriel Restaurant** in Castlegar. Specialties there include four cuts of prime rib and charbroiled or barbecued back ribs. 1432 Columbia Avenue, Castlegar, BC V1N 3K3. (604) 365-6028.

Pass Creek Regional Park, Castlegar-Robson, has a thirty-unit camping facility with beaches. Take road toward Syringa Creek from north end Columbia River bridge,

Syringa Creek Provincial Park, big campground right on Lower Arrow Lake. Take road on north side of Columbia River to its end from Columbia River Bridge, Castlegar. Get there by noon to hope for a spot in high tourist time. Fine for RVs. Follow signs.

Castlegar Museum is in the old railway station of Canadian Pacific Railway built in 1907, local and CPR history. Columbia Avenue in North Castlegar. Open Monday through Saturday, 8:00 A.M. to 5:00 P.M.

Sunfest and chili cook-off the first weekend of June at Castlegar.

Southern Interior Charters takes you **fishing by boat**, guided tours (some overnight) traveling the Columbia River and Arrow Lakes. Best season for trout and char is early spring and fall, kokanee in summer. 561 8th Avenue, Castlegar, BC V1N 1N7. (604) 365-2324.

Fireside Motor Inn (604-365-2128) at the south entrance of Castlegar is a pleasant overnight stop with excellent restaurant. **Scotsman Motor Inn**, (604) 365-2177, in same area offers modestly priced rooms, with sturgeon-sized cinnamon rolls for breakfast.

Trail area:

Trail District Chamber of Commerce, 843 Rossland Avenue, Trail, BC V1R 4S8. (604) 368-3144.

Cominco wants to show you how lead and zinc are extracted in its 3,400-employee **smelter at Trail**. Monday through Friday at 10:00 A.M. retired Cominco workers provide free guided tours. No cameras or video equipment. The tours take two to three hours, there are stairs and long pants are required (no shorts). Ask Chamber of Commerce.

See the Columbia River running swift and free from Trail's waterfront **Gyro Park**, two miles long.

Colander Restaurant, Trail, gives a taste of boarding house days, when throngs of single smelter and mine workers ate at Kootenay Hotel. Angelina Infanti once operated that boarding house, and in 1990 worked for Colander. Today a huge meal of spaghetti and trimmings is modestly priced. Colander is downtown at 1475 Cedar Avenue, always crowded. Take a walk after dinner to the nearby Columbia River.

Terra Nova Motor Inn on Highway 22 downtown has modern hotel rooms, a restaurant, pub and a real nightclub with exciting decor. (604) 368-3355.

Trail Museum of history and sports figures. Near Columbia River bridge on Highway 22 downtown. Trail had a history of intense sports activity, winning championships at hockey especially. Adjacent is the **Cominco Memorial Centre**, a sports and recreational center. Home of the Trail Smoke Eaters Hockey Club. Those single men had to do something besides work.

Silver City Days is about the second week of May each year, an Italian festival with historic overtones. Jet boat races on the Columbia River.

Rossland, site of **LeRoi Mine**, offers mine tours of the LeRoi, also a museum. Last tour is at 4:00 P.M. You go underground into the actual mine and see how hardrock mining was done. Rossland Gold Mine & Museum Complex, Box 26, Rossland, BC V0G 1Y0. (604) 362-7722. A short way west of Rossland on Highway 3B.

Red Mountain Ski Area, just west of Rossland. Four lifts and also alpine skiing. A popular and challenging set of runs. Ski shop. The area has at least three hotels/lodges and a bed and breakfast. **Carolyn's Bed and Breakfast** squarely faces the mountain and has one suite with a fireplace.

Winter Carnival in February brings lively ski crowd, torchlight parade, dancing, tobogganning, ice sculptures and bobsled races—all at Rossland and Red Mountain.

Golden City Days the second weekend of September in Rossland celebrates mining days. Includes can-can dancers and kite flying.

As a ski and summer destination village, **Rossland** has many charming and mountain-style hotels and motels. Restaurants abound. Historic buildings are reminiscent of pioneer days. From Trail the highway is up all the way, for Rossland lies about four thousand feet above Trail in mountains all but deserted now.

Gold Fever Follies, Rossland, plays to amused audiences at the historic Miners' Hall, built by the union serving local gold miners in the early century. It's a drama about the area, not very serious. Main Street of Rossland.

Mountain **biking and hiking trails** are listed in a brochure entitled "Rossland Recreational Trail Map." In mid-September the Rubberhead Classic Mountain Bike Race is held.

The **Creston Valley Wildlife Management Area**, although not in the Columbia River Valley, is a 17,000-acre wetlands near Kootenay Lake between Trail and Creston, and welcomes photographers and hikers, fishermen and canoeists. Towers from which you can see the area without disturbing wildlife. Box 640, Creston, BC V0B 1G0. (604) 428-3260.

U.S. Border to Priest Rapids

CANADA

British   Columbia
Washington   Oroville

UNITED   STATES   Trail

Northport

OKANOGAN R.   KETTLE R.   COLUMBIA R.   PEND OREILLE RIVER

Riverside   Kettle Falls
Omak   Colville
Okanogan   COLVILLE

Mountains   OMAK LAKE   INDIAN   Gifford
                                                              FRANKLIN D. ROOSEVELT LAKE
(To North Cascades Hwy.)   CHIEF JOSEPH DAM   Inchelium
Brewster   Nespelem   Hunters

LAKE CHELAN   Pateros   GRAND COULEE DAM   Coulee Dam   RESERVATION

Cascade   Chelan   Bridgeport   NORTH DAM   SPOKANE RIVER

WELLS DAM   Grand Coulee
DRY FALLS DAM   BANKS L.   Electric City
ROCKY REACH DAM   Spokane
WENATCHEE RIVER   DRY FALLS   Coulee City
Wenatchee   Dry Falls

ROCK ISLAND DAM   Ephrata

North   COLUMBIA   MOSES LAKE
Ellensburg   Moses Lake

Vantage
                                POTHOLES RESERVOIR

WANAPUM DAM

Mattawa   RIVER
Yakima   HANFORD
                     RESERVATION   RIVER
YAKIMA   PRIEST RAPIDS DAM   SNAKE
INDIAN
RESERVATION   YAKIMA RIVER   (Tri-Cities)
                        RIVER   Richland   Pasco   Whitman Mission
                              Kennewick   Walla Walla
                                    WALLA   WALLA R.

THE COLUMBIA FROM CANADA
TO THE TRI-CITIES

L E G E N D

– – –   International Border
– · – · –   Reservation
●   Community
⌂   Dam

5   0   10   25

Scale in Statute Miles

1991 David Jungkuntz

N

South of the Border

Little has changed today along this free-flowing turbulent stretch of water from Castlegar to the upper reaches of Lake Roosevelt near Northport, except that powerful boats whisk water skiers along the deadly whirlpools. One skier said with an evil grin, "You can look right down into the dark center hole, and it makes it more fun."

Twenty miles south of the border, the hamlet of Little Dalles was settled about 1865 to serve as the southerly terminus for riverboat traffic. No sensible riverboat captain regularly challenged The Dalles below town, a washing machine of a rapids. However, when the *Forty-Nine* was launched near The Dalles in 1865 to serve Big Bend prospectors, its captain, Leonard White, did challenge The Dalles rapids to rocket downstream and dock in front of old Fort Colvile to pick up Christina McDonald for this premier voyage. (Her father Angus saluted the sternwheeler with a volley from a little brass cannon.) Little traffic ensued after White's few trips until the Canadian Pacific Railway came to Revelstoke and interest was rekindled in the Columbia River area.

To tap the growing north/south traffic, D. C. Corbin swiftly extended his Spokane Falls & Northern Railroad to Little Dalles by 1890, where he connected with riverboats of the Columbia and Kootenay Steam Navigation Company. Responding, also, to the profitable mines at Rossland (Red Mountain) in British Columbia, Corbin hastened to extend his railroad ten miles north in 1892, where the resulting new settlement, Northport, eclipsed The Dalles. From there the logical course toward Red Mountain was across the Columbia and up Sheep Creek Canyon.

Angry Indian police were guarding the far shore against encroaching would-be settlers. The Congressional Act of July 1, 1892, restored the north part of the Colville Reservation to the public domain but provided for initial allotments of 51,653 acres to 660 Indian people, before non-Indians could apply. It took a senate bill to grant permission for the railroad to cross the land.

While Corbin's railroad proceeded, a stage line ran between Northport and Rossland, and the steamer *Lytton*, Columbia and Kootenay Steam Navigation Company's early sternwheeler, operated between Northport and Trail.

Meanwhile, entrepreneurs were constructing the Northport Smelter, opened for business in 1898, especially hoping to process ore from Rossland's LeRoi Mine and beat out the Trail Smelter. While Corbin's railway supplied ore, the Northport Smelter prospered, employing about two hundred men initially, six hundred at its zenith. The sound of saw and hammer was constant as two thousand people struggled for housing. By 1904, the Trail smelter had won out, and there was insufficient ore to feed the furnaces.

As suddenly as it began, Northport became a virtual ghost town, flickering to life briefly in 1915, when the smelter processed lead. The only significant mining was for gold; transient Chinese worked the Columbia River bars, and the outlines of their unique "washings" or gravelly flumes are still visible. A sawmill, logging companies, farms and orchards kept Northport alive for a few hundred residents. All that remains of the old smelter is its smokestack on the sawmill grounds.

During prohibition days such border communities were accustomed to strangers in autos or pack trains passing through the back roads. A most innovative bootlegger sent cargos down the Columbia from Canada in sealed hollow logs especially marked so a waiting American accomplice could identify them and pull them in.

At China Bend one evening, two men requested the ferry operator to take them across as fast as possible. It was too windy to be safe, the operator said. The fidgeting passengers offered the operator big money if he would risk it. When the wind died down a little, the operator made the trip, receiving $25, big money, indeed.

Cable ferries linked small communities on either side of the river. Such transport across the Columbia could be adventurous. Cables could break, stranding passengers in midstream until someone came by rowboat to rescue them. A high wind or extra-strong current could cause the ferry to revolve completely and make braids out of the cable. Where cable ferries were not available, settlers (even young children) rowed across the river to socialize, with little thought as to what could happen should they be swept downriver into the rapids or over Kettle Falls.

On one occasion a cable ferry did break loose entirely and hurtle down river. Twenty-seven miles below lay Kettle Falls, a 20-foot drop. That evening at Marcus, just above the falls, Carl Brauner was fixing dinner when he heard pounding hoofbeats. A wild-looking man threw himself off his lathered horse, crying to Brauner, "Quick, get your boat! The Bossburg ferry is coming down the river with passengers aboard." Brauner raced to his boat and rowed strongly to the middle of the broad river, managing to remove the screaming passengers before the ferry boat fell to destruction over Kettle Falls.

Brauner's home at Marcus was within sight of the decaying buildings of Fort Colvile. Until its official abandonment in 1871 (although various McDonalds lived on there), Fort Colvile was one of the most influential trading posts in the Hudson's Bay Company system.

Sir George Simpson, Hudson's Bay Company governor, ordered the construction of the fort in 1824, upon the earlier recommendation of Alexander Kennedy that Fort Spokane should be replaced. David Thompson of the North West Company and Finan McDonald had built Spokane House as a distribution center ten miles northwest of today's Spokane in 1810 to 1811. The location was delightful for *living*, located in a pleasant valley, but was out of the way for fur brigades, since it was not on the Columbia River. Spokane House personnel moved to adjacent Fort Spokane (Hudson's Bay Company) after merger of the two companies in 1821, and abandoned Spokane House. Now the fort, too, was to be phased out.

Thus, in 1825, Fort Colvile began to rise about a mile above Kettle Falls in a broad valley protected from wintry winds by low mountains. Construction was entrusted to John Work, a tough, capable man living up to his name. He and his crew completed enough buildings that Spokane personnel could move.

The complex closedown of Fort Spokane took place in March, 1826. Two strings of packhorses, one of sixty-two animals, the other of eighty, augmented by several boats, transferred everything. Employees unscrewed the iron hinges from doors. The formerly lively post became a shambles overnight, and friendly Spokan Indians viewed the move with consternation.

Construction continued over the next few years. The trading post itself was a wooden fort enclosed with high pickets. At one corner there was a blockhouse or bastion with a four-sided roof and three portholes for rifles and another for the cannon, a small, ineffectual piece never fired in anger. The factor's home was a relatively substantial place with a large living room warmed by an odd adobe fireplace so narrow that one could insert logs only vertically. There were offices, storage areas for furs, storage granaries, a blacksmith shop, a carpenter's shop, two houses for visitors, an Indian hall to shelter native dignitaries who came to call, trappers' barracks and other structures. Outside the stockade were extensive farming areas, barns, servants' housing, bakehouses and a boathouse.

Responding to Simpson's orders that forts should be frugal and grow their own food, post personnel planted fields of potatoes, vegetables and grain between the river and the chalky-white limestone bluffs. The Catholic fathers at St. Paul Mission operated a school, available to all, especially Indian children; and in 1863 Mary Meyers opened a school on the Colville River for white and mixed-blood children.

In his memoirs, Ranald, the son of Archibald McDonald (Chief Trader 1834 to 1842, Chief Factor 1842 to 1844), remembered the gracious parties in the commodious dining room of the fort, when the supply boat or the semiannual express came from Fort Vancouver or York Factory. Guests were pampered from a richly stocked cellar of liquors and a groaning pantry of meats and vegetables. Those invited might include hunters, Indian chiefs, Hudson's Bay Company inspectors, trappers, all seated in order of importance, his father at the head of table, women and children at the foot. From newspapers and letters received in the express, Archibald often read aloud to those hungry for any information about the world beyond the Columbia River.

Below the fort the river quickened to enter a canyon leading through rock-strewn rapids to two great falls. The main torrent swirled boulders around with such force that they wore depressions like kettles in the rocks, hence its name Kettle Falls or, in French, *Les Chaudières*.

Kettle Falls was the most revered Indian fishing site on the upper Columbia River. A rich variety of tribes, cousins from ancient days, lived all across the boundary country—Spokan, Lake, Nespelem, Okanogan, Sanpoil and others. In late June, these tribes and distant visitors gathered on the west bank, the fishing preceded by the First Salmon Dance. Presiding over the assemblage was a salmon chief, whose sacred duty was to apportion equitably all salmon caught. A number of salmon were allowed to pass above the falls to spawn upstream. Then the salmon chief directed a fisherman to catch one fish, boil it and let him taste it. If all was well, the salmon chief approved the start of fishing.

The Indians used spears or uniquely shaped baskets of willow, about 4 feet deep, 5 to 6 feet wide, 20 feet long. Salmon attempting to leap up through the falls usually fell back several times before attaining the top. Fishermen thrust the baskets beneath the falling salmon, and when the catch filled the basket or became too heavy to handle, they dumped it out on shore. Waiting hands butchered and salted down the fish in containers or hung them on drying racks.

A spear fisherman stood precariously on a platform hanging out over the river, spear poised. Spears and gaffs had an ingenious "fail-safe" character so that, if the fish were too weighty, the spearhead would detach and play out along a strong cord. Otherwise, the fisherman might be yanked into the river, a foaming caldron.

Witnessing Indian fishing in 1860, Lieutenant Charles Wilson of the Royal Engineers said that two men stripped and jumped into the water beneath the falls, where they knocked the caught salmon senseless and passed them to handlers on shore. The men stood right in the falling water, half-drowning.

Salmon-gathering time was not all work. Dancing, stick or bone games, and horse racing filled idle moments. In later years when settlers had formed the towns of Kettle Falls and Colville, Indians (and sometimes settlers) raced through the streets of town. A popular event was the salmon relay. A contestant grabbed a big live salmon up to 30 pounds from a trough, ran 100 yards with the struggling and slippery fish, then back to the trough. Often salmon and contestant wound up rolling around together in the dust.

When construction began on Grand Coulee Dam in 1933, the Kettle Falls salmon runs began to fade. In 1940 the Indians held a poignant "mourning ceremony" to mark the loss of the traditional fishing ground, since fish cannot go upstream beyond the dam. At the Colville Tribal Museum, Grand Coulee, one may see replicas or original baskets and spears, and fishing scenes painted from memory. An Indian historian and tribal volunteers answer questions.

Heavily intermarried, the Indians and settlers have a remarkably amicable history—especially since the initial behavior of the intruding Americans was sometimes unsavory. In pioneer days Indians and settlers starved together when times were tough, and worked together at logging and ranching—in fact, often the "Indians" were the "cowboys."

Among the earliest settlers of Kettle Falls was Carl Brauner, rescuer of the cable ferry passengers. He came from Austria in the 1920s to work on the Columbia River, building a tough rowboat to catch drift logs—logs that escaped from booms far upriver or trees that fell into the river naturally. During high water the logs might have come all the way from the Pend Oreille River in Idaho or from the Columbia's Big Bend country. He boomed them and sold them to a mill on the Kettle River.

So turbulent was the Columbia River that logs would "jump out" of standard booms. Brauner screwed a metal eye into each log and threaded chains or ropes through to hold them in. One spring, as Brauner attempted to tow a log boom into the mouth of the Kettle River, the engine on his 26-foot boat quit about a half-mile above the falls. Stubbornly refusing to lose the boom and boat over the falls, Brauner jumped into the icy spring water to replace a key in the propeller.

This intrepid pioneer also ran the Marcus cable ferry for a decade. He was known to climb over the river on the cable, hand-over-hand, to replace the pulley when it fell off.

The site of Fort Colvile is now a broad circular bay. The centripetal action of the river has deposited up to seventy feet of silt there along a bank. During a recent low water period, the river cut into the silt banks and drew it back into the mainstream. Bill Brauner, Carl's son, who runs the family logging operation and was on the city water board, said, "The water was thick as soup going over the falls for almost a month. The town of Kettle Falls fought to sort out the sand and silt from the drinking water, and save the pumps from being damaged by the sand."

Periodically water levels in Lake Roosevelt retreat so that Kettle Falls is uncovered, its roar heard again with nostalgia by nearby residents. In 1976, exceptionally low water uncovered the site of Fort Colvile and old fishing camp areas, yielding a rich harvest of artifacts.

When Lake Roosevelt backed up behind Grand Coulee Dam, the original town of Kettle Falls had to be moved to higher ground. Near the town's original site today is an extensive campground and a new marina and boat rental facility (including a few houseboats).

Nearby, Boise Cascade's plywood mill employs about four hundred people in the region, a successor to several smaller mills. The logs come in by truck, not river boom; the river is used only for occasional log storage. The plywood process uses, not large logs, but those 7 to 20 inches in diameter. They are peeled down to veneers of 1/8 to 3/16 inch for exterior sheeting.

Adjacent to Boise Cascade is the Washington Water Power Generating Station, environmentally exciting. When the state's residents became concerned about environmental factors, wigwam incinerators burning tons of sawdust generated by sawmills were pinpointed as polluters. In 1983 Washington Water Power, the private utility for northeast Washington, installed a plant to generate power from sawdust, the first in the United States. Trucks haul waste wood and chips to the plant for burning in a closed system (the resultant ash is captured), creating steam to run turbines for power generation—an output currently that can serve twenty-three thousand residential customers per day. Like the Trail smelter, which alleviated pollution by turning sulphurous emissions into useful fertilizer, the new generating plant turns potentially wasted or damaging by-products into "good" channels.

In 1921, two adventurers made trips down the 1,214-mile length of the Columbia River. Lewis R. Freeman was accompanied by a photographer to make a movie of the trip and got away first. M. J. Lorraine, age sixty-seven, did it in a rowboat just for fun weeks later, reading Freeman's feature in Sunset Magazine when he passed through Northport. Both men wrote books that reflected great respect for the seemingly endless series of rapids between Kettle Falls and Pasco at the time. It is interesting to touch on their travels before relating the saga of two major dams that would seriously change the channel of the Columbia River—Bonneville Dam on the lower Columbia, Grand Coulee on the upper, the latter to drown Kettle Falls.

Freeman traveled as far south as Hunter's, seventy-five miles below the border, with riverboat pioneer Captain Frank Armstrong as his guide. The men spent their last night together in a farmer's barn, where belled cows kept them awake and licked their faces.

As Armstrong's replacement locals suggested (always with a devious grin) a river pilot, Ike Emerson. After much difficulty, Freeman did locate Emerson and found him to be quite a character but seemingly capable. Emerson suggested that Freeman and the photographer should throw their boat atop his lumber raft to go through Hell Gate Rapids (below Hunter's). The raft was 100 feet long, 30 feet wide and stacked several feet high with cordwood for downriver markets. Through the stacks one could see the river, flowing darkly beneath. Onlookers told morbid stories of those who had failed to manage Hell Gate. As if to emphasize the dangers awaiting them, Emerson's youthful helper fell into the river first thing, disappearing under the raft, only to come up safely at the rear and clamber aboard.

En route downriver toward Hell Gate, Freeman reported that "the sun painted the sky and the weird pinnacles and bluffs of the bleak shore with colourings brighter and more varied than any I had believed to exist outside of the canyons of the Colorado and the Yellowstone. Saffron melting to fawn and dun was there, and vivid streaks that were almost scarlet. ... A fluted cliff-face ... flushed a pink so delicate that one seemed to be looking at it through a rosy mist." (Lewis Freeman, *Down the Columbia* [New York: Dodd, Mead and Company, 1921], 249.)

The dramatic 1,000-foot face of Whitestone signaled the approach to Hell Gate—"a pair of black rock jaws, froth-flecked and savage ... closing together in an attempt to bite the river in two." A long black reef, jutting out from the left bank, choked the river into a narrowing channel against a rocky wall, the water shooting between the two obstructions to split against a rock island 100 yards farther down. Thereafter, it negotiated a Z turn.

Emerson had built an oversized sweep to steer the raft, its handle a 4-inch in diameter wooden piece about 20 feet long. A motor launch steadied the head of the raft. Freeman's impression of the whole wicked rapid was blurred activity ... the water of the black-walled chasm ricocheting off the basaltic walls, a foam geyser of water tumbling over the stern, which swung broadside and straightened out with mighty efforts on the sweep. And then they were through.

Elderly Lorraine, an unruffled pragmatist somewhat smug about his ability to handle any kind of water, also wound up at Hunter's in late September. About a mile below, he was hit suddenly with a wall of wind that sent sand flying and whipped up the river into whitecaps. Dust from the Big Bend farms obscured the sky (a condition the author experienced there in 1990). Retreating to shore, Lorraine spent a fitful night. In the morning he found that his boat had broken loose with all his possessions aboard, even his camera and typewriter. After searching all day along the shores, he found the boat six miles down river, her mooring line luckily caught on an obstruction. Nothing was lost.

When Lorraine reached the infamous Hell Gate, he approached it stern-first in his heavily built rowboat and slid quickly through the opening. He deliberately steered his craft toward the perpendicular wall Freeman mentioned, skillfully turning when 100 feet away, running across the rushing water bow first. Again he turned the rowboat stern-first and came out of the rapids without shipping a drop of water.

After further such adventures, Freeman finished the long journey at Portland. Lorraine went all the way to Astoria; his last view from his battered boat was the white crest of Mount St. Helens hanging above the river like a cloud.

CHAPTER 9

Primeval Times
and Indians

A hundred miles below Kettle Falls, the mighty Columbia River's destructive force was turned into electrical power generation with the completion of Grand Coulee Dam between 1941 and 1951. It was here that the original Columbia River once changed channels.

Witnessing the power of an ordinary river is an awe-inspiring experience—the grinding and churning of massive floes as big as a house, when river ice breaks up in spring—the deafening thunder of falls—the unstoppable power in flood stage, over its banks, relentlessly tearing apart houses and stores, ripping away big chunks of earth and toppling trees. Think, then, of the power of the primeval Columbia River of central Washington, many times the size of today's river. (Modern place names are used for orientation.)

The early Columbia River drained glaciers through present channels. As the river came south past Kettle Falls, it was shunted westward by the massive Columbia Plateau or scablands, to skirt its edges. The North Cascades caused it to veer southward again, a channel described in Chapter 1, *Discovery*.

These scablands were formed by lava upwelling like a fountain in southeastern Washington. The lava extended from slightly below Colville into Oregon, from beyond the Idaho border to send fingers oozing through the North Cascades Mountains all the way to the sea. Over and over the black basaltic material overflowed, spreading over the Columbia Plateau more than a mile thick. Then in the Pleistocene Epoch vast fields of glacial ice, no doubt blue-white and beautiful like the glaciers of the Cascades today, pressed forward to cover British Columbia and Washington in an irregular pattern. Ancient Lake Columbia filled the trench now occupied by Lake Roosevelt. A long finger of glacial ice, perhaps 5,000 feet thick, moved down the Okanogan River

Valley across today's Bridgeport and overran the plateau as far south as Coulee City, blocking the course of the ancient Columbia River. Forced aside it turned south, wearing itself new paths.

A new era began, the earth warmed, and glaciers began to retreat unevenly. To the northeast the enormous Lake Missoula had developed behind an ice dam. It eroded the dam and sent a torrent too massive to comprehend catapulting oceanward. The evidence is there in central Washington.

Crashing down the Spokane River channel, the waters came with unimaginable force into the Columbia above Grand Coulee. Blocked by the ice barrier at Bridgeport, the rampaging waters turned into the alternate southward channel of the Columbia, taking advantage of a natural fault to rip out weakened chunks of basalt and carve the coulees indenting central Washington State. First came the excavation of Grand Coulee, extending twenty-one miles south of today's dam, its virtually sheer walls more than 800 feet high in places, exposing the strata to be easily read by geologists.

The flood spread out briefly, then plunged seaward again over a falls three and a half miles wide, dropping more than four hundred feet. (Niagara Falls is one mile wide and drops 165 feet.) It must have washed away rhinoceros, woolly mammoth, mastodon, the great lion, short-faced bear, sabre-toothed tiger and more in its unchecked rush, for fossils of some have been found along the channels. The basin it scooped out holds a pathetic remnant of water as several small, extremely deep lakes. There at Dry Falls, standing at cliffside, one can imagine the torrent, the awfulness of that flood.

The water continued down a narrowing fault, carving out the coulees and lakes we know today—Sun Lakes, Soap Lake, Moses Coulee, Moses Lake, Potholes Reservoir. The flood became a temporary lake from the Cascades to Lewiston, Idaho, covering Pasco's site with 800 feet of water. Eventually it wore away the Wallula barrier and, in a cataclysmic rush, turned westward, widening the Columbia Gorge through the Cascade Range, and emptied into the ocean. The site of Portland was under 400 feet of water.

Most scientists believe that disastrous floods recurred from a freeze-and-melt, melt-and-freeze cycle on Lake Missoula. At any rate, when ice near Bridgeport melted, leaving behind large boulders scattered randomly on the dry plateau, the Columbia River resumed its present channel.

Grand Coulee, then all but dry except during rainy seasons, had a stark and frightening grandeur of its own, described best by Alexander Ross in 1855:

The sight in many places is truly magnificent: while in one place the solemn gloom forbids the wanderer to advance, in another the prospect is lively and inviting, the ground being thickly studded with ranges of columns, pillars, battlements, turrets, and steps above steps, in every variety of shade and colour. ... Thunder and lightning are known to be more frequent here than in other parts; and a rumbling in the earth is sometimes heard. According to Indian tradition, it is the abode of evil spirits. ... It is the wonder of Oregon. (Alexander Ross, *Fur Hunters of the Far West* [Norman: University of Oklahoma Press, 1956], 31–32.)

Today the Grand Coulee's battlements are reflected in the deep blue water of Banks Lake, the vistas akin to those of Lake Powell in Arizona/Utah on the Colorado River. The massive rock formation, Steamboat Rock, formerly sailing through a dry wash, is more fittingly almost surrounded by water.

Around the perimeters of the hot, dry Columbia Plateau, aboriginal people thrived, arriving eight to thirteen thousand years ago on some sites. Northwest Indians said of themselves only that they came "from the north." In Columbia River country the tribes belonged to two distinct linguistic families—Salishan, the more northerly and coastal, and Sahaptin from south central Washington on.

Two decades after Gray startled the Indians of the Lower Columbia, David Thompson and Finan McDonald came in from the north to establish Spokane House to trade with the Spokans and Coeur d'Alenes, as mentioned earlier. Relationships with the Spokans were amiable; they were a largely peaceful people living in a richly endowed land.

Several Indian tribes or bands lived periodically along the Columbia River, moving with the seasons to customary fishing sites, hunting camps, root-gathering places and permanent winter camps. Few called any one specific place "my land." Indigenous to northern Washington were Salish-speaking Okanogan, Sanpoil, Nespelem and Lake. Despite often shabby treatment by white people, more by the transients than the governmental figures, these Indian people were staunch friends and still today point out that they never warred on Americans. The painful process of accepting an encroaching culture unquestionably was eased a little by earlier contacts with Hudson's Bay Company and North West Company fur traders.

David Thompson of the North West Company tells of meeting the Indians on his first Columbia voyage. About 70 miles below Kettle Falls he met the Sanpoils, commenting on their foods, including camas and a small onion, plus moss bread (considered by the Indians as the last resort before starvation) and their hunting practices. To catch deer, thirty or forty persons gradually encircled a herd until a signal came to start shooting them.

Near Box Canyon he encountered Nespelem Indians, who were taller and fairer. He noted that the women daubed their faces with red ochre and the men painted a stripe down the parting in their hair. At the mouth of the Methow River he met the Methows, cautiously friendly.

At the Wenatchee River and south to Priest Rapids, Thompson met Indians who apparently had not seen a white man before. They examined Thompson with wonder, even feeling his leg to see if he was real. Beyond that point, Thompson entered the Sahaptin-speaking country, and his interpreters were replaced.

The Salish Indians exhibited few or no warlike weapons, and usually were friendly. In 1841, in Canadian Okanagan Indian country, when an Okanagan killed an Hudson's Bay Company trader whom he wrongly blamed for his father's death, Okanagan Chief Nicola thundered out against the perpetrator: "The winter is cold. On all the hills around the deer are plenty; and yet I hear your children crying for food. Why is this? You ask for powder and ball. ... The powder and ball he gave you that you might get food ... you turned against him. ... I cannot look at myself in the glass, I cannot look at you. ... Wherefore did you kill him?" (Quoted by Sister Maria Ilma Raufer, O.P., in *Black Robes and Indians* [Milwaukee: The Bruce Publishing Company, 1966], 21.)

Chief Nicola's father, Chief Pelka-mulox, once said to the white traders: "You are my white children, and I do not want to lose you. I want you to live in my territory. I have a big country, big enough for all of us and for our children and our children's children. ... As long as the waters run and until yonder hill is no more, you and I stay here, your children and my children. " (*Ibid.*, 3)

The upper Columbia tribes were mariners, not horsemen; they built and paddled canoes where few would go, through the Columbia River's rapids and up treacherous shallows in their commerce and fishing. Not until late in the nineteenth century did horses become important.

Their equally friendly cousins, the Spokans, were inordinately fond of horses. One of the chief horse trading fairs was near the Little Spokane River. The sellers lined up, holding their horses; the buyers started piling up goods until a seller handed over the lead rope. Like the Nez Perce, famed for their racing steeds, the Spokans might stage races as long as five miles over hill and dale.

The Spokans were happy to supply traders with skins, since the payment in guns and metal gave them a chance against traditional enemies, the Blackfeet and Nez Perce. They entered wholeheartedly into the social life of the trading post, learning European-style dancing, and the women adopted the foreigner's clothes. Many traders and trappers, including John McLoughlin and Peter Skene Ogden, married native women. One poor soldier almost lost his head over marrying an Indian bride, only to have her husband come home—understandably furious, but later willing to relinquish her for suitable presents.

Moving like leavening agents throughout the meetings between cultures were the missionaries, Catholic Fathers deSmet, Demers, Grassi, Joset, Ravalli, who established St. Paul's Mission at Kettle Falls and St. Regis near Colville, and the Protestants Cushing Eells and Elkanah Walker among the Spokans. Often they visited their converts by canoe, a dangerous journey at times. In the spring of 1842, when Father Pierre de Smet came to visit the Okanogan Indians, he walked along the Columbia River and watched helplessly as the canoe he had just left was drawn into a whirlpool. Five people were drowned.

The Indian's faith was tested severely in 1853 and 1854 during a dreadful smallpox epidemic. Because most of the white settlers were vaccinated, they did not get the disease, and prostrate Indians (many of whom had declined vaccination) believed the infection was some deliberate ploy of the Americans to reduce their numbers. New Christian converts returned to the dreamer-prophets, Skolaskin of the Sanpoils (his grave is in Keller Cemetery, and his old log church is at Nespelem) and Smohalla of the Wanapums, and their mystical religions. Most of them clung to old ways of dealing with disease—the sweat house and a plunge into cold water, disastrous as treatment of smallpox sufferers. Still the steady hands of wise chiefs kept the peace.

Confusion among the Indians as to beliefs of Catholics and Protestants led to some friction. When surveyors for the railroad and for the Mullan wagon road from the headwaters of the Missouri to the Columbia came with tape measures, the Spokans realized that the white people intended to take some of their lands. They wondered if they had been wise by being friendly. Word came of the Whitman massacre in southern Washington; the Spokans hoped their white friends would not blame them as accomplices.

Then gold seekers in northeast Washington and Idaho capped the uncomfortable changes, bringing liquor that inflamed these previously sober Indians. Many prospectors did not honor Indian lands or ways. Finally, despite the steadfast friendliness of leaders like Spokan Garry, a devout Christian, the Spokans' regard ruptured over the matter of going onto a reservation—not even a convenient reservation on their homelands, but the threat of being moved west of the Columbia.

This was too much. Meeting Colonel E. J. Steptoe in May 1858, while he marched north from Fort Walla Walla to placate the Indians, the Spokans and allied bands soundly beat him in a well-executed attack.

Three months later, the Spokans, aligned with bitter Nez Perce, Coeur d'Alenes and others, were decisively defeated by Colonel George Wright in bloody battles at Four Lakes and Spokane Plains. Afterward, the American force shot hundreds of Indian horses. Relenting somewhat later, the authorities did establish a reservation along the north bank of the Spokane River, part of the Spokans' original homeland, although a small group of Spokans chose to go to the Colville Reservation west of the Columbia River.

At least one military man, General W. S. Harney, formerly an avid Indian opponent, spoke mercifully about the necessity of protecting the remaining Indians *from* the unscrupulous white miners and settlers, not *vice versa*.

Schools eventually came to the reservation, the most beloved teacher sent there being Helen Clark, a Quebecois, who taught at Wellpinit between 1894 and 1899. She was protector and friend to her charges and once said indignantly, "Every white man seems to think that it is his legitimate privilege to ... trick an Indian in any kind of a trade or business transaction, and as a rule they have very little confidence in the white man's honesty. I tell them I am ashamed of my people." (Quoted by Ruby and Brown in "The Spokane Indians" from *Lincoln County Times*, March 20, 1896, 7.)

Meanwhile, to trade with the Indians living farther west, the North West/Hudson's Bay Company Fort Okanogan served the area between 1814 and 1848. The fort was superbly situated on a promontory overlooking the confluence of the Okanogan River and the Columbia near today's Brewster. There the fur brigades transferred from Columbia River canoes to pack trains to supply posts at Kamloops and Alexandria (near Prince George). With the establishment of the forty-ninth parallel as an international border in 1846, Hudson's Bay Company moved its headquarters to Fort Langley north of Bellingham, Washington, on the Fraser River, and abandoned the Okanogan post (and others).

Okanogan Indians were friends of Fort Okanogan personnel. Clerk Ross Cox told of an eerie prediction by a Chief Ye-whell-come-tetsa that wolves would come after the post's horses. Discounting the premonition, Cox went about his business, but the very next night wolves killed five horses. Grimly, Cox and a hunting party went after the wolves and among those shot was a monster white wolf estimated at over 125 pounds. Cox gave the skin to the chief, a special treasure, because the insignia of an Okanogan Indian chief was a white wolf-skin, fantastically painted with figures, the head and tail decorated with bears' claws and animal teeth, suspended from a pole near his lodge.

In 1858 and later, miners traveled past Fort Okanogan's derelict remains on their way to the fabulous gold fields of Barkerville (Canada),

300 miles north of the border. More sagacious adventurers drove big herds of cattle north to feed them.

The sheer numbers of a large party moving north in 1858 were alarming. The party under David McLoughlin (son of John) moved north from Walla Walla, bound for Barkerville. South of the border at a defile thereafter called McLoughlin Canyon, the party walked into an ambush by Indians encouraged by Chiefs Moses and Sarsapkin. Six men fell in the first volley. Taking cover, the miners held their own until nightfall, escaping across the Okanogan River. A day or two later, they were attacked again, but Chief Tonasket came to stop the fighting.

Then, all Indian-settler relationships became strained in the Columbia country. Government representatives attempted to conclude treaties with hostile Indians and to fashion reservations for many. The bands called "Colville" today did not sign any treaties but eventually accepted a reservation that extended from the Columbia River on the south and east to the international border on the north and to the Okanogan River on the west. Later agreements would pare the reservation.

As Indians moved, willingly or not, to reservations, governmental authorities were often confused about their tribal backgrounds. Disparate people were assigned to the Colville Federated Tribes, often likened to "Colville United Nations." Tribes had differing customs, religions, governments and languages. Two groups especially were foreign to the others—the Moses Indians and the Nez Perce band of Chief Joseph.

Moses' people came from near Wenatchee, around Rock Island Rapids, and were intermarried with Entiat and Yakima bands. They considered lands in Douglas and Grant counties as their own, south of today's Colville Reservation. They also had signed no treaty or reservation agreement. In June 1877, Chief Moses agreed to move to a reservation if he could help to select it. Certain lands were proposed in May 1879, at a most colorful gathering at the Wenatchee and Columbia rivers that included Territorial Governor Elisha P. Ferry; General O. O. Howard, the military leader; local trader and settler Sam Miller and "Dutch John" Galler; Chief Moses, Chief Innomoseecha of the Chelan band; Chief Harmelt of the Wenatchi (original spelling); and hundreds of Indians and troops. The gathering was described by Lieutenant C. E. S. Wood:

> Hour after hour the Indians arrived, singly, by families, bands, and almost by tribes, trooping in with herds and loaded pack animals. ... The tepees of buffalo-skin were put up, the smoke of many campfires arose, and the hillsides became dotted with grazing ponies. All the life was barbaric. ... The shy women in buckskin shirts and

> leggins (riding astride), their saddles hung with bags, strange utensils, and sometimes the papoose swinging in his swaddling cradle at the pommel; wild-eyed, elfin-haired, little bronze children, perched naked on top of some bales of household goods. ... In the train came the grave, anxious looking men in fur mantles or loose buck-skin shirts, or with yellowish copper-colored, naked bodies, and only the breech-clout and fringed leggins, their hair loose or braided, and their faces painted black, red, yellow, white. ... The ponies ... sometimes gay with interwoven feathers, and sometimes ears, tail and mane all cut close to the body. ... Then the camp ... its color, its gorgeous setting in the evergreen and snow-clad hills; the eternal snow peaks high in the air against the blue sky. ... (Lt. C. E. S. Wood, "An Indian Horse Race," *Century Magazine* 33 [November 1886–April 1887], p. 448.)

The Indians listened but made no decision, preferring to stay where they presently lived until forced to move. Besides, they had brought their horses to the council—the best to be found—for wildly competitive horse races on the broad council plain.

Later in 1879, Moses approved a reservation centered on the west side of the Columbia River, but by then, miners were flocking into the upper Methow River Valley where gold in paying quantities was found. Many Wenatchi, Chelan and Wapato bands stayed where they were. Chief Moses collected rentals from squatters on his new reservation for awhile. In 1884, he sold the reservation back to the government, and his band was assigned to the Colville Reservation.

During Indian negotiations with the government, Moses was represented as a chief of the Okanogans, absolutely incorrect and resented by the latter. A Colville Tribes historian suggests that the government needed a "chief" with whom to deal, not several leaders, and seized upon the personable Chief Moses.

The Moses and Wenatchi bands, at least, were Salish-speaking and were akin to the locals. After the famous flight of Chief Joseph and a band of Nez Perce from the U.S. cavalry, the defeated group was sent to Oklahoma. Most miserable there, Chief Joseph's band agreed to live on the Colville Reservation, to which Chief Moses invited his old friend, Chief Joseph, in December 1885.

The other tribes indigenous to the Colville lands were outraged; they said it was the Nez Perce who, long ago, raided their lands and killed many of them along the Columbia River. Furthermore, the Nez Perce are not of Salish but of Sahaptin language. The proud old Chief Joseph lived his life out among hostile "friends" on the reservation.

Nonetheless, a memorial to him stands near Nespelem, Colville Federated Tribe headquarters. To the south, the Columbia dam quelling Box Canyon's rapids is Chief Joseph Dam.

Today the Colville Federated Tribes with college-educated leaders and sophisticated management techniques operates a timber mill, extensive logging operations, a very successful rental service of large houseboats on Lake Roosevelt, a first-class restaurant at Seven Bays Resort on the lake, and other enterprises. Former tribal differences have lessened. A usually easy relationship prevails with the white settlers and business people around and within the reservation; after all, large numbers of the indigenous peoples were intermarried with Europeans (Hudson's Bay men) and with later American settlers.

On festival days, though, the spectacular finery comes out of mothballs, the feathers are brushed and the leggings are donned. The drums set up their hypnotic beat, and half-remembered chants begin. Old stories come alive of days before the Americans came to make "Americans" of them, the country's aboriginal people. It is well that they do remember and revere their tribal arts.

During the 1890s and early 1900s horses helped struggling boats traverse through rough stretches of river currents. From an original oil painting by Frederick L. Hubbard entitled "Extra Horsepower." Used by permission.

Uncertain Times

In eastern Washington, the earth itself was changing. Between 1872 and 1906, earthquakes were puzzlingly frequent. It all started out with a real shaker on December 14, 1872, that brought down an entire bluff north of Entiat, blocking the Columbia River for several hours until pent-up water broke through. One can imagine an Indian's astonishment, coming to the river for water that day, only to find it completely dry! The formation left behind—Ribbon Cliff or "Cock Shoot," "Broken Mountain" as the Indians called it—is clearly visible today.

Stinking sulphur water spewed over food supplies of nearby Chelan Indians, and yawning cracks opened and closed in the earth. For a time a tremendous geyser shot up at Chelan Falls adjacent to the river, subsiding into springs. Nineteen miles up Lake Chelan a water eruption sent 6-foot waves toward shore, washing a small boat onto the rocks. Throughout the following year there were frequent aftershocks. Smohalla, the dreamer prophet, had predicted that the Great Spirit would show his displeasure by shaking the earth. Terrified Wenatchi Indians fled to the Wenatchi trading post run by Sam Miller, asking him to read from the magic black book, the Bible, while others turned to Smohalla. Again in 1887, there were three days of severe earthquakes, recorded by settler James C. Bonar, "I can hear [the cannonading] and feel the jar of the earthquake nearly every hour."

Robert Byrd, in his annotations in *Lake Chelan in the 1890s*, speculates that earthquakes may have lowered the lake bed. He tells of a Spokane visitor to Stehekin in 1891 who mentioned seeing extensive Indian petroglyphs on smooth rocks at the head of Lake Chelan, figures of war parties and large animals. They were so high on the cliffs that they must have been painted from a canoe at a time when the lake was higher.

In 1906, above the present Keller Ferry site on the Columbia River, a cliff gave way under an Indian on horseback, carrying them across the river unharmed, but damming the Columbia for a time.

The Indian unrest described in the previous chapter led to establishment of forts on the Columbia, along what is now Lake Roosevelt—Fort Colville (not the Hudson's Bay Company fort) fourteen miles southeast of Kettle Falls, and Fort Spokane on a pleasant bluff above the confluence of the Spokane and Columbia rivers.

To protect the crews surveying the international border, Fort Colville was established in June 1859, under orders of General W. S. Harney, commander of the Department of the Columbia. Major Pinkney Lugenbeel came with a battalion of the Ninth Infantry to do the job. Lugenbeel found that the Spokans were peaceful and wanted only to obtain farming tools, medical supplies and missionaries. When his troops (regulars) were ordered into the Civil War, they were replaced with more rowdy volunteers, Companies C and D, Second Infantry, California Volunteers. They were unruly and frequently drunk.

Unscrupulous traders set up distilleries and shops at nearby Pinkney City, a sordid civilian village growing up near the fort, illegally selling liquor to the troops and to the Indians. Prostitution thrived there, with diseases shared by Indians and soldiers alike. The squalid situation was not aided by Indian Agent W. P. Winans, unpopular with the Indians and accused of dealing in liquor himself.

One terminus of the new military road from Walla Walla, Fort

Visible Indian art on rocks.

Colville served as a distribution point for government supplies to Indians and, most notably, as a site for conferences between Chief Moses and government representatives during the treaty period. In 1878, troops were sent to a temporary encampment on Foster Creek and the Columbia, then on to Camp Chelan.

Fort Colville was awkwardly located for dealing with the Spokan Indians on their new reservation. To replace it, Camp Spokane (or Fort Spokane) was established in 1880 at the junction of the Columbia and Spokane rivers, close to the Spokan Indian lands. By 1883, when General William T. Sherman visited Fort Colville, it was largely decommissioned.

Fort Spokane proved to be a substantial and long-lasting installation, every inch the military post with West Point lieutenants, disciplined troops and extensive drills. By 1890, there were fifty sturdy buildings, including officers' quarters, barracks, recreation hall and hospital.

Nevertheless, duty there was dull, and the vastness of the area was intimidating—especially to soldiers from the East. There were desertions each spring. To enliven the deadly routine, for there were no wars, sergeants periodically led their troops on long field trips to work off excessive frustrations. The first wilderness survival programs were staged out of forts Colville and Spokane, where recruits would be "abandoned" in the wilderness to live off the land for a period of time.

On the cultural side, visiting dramatic troupes performed, grandly formal dances were held, and lecture series on tactics and other military matters were given for officers. There was a well-stocked library.

Of historic importance was the ministering by fort personnel to Chief Joseph and his band of Nez Perce immediately after they were assigned to the Colville Reservation. They encamped across from the fort, bitter, disillusioned, ragged and hungry, estranged from the other Nez Perce at Lapwai, surrounded by resentful local Indian bands. The Colville Indian Agent was suspected of embezzling supplies. Lieutenant Colonel Joshua Fletcher, commander of the post, angrily denounced the situation and attempted to get his superiors to act against the agent, which they finally did. Supplies to feed these wretched people were slow in coming, and Fort Spokane officers fed the Nez Perce from their own stores. Eventually the band moved over to Nespelem.

When the Spanish-American War broke out in 1898, the troops from Fort Spokane were sent into action, and the government abandoned the military post by 1899. In 1902, facilities were remodeled for use as a boarding school for Indian children. At first only about a hundred students enrolled, but more came upon the encouragement of the Spokan chief, who had asked for a school near his reservation. A health service was established, ministering to Indians until 1929. To occupy some of the vacant buildings, the Colville Indian Agency moved its offices to Fort Spokane. In 1914, the agency moved to Nespelem, and the school closed.

Four buildings survive today, including the old administration building facing the parade grounds. The grounds are open to the public as a national park.

Indians and settlers alike began to log the forests to supply sawmills such as the Lantzy Mill above Fort Spokane. They brought the trees to the Columbia by horse team for booming to the mill. After the Lantzy Mill converted the logs to rough lumber, they sent it to the railhead at Bridgeport by chaining lumber on rafts propelled only by the Columbia current. Near Whitestone, a cliff that resembles a grape-fruit bisected with a knife, the Lincoln Lumber Company Mill opened, later managed by Crown Zellerbach. Operations ceased there in the 1980s, leaving only stark foundations on the shore of Lake Roosevelt.

The mariners who muscled the lumber rafts and log booms to Bridgeport installed oversized sweeps to help them steer through the rapids and around the curves. In Box Canyon above Bridgeport there were deep subcurrents. Booms would break up, the huge logs spinning around and going completely under water to emerge far downstream. One mill owner built a fin boom (an angular guide) to bring drifting logs into his sawmill. He worked with a logger upstream who stockpiled logs until the spring runoff floated them, but the mighty Columbia propelled the logs right over, around and under the fin boom. Despite several configurations, the idea never worked. Later, powerful tugs were added to pull booms downriver to the sawmills. Only one tug remains on Lake Roosevelt to serve varying needs.

On the windswept Columbia Plateau, a wilderness desert, nutritious bunch grass grew thigh-high from Davenport to Wenatchee, Mansfield to Pasco. Prospectors in the North Cascades foothills and along the border were hungry; in response, the area became cattle country, a frontier "Wild West." Cattle were driven northward, crossing the Columbia by swimming or ferry near Bridgeport and herded on to Conconully, Ruby or Republic.

This popular ferry was run by "Wild Goose" Bill Condon (Samuel Wilbur Condit), who got his name by mistakenly shooting tame geese. He established a reliable ferry in 1884 across the Columbia in Nespelem Canyon about twenty miles below today's Grand Coulee Dam (a location recommended by Lieutenant Thomas W. Symons during his reconnoitering trip on the Upper Columbia River in 1881). By 1889, Condon Ferry had a hotel, store and saloon, and was an official stage stop and post office.

Condon was quite a ladies' man, and this was his eventual undoing. In a classic love triangle, middle-aged Condon befriended and fell in love with a younger woman, who fell in love with a younger man. One day, when Condon was absent, she moved over to her lover's cabin. When Condon returned home, he calmly made out his will, then marched over to the cabin to take his sweetheart back. In the resulting melee, he and the lover shot each other dead before the woman's eyes.

After Condon's death, relatives and friends continued to operate the ferry until 1929. In "Gold Historian," John Weber told of seeing the old ferry cable during the Columbia River flood of 1948. Investigating loud rhythmic booming sounds, he saw that the center portion of the sagging cable was below water. The strong current swept the cable downstream where, "tight as a bowstring, it would clear the water and arc back upstream 40 to 50 feet, striking the water with the noise of thunder." Debris subsequently snapped the cable.

One by one the old ferries met similar fates. The only ferries remaining today are the Keller Ferry and a ferry from Inchelium to Gifford, both on Lake Roosevelt. The latter, the *Columbia Princess*, was brought from Everett, Washington, in 1981, up the Columbia and Snake rivers to a point where it was taken on a tractor trailer to Lincoln on the Columbia. It was the widest load ever moved on the state highways.

Some of the best ranchlands were right in Grand Coulee, where small springs bubbled up to water the stock. Near Steamboat Rock was Devil's Lake, so named because any drowned bodies never rose to the surface. In this picturesque region one of the largest spreads in Washington thrived, the Steamboat Rock Stock Company, later called Lincoln Stock Farm. At least five hundred head of whiteface cattle grazed on native grasses supplemented by alfalfa hay grown on irrigated land. Often important guests came to stay, and Chinese cooks served superb dinners to guests in formal attire. The Stock Farm's trees, flowers and handsome buildings are now under the waters of Banks Lake.

Far from being totally barren, the Coulee was home to carpets of flowers; under the willow trees grew wild columbine, roses, iris, violets and wild mint. Service berry (when dried, a staple food of the Indians) grew profusely. There were blue lupine and gold balsam root. The Coulee area is on the Pacific Flyway, serving trumpeter swans, night hawks, ducks and geese. This area is enhanced today by marshes on the shores of Banks Lake.

Isolated as they were, children of the ranchers grew up on horseback, and their animals were friends. One family raised an abandoned sandhill crane. Because of his aggressiveness, he was boss of the farmyard and was dubbed "Nero." When the family went off to Wilbur for supplies, Nero—with a wing spread of 7 feet and looming as tall as the wagon bed—insisted on going, too, walking beside the horses or flapping his wings to catch up. Teams meeting this apparition often bolted in wide-eyed terror.

One of the most successful horse ranches was operated by Cull White north of the Columbia River on the Colville Reservation. He purchased horses and broke them to sell to the U.S. Army. Another was Peter Dan Moses, carrying on the family tradition, as his uncle Tse-Chil-a-wax of Ephrata was said to be the greatest horse rancher in Western Indian history, selling three thousand horses to incoming settlers. Such prolific herds of fine horses and cattle were bound to attract thieves and rustlers, the most infamous along the Columbia being the Fiddle Creek Gang and Texas Jack.

Times were tough enough without the pilfering; blizzards howled across the uninterrupted plains, killing horses, cattle and people. (In 1916, the snow was 6 feet deep near Waterville.) Water holes froze, so cattle went thirsty. And the cattle were wild as deer. Pioneer Emry Vance told of rounding up twenty-five head of wild steers on the reservation and trying to get them onto "Wild Goose" Bill's ferry. Three men had managed to get the spooky cattle near the ferry, when the operator started to hammer on a board, then dropped some lumber. The cattle scattered wildly into the brush with the cowboys in hot pursuit. When the herd was reassembled and approached the ferry again, the operator called out to the cowboys. The sudden noise sent the herd, nostrils dilated with excitement, back into the brush.

As ranchers scratched the scablands to grow hay, farmers watched with interest the verdant crops that emerged. In the south part of the plains, farmers tried growing wheat early, but it was not until around 1890 that dirt farmers drifted into the plains between Chelan and Grand Coulee near Mansfield, where huge boulders lay tossed about by a giant's hand, the terminal moraine of the ancient glacier. Grain crops fairly leaped out of the ground, but that was a siren song for farmers; out of the sky came grasshoppers and hailstorms. Winds lifted the fine glacial silt into the air in dust storms that were like the night. Along the Columbia near the Methow River, a pioneer boy dug cricket ditches filled with water to protect crops, emptying shovel-loads of crickets from the ditches each night.

Lulled by the usually moderate climate, settlers were unprepared for renegade winter storms whistling down from the frigid north, freezing the fall wheat in the ground and the animals above it. Yet there were enough good years that dry land farming proved prosperous; soon this great Columbia Plateau waved with wheat. The next problem was how to get wheat to market. The Columbia River became the highway.

Until adequate railways were built, farmers hauled their sacks of grain to the river where sternwheelers docked to transport them to railroads. The river between Grand Coulee and Wanapum growled along between bluffs 1,000 to 2,000 feet high; passes to the water's edge were few and agonizingly steep. Soon someone dreamed up the idea of building chutes from the canyon rim down to water level. These chutes were similar to large stovepipes, but the wheat hurtling down the pipes created such friction that it arrived scorched at the boat. Engineers tried baffling to slow it down, and eventually the methods worked well. One wheat tramway came down the bluff south of Waterville to Orondo's docks, serving farmers well into the twentieth century.

A virtual parade of grain boats joined the complex fleet of passenger/freight steamers plying the Columbia. Among the grain ports above Rock Island were Chelan Falls, Virginia City (about half a mile south of Brewster), Central Ferry, Orondo, Troy and Wenatchee.

Basically, navigation was not practical between Pasco and Wenatchee because of the Priest, Cabinet, and Rock Island rapids. Boats plied the river from a port above Rock Island Rapids to Brewster and Bridgeport, even though the connecting trail from the railroad at Ellensburg was so steep that teamsters attached logs to their wagons on the downhill grade to slow the descent. Boats tended to carry mining and general supplies upriver, and ore, grain or animals downstream.

Joining the two sternwheelers late in the century were smaller boats, some that regularly went to Okanogan (and even farther in high water), including the *North Star*, *City of Wenatchee* and *Echo*. How the steamers made it through rapids was accurately, if ecstatically described by passenger Dora Tibbits Casey (at the Methow Rapids):

> The scene, too, beggared description. Just the first streaks of dawn coming over a desolate-looking plateau to the east. ... To the west the frowning mountains, and ahead, jagged rocks, almost filling the river bed, some towering several times higher than the smoke stack of the boat ... whirlpools only surpassed by those below Niagara Falls. ... [Passage upstream] was possible by carrying a cable attached to the winch on the deck up to the guide rings ... anchored in large boulders. ... With the donkey engine turning the winch and slowly winding up the cable, the boat would not only be kept on her course, but her engines assisted in carrying the load up against the strong current. (Dora Tibbits Casey, "Reminiscences of a Ranch Woman." Unpublished manuscript, Binder 1, December 30, 1930, at North Central Washington Museum, Wenatchee, Washington.)

Casey compared the scene to the eerie feeling one might have when an iceberg loomed in the fog.

Not far south of the Methow Rapids, Chelan Falls was the Columbia River port at the foot of a 375-foot waterfall, culmination of the three-mile Chelan River, shortest river in the state. It forms the overflow from Lake Chelan.

The lake extends fifty-two miles into wilderness; even now there are no roads to its head; from Stevens Pass (Wenatchee to Everett) north almost 150 miles, only one road transects the mountains.

A steamer, *Belle of Chelan*, was placed on Lake Chelan in 1889, then as its successor is now, a tourist boat taking sightseers up the lake, over 1,500 feet deep in places. At the head of the lake surrounded by the crags of the North Cascades Mountains, the luxurious Field Hotel operated until the Chelan dam raised the water level and inundated it. Most passengers stayed at least one night there.

Land travel from Chelan to Wenatchee was impractical, but the settlement was only a small collection of farms and houses at that time. In 1885, the news of railroads building between Spokane and Seattle sparked land speculation. Seattle attorney Thomas Burke, L. C. Gilman, G. M. Haller and others bought 700 acres around Wenatchee in 1888, platting it into 100 feet by 30 feet lots priced at $100, land that cost them $10 per acre. Before many lots were sold, the Great Northern had acquired the railroad being built from Spokane, and the Wenatchee land company sold one-fourth of its lots to them, a shrewd move that merged their interests with the railroad's aims.

The railroad came to Wenatchee in October 1892, crossing the Columbia River on the sternwheeler *Thomas L. Nixon*. East and west links joined at Scenic on January 6, 1893, near the summit of Stevens Pass. Responding to the new rail connection, the southerly terminus of the sternwheeler fleet moved to a wharf at Wenatchee. When the Columbia froze over, boat crews dreamed up bizarre entertainment. One night a crew member won a quart of whiskey from a bet that he could run across the river and back stark naked.

With the commencement of rail service north, riverboat traffic declined. Three boats had been wrecked in rapids by 1906, and the final blow was delivered in July 1915, when the *North Star* (Columbia and Okanogan Steamboat Company) caught fire at her berth in Wenatchee, taking the *Columbia*, *Okanogan* and *Chelan* with her in the blaze.

At Wenatchee the railroad's arrival was the impetus for fruit growing to become a major industry. One pioneer grower brought a load of trees on muleback all the way from The Dalles to Wenatchee. At the Columbia River an onlooker watched in amazement as a queer procession swam across—mules tied together, appearing like a floating island of trees, and the owner swimming behind by hanging onto the last mule's tail. Orcharding had a long way to go.

Until convenient irrigation and transportation, though, settlers planted apples, peaches and cherries in backyard plots for their own use. The irrigation canal built by Jacob Shotwell in 1891 was the first in the Wenatchee area, utilizing water from the Wenatchee River that empties into the Columbia.

Shotwell and a partner, Arthur Gunn, organized the Wenatchee Water Power Company in 1896 to expand the irrigation service but ran out of funds. The Great Northern Railroad held their bonds and found itself owning the project. A new group opened the Highline Canal, which still runs through the city of Wenatchee. Other systems followed to water lands in Wenatchee, Malaga and Manson.

The apple growers had "a bear by the tail," a fledgling industry that would place the lands along or near the Columbia River as the nation's prime area for fine apples, plus other fruits. The path to success was fraught with problems, however.

A tree took ten years (far less now) to bring forth fruit; depletion of nutrients in the soil was not understood clearly, quality fertilizers were unavailable and national marketing had to be learned. Pests were unwelcome settlers—aphids, which were unsuccessfully treated by dipping young branches in soapsuds, and codling moths, treated with arsenate of lead. Today, safer pest-control methods prevail.

The early picking and handling process was crude and was streamlined over the years—from metal pails to bags for less bruising, from hard boxes to "totes" (big plastic bins that could be handled by machine), from hand-sizing in arbitrary grades to machine grading.

No one grower could handle the marketing into national stores; cooperative marketing was developed, then better storage and refrigeration. Curiously, the first exports of apples went—not to the East

View of Wenatchee sketched in 1904 from the east side of the Columbia River. Lithograph of a sketch drawn by Edward Lange, Great Northern Railway owner James J. Hill's personal artist. Used by permission of North Central Washington Museum, Wenatchee, Washington.

Coast—but to Australia, Japan and England. Domestic demand grew later. In 1913, north-central Washington shipped 4,100 rail cars of fruit, in 1915 the area shipped 5,400 cars and more than three times that in 1923, but stores were unhappy with quality. Refrigerated rail cars had been diverted for military use during World War I, and without them, apples froze in winter or overheated from unreliable amateur heating systems.

Problems were ameliorated with the establishment of Wenatchee as a Great Northern Railroad division point and in 1923, with formation of the Western Fruit Express Company to schedule cars more efficiently.

As sweet-smelling fruit orchards spread over the benches of the Columbia River and its tributaries, the expense of irrigation and the need for a reliable source of water were constant concerns of growers. No practical way had yet been found to tap the vast water resources of the Columbia River, because it lay in a deep canyon, requiring installation of powerful pumps to raise water to the farmlands.

Rufus Woods, editor and publisher of the *Wenatchee Daily World* newspaper, electrified readers all the way to the national wire services in 1918 by airing a proposal by William Clapp, an Ephrata lawyer, for a dam to divert part of the Columbia River into the Grand Coulee and southward. Clapp's figures were incomplete; experts said that had his initial plan been implemented, the impounded water would have raised the Columbia 170 feet at the Arrow Lakes in British Columbia. The article was very influential, however, in stirring the imagination of local interests, politicians and government officials, who argued for the next fifteen years before a practical dam plan began to become a reality.

Grand Coulee Dam

Today there are fourteen dams on the Columbia River from headwaters to ocean. Of these, Grand Coulee is the world's largest concrete structure. The bulky barrier stands 550 feet above bedrock, 350 feet above downstream water level. The total length of the dam is 5,223 feet. An incredible 11,975,521 cubic yards of concrete compose the structure, and more than 38 million yards of material was excavated to prepare the site. The total generating capacity of the dam is nearly 6.5 million kilowatts, enough to serve the entire Northwest and occasionally sell power beyond. Transmission towers march away from the dam like children's stick figures, arms uplifted, their lines shimmering against the stark landscape. Besides generating power, the waters irrigate more than a half million acres of land in Washington's dry but lava-fertile plains.

The system includes 333 miles of main canals, 1,959 miles of lesser canals and 2,761 miles of drains and wasteways. Three huge reservoirs store the Columbia River's waters to be returned to the dam for power generation as needed, but mostly used to irrigate agricultural lands. These are Lake Roosevelt, Banks Lake and Potholes Reservoir— 128,000 acres of lakes for the public to enjoy and on which wildlife thrives. Indeed, three times that acreage is managed to provide suitable habitat for fish and wildlife.

Beyond the statistics, which are necessary to fathom the immensity of the project, there are fascinating stories of political machinations and human adaptability. As early as 1903, the U.S. Reclamation Service considered proposals for a dam or for irrigation by tapping into the Pend Oreille or Spokane River and bringing water by gravity flow to a reservoir in central Washington. In 1918, Ephrata attorney William H. Clapp advanced a plan to use Grand Coulee as a natural storage basin. A dam would divert Columbia River water southward through Grand Coulee in the old Missoula flood channel. Both plans had backers and adversaries, equally feverish. However, the accounts in the *Wenatchee Daily World* and in the national news caught the attention of governmental groups. In 1919, the Washington State Legislature created the Columbia Basin Commission and appropriated $100,000 for a study of the two proposals. Panama Canal builder, Major General George W. Goethals, was hired to make a study of the situation and came out in favor of the gravity flow plan from the Pend Oreille.

Most Washingtonians credit James O'Sullivan, a contractor who came from Michigan to work out of Moses Lake in the 1920s, with dedicating his life to make the present Grand Coulee Dam a reality. He worked for minimal pay, talking to whomever would listen, neglecting his business to lobby for the dam—which he believed with the fervor of a messiah would make a garden of the barren scablands. Rufus Woods, through the pages of the *World*, focused attention on the proposed project.

Clearly the expense would require the project to be funded federally, and in 1926, Washington Senators Wesley L. Jones and Clarence C. Dill tried to secure a $600,000 appropriation for a serious study. When opposition seemed overwhelming, Jones quietly placed the appropriation request into a rivers and harbors bill, where it passed undetected

Dry Falls State Park below Grand Coulee in Washington. The ledge is where a cataclysmic waterfall rushed over during a break in the ice dam during the Pleistocene Era.

by the opposition. Major John S. Butler of the U.S. Army Corps of Engineers was directed to make the study, started in 1928 and completed in 1931, at a cost half of that appropriated. Butler favored Clapp, Woods and O'Sullivan's plan over the gravity plan.

Washington proponents continued their media and speaking campaigns. National newspapers and magazines scoffed. In a national magazine, a writer said insultingly, "All this dam would do is provide water for thirsty jackrabbits and for light bulbs in Indian tepees." Adversaries referred to the town of Ephrata as "that Dam University." Opponents included private power companies, which preferred to initiate developments at Kettle Falls on the Columbia River.

Curiously in 1929 and 1930, a pitiless sun shone down on drought-ridden central Washington. Advocates of Grand Coulee Dam pointed out that the Columbia River and its tributaries were fed by Rocky Mountain glaciers usually unaffected by such weather vagaries.

The fine silt peculiar to the Columbia areas blew suffocatingly across the plains. In April 1931, 600 miles out at sea, passengers on a Honolulu-bound ocean liner, reported being enveloped in a huge cloud of this dust.

The Great Depression had set in—bad news but good news for the dam project. In 1933 President Franklin D. Roosevelt made Grand Coulee Dam a project of the Public Works Administration. The Bureau of Reclamation was to supervise the dam-building, headed by Frank A. Banks, construction engineer. He and a small cadre of engineers drove survey stakes on the Columbia River's banks on September 9, 1933. The State of Washington allotted $377,000 to do preliminary work on the site. Initial offices and residence complexes were at Almira, twenty-one miles south.

The news spread rapidly across the nation. WORK, PAYING JOBS were to be had in Washington. In came the unemployed, the destitute, the ragged, hungry men willing to work in a country devoid of jobs. Some came in, on and underneath rail cars with a sandwich and a canteen, or nothing at all to exult in obtaining jobs, eking out food supplies while awaiting their first paychecks. In 1932 there were six people living at Grand Goulee; by 1933 and 1934, there were seven thousand men and a handful of women.

There were no facilities for these people. Dormitories and homes came later. Overnight a shack and tent town covered the rocky, rattlesnake-infested ground that today is the pleasant town of Grand Coulee. Fortunate were the Colville Tribes workers who came, for they could go home at night.

With eager workers and capable engineers the work moved swiftly. The original contractor in 1933 for the first stage of the dam was the acronym MWAK, a merger of several firms, chief among them Silas Mason Construction Co., the Walsh Construction Co. and the Atkinson-Kier Co. In 1938, the second stage of the dam went to Consolidated Builders, Inc., another joint venture.

Before workers could excavate the river bed, they built cofferdams to divert the Columbia River from its channel. Geologists drilled six miles of test holes to check the bedrock, while surveyors assessed just how much of the uplying lands would be flooded. Ten entire towns had to be moved or razed. Parts of the dam project were carried out by the Works Progress Administration and Civilian Conservation Corps, both governmental programs to furnish jobs for the unemployed. Construction began on a railroad spur and a highway from Coulee City.

In 1935, unstable wet clay on the east bank slid like grease into the excavation and refused to be stemmed. Through an ingenious method of inserting pipes into the bank, then pumping freon gas in to freeze the wet earth, the area was stabilized until concrete pouring could be completed. The broad footings were installed, 450 feet thick.

After construction of a tramway to haul cement into place and the building of forms, the waffle-like sections of the dam began to take shape. Over twenty-thousand interlocking segments were poured, from 25 feet by 44 feet, to 50 feet by 50 feet. The lowest forms were anchored by diagonal rods imbedded into the rock. Concrete was dumped in layers, each successive layer vibrated out by air-powered machines. To cool the concrete to "setting" consistency, pipes were installed through which cold river water coursed. The pipes remain within the structure.

It was on this operation that a particularly horrifying accident ensued. Two men operating the vibrator machines were buried up to their armpits when the crane operator above dumped a load of concrete on them. As rescue efforts escalated, every time a man was moved, he sank deeper—much like quicksand. Finally the wall of the form had to be removed, the concrete spilling out, to release the men. Both lived but one was a complete invalid, the other badly injured and leaving the job.

On any construction job there are accidents, since the work is inherently dangerous; seventy-seven men died during building of Grand Coulee Dam, most from falls or dropped objects. Charles Chase Parsons was appointed Safety Inspector for the project in 1940, his job to monitor conditions, instruct employees and train a "Mercy Squad." The job included monitoring field crew problems of rattlesnake bites and tick fever; snakes were so bad on a reservoir site that work was delayed one summer until hibernation time.

Soon after the project started, homes were erected for the engineers on a ledge above the Columbia River, called "Engineers Town," and later renamed Coulee Dam. Across the river was Mason City, named for the construction company, now part of Coulee Dam. Elmer City, called Elmerton at first, grew up downriver. Grand Coulee in a stark valley a mile south was the shacktown home of most workers.

Notorious women appeared almost immediately at Grand Coulee, attracted by the prospect of several thousand single men. On a Saturday night, or any night, really, B Street was wide open. The red light houses operated openly, saloons were crowded. A Grand Coulee resident says, as children, he and his sister used to go to the First Aid Hall on Sunday mornings to size up the previous night's injuries—lines of men with black eyes, broken bones or needing other medical attention.

Another oldtimer said he was sent to a house to replace a broken window early one morning; when he rang the bell, a blowsy woman answered and declared plaintively, "My gosh, you guys even come at this hour!" The startled youth protested, blushing to his hairline.

"Good" women began to arrive and found their determination to live with their men a challenge. Lots in Grand Coulee were platted 25 feet by 70 feet and, since some shacks were built prior to surveying, there were odd-sized properties. Most husbands built one- or two-room homes plus an outhouse, and while running water was soon provided, at first it came from big tanks on a truck. Electricity was yet to come; kerosene or Aladdin (gas-powered mantle light) lamps were customary. The iceman came. The grocery store was in a tent. Near the damsite in 1933, the Trading Post of E. A. Betz and William Rosholt opened for business on a large wagon. Later it moved to Grand Coulee, billing itself as the "Biggest Little Store by a Damsite."

Fires swept through the packed community, crammed between bluffs; over and over, the tar paper and wood shacks exploded into flame in the dry desert air. During the late 1980s Grand Coulee workers intentionally burned about 150 vacant shacks still marring the local landscape.

Dust was the worst enemy. One woman said she checked on her sleeping baby and was horrified to find even his eyelashes heavy with dust. The silt of the Columbia River moved around with the slightest breeze, and no one ever really felt clean.

The only restaurant in town served a limited menu of pancakes for breakfast, stew for lunch and steak and greasy French fries for dinner. A Mexican man sold tamales from a pull cart. Dining out was not attractive.

Yet, "we were all in the same boat," says Edith Lael, a Grand Coulee resident, "and we didn't mind. We had a real community spirit." Bored housewives and children formed a library and Girl and Boy Scouts, gave card parties and formed horseback clubs—one of which, the Ridge Riders, thrives today. Money for the first schools came from donations, and when it was learned that the greatest sums contributed came from the ladies of B Street, some huffy parents wanted to keep their kids out of school.

Contractors built dormitories, mess halls, recreation rooms and a hospital as soon as possible. Today one of the dormitories is Four Winds, a bed and breakfast house, and the Bureau of Reclamation's engineering office is the Coulee Dam city hall.

While workers built the dam, other workers cleared the lands upriver. They lived at riverside camps or barges with barracks. Kettle Falls and Marcus were moved to higher locations. Peach, Fruitland, Lincoln and others were razed, never rebuilt. Workers dismantled or burned structures down to the foundations, leaving no loose lumber, and cut all trees and shrubs. Finally, a huge cable was dragged between two tractors or horses to scrape all vegetation possible from the land, leaving nothing to float to the surface and cause trouble. The Columbia River Valley looked as sere as when the prehistoric flood roared down to scrape everything clean.

In 1934, President Franklin D. Roosevelt came to see the growing big hole into which the government was pouring money, and again in 1937, to review progress. Then twenty thousand people lined the streets and cheered their leader. On May 11, 1950, Harry Truman came to dedicate the dam and unveil a plaque naming the reservoir "Lake Roosevelt."

The dam was nearing completion when the Japanese bombed Pearl Harbor in December 1941. War-footing security measures were taken at Grand Coulee. Two months before Pearl Harbor one 108,000 kilowatt generator had been placed in service; to meet the sharply escalating demand by manufacturers for power, two generators scheduled for still incomplete Shasta Dam in California were installed in Grand Coulee. This boost provided the power needed, also, for Richland's Hanford Project. After the war, Shasta got its generators back and Grand Coulee received larger new ones. By 1951 the dam was the largest hydroelectric facility in the western hemisphere.

Once World War II was over, attention was turned to irrigation. Involved were Banks Lake that fills the Grand Coulee virtually wall to wall; Potholes Reservoir south of Moses Lake formed by O'Sullivan Dam on Crab Creek; and Main, West, East Low and Potholes Canals. A complex system of pumps moves water from the Columbia River to Banks Lake, which feeds irrigation canals as required. A portion of runoff or waste water returns to the system for reuse. When Grand Coulee Dam has need of stored water for power generation, the system reciprocates by returning water for power generation.

When irrigation systems were in place, the federal government advertised farming lands it owned. Between 1948 and 1967, screened buyers drew lots to buy 1,157 farm acreages of varying sizes. Veterans were given preference. Today about a third of the lands are devoted to raising alfalfa hay, the balance in potatoes, corn, various seed crops and wheat. The agricultural production has spawned processing plants and feedlots.

As Franklin D. Roosevelt Lake (commonly referred to as Lake Roosevelt) covered the clean-scraped land, a biologist's study theorized that fish could never live in the lake because of insufficient food. Perhaps at first that was true. But as the years went by, nutrients washed back into the lake, the sun shone and grasses grew in shallows. Fish began to appear in the lake in ever greater numbers—trout, kokanee or landlocked salmon and walleyed pike.

In 1984 Thomas R. Jagielo noted in his master's thesis that there was considerable plankton in Lake Roosevelt and Banks Lake, favored by young rainbow trout. Bruce Smith, eastern director of the Washington State Fish and Wildlife Department, introduced to Lake Roosevelt residents a man who operated fish net hatcheries in western Washington. Smith wanted volunteers to try raising trout in Lake Roosevelt.

An eager volunteer was Win Self, a real estate developer of Seven Bays, a residential community, marina and restaurant (the latter operated by Colville Federated Tribes) about forty miles above the dam. Bucking many who believed the project would not work, Self invested about $1,500 of his own money in nets and supplies; Fish & Wildlife furnished the small fry. The fish thrived in their net pen near

View of the Grand Coulee Dam in early morning from above the dam.

the marina, fed and cared for by Self and volunteers. A few miles upstream at Hunter's, high school members of Future Farmers of America installed more net pens as a school project, feeding and caring for hatchlings, aided by public donations.

Today four students are enrolled at Eastern Washington University in Cheney to study fisheries management. Other net pens are installed at Kettle Falls and Banks Lake. Self alone has sixteen nets on the lake now, all as a labor of love. Fish & Wildlife and Colville Tribes supply fry. These grass roots efforts have caused four hundred thousand trout to be released in 1990 and, it is hoped, five hundred thousand in 1991. In addition, a pilot project for twelve thousand kokanee is underway. Self and the Hunter's kids believe that "everyone has to become involved and not expect the government to do everything, that it takes individual effort to get things done."

An Eastern Washington University scientist has tagged some fish and will keep records of where they are found. Significantly, the tags have shown up in the lower Columbia River, indicating that fry have gone through Grand Coulee's giant turbines without injury.

That was the fortuitous partnership forged in 1933, of government money for a vast dam project and of volunteers willing to help ameliorate problems.

Pioneers and Archaeology

Water from the Columbia River indeed made Washington State a bread basket for the nation. Grains and vegetables grow profusely in the odd patterns dictated by irrigation machinery—circular, rectangular or between ditches. Along the river itself, orchards thrive on the benches and in the valleys, protected by bluffs from the chill winter winds, the temperature further moderated by the large volume of river water. The volcanic soil and long growing season (135 to 175 days) complete the ideal conditions for apple culture, enabling Washington to market over half the nation's apples by 1990.

Commercial orchards appeared about 1850 near Oroville, and at the Ahtanum Mission and Fort Simcoe in Yakima Valley in the 1860s. Although there are a whopping eight thousand varieties of apples, Red Delicious, Yellow Delicious and Granny Smith comprise ninety-seven percent of the crop. Orchardists graft buds from a parent tree onto rootstock to duplicate the parent, some rootstocks dating back two thousand years, according to the Washington Apple Commission.

Despite the moderate climate, frost is an ever-looming danger. Some growers use giant wind machines and occasionally heaters. Others turn on sprinklers; when water turns to ice on the trees, it protects the buds at the freezing point.

Until the development of controlled atmosphere storage methods, ripening apples were rushed into insulated warehouses, opened to cool down by night and closed tightly to resist daytime heat. Archie Van Doren, a "local boy," worked with Robert Smock in 1940 on the theory of controlled atmosphere storage for fruits as his project for a Ph.D. in horticulture from Cornell University.

An apple uses oxygen as it ripens; thus, if you limit the amount of oxygen, the ripening process slows or virtually ceases. Van Doren returned to Wenatchee in 1956 and persuaded an orchardist to install the necessary machinery—a gas-tight room kept at 30° to 32°F from which 97 to 98-1/2 percent of the oxygen is removed. The spring after storing apples in a controlled atmosphere facility, the orchardist sold apples at the New York Fruit Auction for $14 a box, instead of four or five dollars. The process is now in common use. It can be used for preserving bananas and floral products, as well.

Van Doren also developed a chemical thinner. When a tree blossoms, it develops a king bloom in the center and several side blooms. After the bloom opens and is pollinated, if sprayed with this substance, side blooms fall off, leaving the strong main blossom only. Hand-picking of side blooms is extremely expensive as an alternative. In 1966, the Washington Apple Commission honored Van Doren for his contributions to the industry.

In 1929 Wenatchee orchardist Herman Ohme envisioned an oasis near his home on a sere bluff overlooking the Columbia Valley. He brought in alpine shrubs and evergreen trees to shade the barren land and planted lawns. Over the decades the family has built rock-lined paths and a pool "so the kids could learn to swim." In 1939, yielding to popular demand, Ohme Gardens was opened to the public. The nine-acre garden is ranked among the top gardens of America.

From Ohme Gardens on a bluff above the river looking south over Wenatchee and the Columbia River.

An extensive interlocking park and trail system marks the western shore of the Columbia River, built by Chelan County Public Utility District (PUD), portions leased to the City of Wenatchee and the State of Washington for management. There is a wilderness wetlands. The trail adjacent to a 100-acre protected marsh is closed during eagle nesting season.

A great deal has been done to recognize heritage and restore riverfront use all the way from Chelan to beyond Wenatchee. Old-timer Kirby Billingsley of the *Wenatchee Daily World*, now incapacitated, was a champion of the idea "Selkirks to the Sea," for creating riverfront parks, trails and information sites along the entire length of the Columbia. While his concepts have not been totally implemented, there has been marked progress toward his goal. The Oregon Historical Society is promoting a Lewis and Clark Trail along the Columbia and a Clatskanie Canoe Trail among the islands in the river between Rainier and Cathlamet.

Not marring the scenery in any way, a gold mine exists inside the Wenatchee city limits. For decades prospectors came through Wenatchee, passing by the real lode. Today the Cannon Mine, Asamera Minerals, Inc., mines and processes gold *inside* a mountain so quietly that there are residents who do not realize it exists, the second largest underground gold mine in the United States.

A different kind of dig excited archaeologists in 1987. In an orchard above the Columbia at East Wenatchee, during the installation of an irrigation line, men turned up the largest fluted stone projectile points ever found (up to 9.25 inches long), mostly struck from agate. Stone tools and bone artifacts subsequently uncovered date back to the Ice Age, ten to twelve thousand years ago. The site is one of seven known Clovis sites in North America, the Clovis people entering the area about eleven thousand years ago, possibly over the Bering land bridge.

Additional excavations are being made under the direction of Dr. Michael Gramly, Curator of Anthropology at the Buffalo Museum of Science, in cooperation with the North Central Washington Museum of Wenatchee, where the artifacts are housed. If human bones are uncovered, they would comprise the earliest-known humans of North America. However, representatives from the Colville Federated Tribes, Yakima Nation and others question the propriety of disturbing human remains of any age.

The deep, primeval-appearing river canyon from Brewster/Bridgeport almost to Richland is a remarkable heritage site. Clearly these areas were inhabited heavily back into prehistoric mists. In a Moses Coulee cave, a stone pipe was found in a wooden case carved with figures similar to those on petroglyphs, also a stone knife with a charred wooden handle bound by sinew. Near Orondo just north of Wenatchee is an early rock shelter of primitive people, well above the current river level. There is evidence of an ancient earthslide near Wenatchee, another near Malaga; both may have dammed the river for a time, like the more recent 1872 Entiat slide. The area once was heavily forested with many edible plants and inhabited by primitive animals; among artifacts found are molars and parts of tusks, the huge femur of woolly mammoth and evidence of a cameloid creature.

While building the Milwaukee Railroad from Othello to Beverly, near today's Wanapum Dam, workers found a natural ice cave in which they stored foodstuffs. In the Columbia River above Priest Rapids Dam, a sequence of drawings on a rocky island was thought to depict creation and was called Genesis Rock.

Before rising waters from a succession of smaller PUD dams (Wells, Rocky Reach, Rock Island, Wanapum, Priest Rapids) buried significant artifacts, engineers frequently removed sections of boulders sporting petroglyphs and pictographs to museums within the dams. Bushels of arrowheads were removed and preserved.

Providing ideal storage for artifacts, the Wells, Rocky Reach and Wanapum dams have extensive galleries within each structure. They contain rock exhibits, geologic explanations, artifacts and historic photos and displays reviewing pioneer life, the rich riverboat history and gold mining. These dams have fish ladders (with public viewing areas); a thriving fish hatchery at Wells Dam contributes fingerlings to the river system.

Downstream from Rock Island Dam, from which a huge Alcoa plant and other industries receive their electricity, the Columbia River flows for thirty miles through a magnificent gorge unattainable except by boat or a road at the resort of Crescent Bar. On the old river bed were sand layers, topped by lava that cooled rapidly into angular six-sided columns, above which is lighter, more gaseous material called vesicular lava. The cliffs eroded to create weird formations and towers not unlike those at Bryce Canyon, Utah. The erosion is speeded by waters that leak into the basalt, then freeze and expand to fracture it. Early river travelers marveled at a large petrified tree upright on a high ledge, still there in the gorge.

Looking at the harsh landscape, one is overcome with the odd feeling that he or she has taken a wrong turn in time and wound up in a past eon when the earth was in a formative stage.

On the river's west bank at Vantage, the Gingko Petrified Forest State Park and Interpretive Center is surrounded by major petrified wood sites. In ancient times the Columbia River here was more than 8 miles wide and 600 feet deep. At least two hundred species of wood have been identified as growing in or near the swamps sixteen million years ago, among them oak, maple, hickory, gingko and—in the higher elevations—the great sequoia tree.

As described earlier, lava oozed repeatedly over eastern Washington. Between two of such outpourings, a big lake formed where Vantage is now. Trees then growing along the ancient Columbia fell over and sank to the bottom of the lake. Again the lava came and overcame the lake, covering the logs. Intense chemical activity and lack of oxygen caused petrification; different minerals present created the varying colors of the petrified woods. In a later period the land rose, leaving the desertlike area we know today, draining into the Columbia, the tilting and fracturing bringing petrified materials closer to the surface.

During the Depression of the 1930s, Civilian Conservation Corps (CCC) workers excavated petrified logs in the park for public viewing. The main site is two miles from Vantage, where there are hiking trails on the brown, sage-covered hills that rise like bubbles above the desert. An old-timer claims the ability to find petrified wood by "witching," as some people find water by "water witching." Scientists question this ability, but there is no denying he has found logs buried as deep as six lava flows beneath the surface.

In the Interpretive Center (closed except by appointment in winter), one may view a film and see wood exhibits. Debby Hall, interpreter, says that fifteen varieties of gingko trees grew nearby after the Ice Age, the only known place outside of China. Chinese used gingko seeds for medicine and religious rituals. Ten seeds were supposed to make one slightly intoxicated but were beneficial for kidney, liver and respiratory diseases, and some claim they reversed the onset of Alzheimer's disease.

The area is a virtual wind tunnel. Locals joke that "when the wind stops, everyone here falls down." The sudden onset of wind is no joke, however, for boaters and pilots in the area. The wind has even blown railway boxcars over.

During winter when the winds seemingly carve knife paths through one's skin, animals flock to the sparse river bottoms beneath the Gingko Interpretive Center. One year the State Patrol closed Interstate 90 for a time to protect a herd of 150 elk bent on crossing the freeway. Gingko's groundskeeper even saw an infrequent gray wolf in 1989. In 1985, during severe weather, elk, deer and smaller animals, including a rare albino fawn, came to seek shelter; with no food, they browsed on Vantage residents' trees and shrubs. Kind ranchers came with pickup loads of hay to rescue them from starvation. In recent years the Department of Wildlife has developed a grain and hay pellet for such emergencies.

The Columbia River's basaltic banks begin to diminish south of Vantage. Before Wanapum Dam and Priest Rapids Dam quieted the rapids, a small band of Wanapum Indians made their home around the southeast bend of the river, living primarily from the marvelous bounty of fish in the river. When explorers and settlers came to Washington (then Oregon Territory), Smohalla led the Wanapums, a highly religious and peaceful people, in the Dreamer religion. Its precepts were diametrically opposite to the ways of aggressive pioneers. Smohalla said:

> My young men shall never work. Men who work cannot dream and wisdom comes in dreams. ... You ask me to plow the ground. Shall I take a knife and tear my mother's bosom? You ask me to dig for stone. Shall I dig under her skin for her bones? Then when I die I cannot enter her body to be born again. You ask me to cut grass and make hay and sell it, and be rich like the white man, how dare I cut off my mother's hair? (Taken from display at Wanapum Dam Visitor Center.)

The Wanapum priests inspired Alexander Ross to name the rapids of their home "Priest Rapids." (There were two Priest Rapids on the Columbia River, the other north of Revelstoke.) The Wanapums were a peaceful people, never warring with anyone. Sahaptin-speaking and related to the Yakimas, Nez Perce and Cayuse, they lived in tule mat houses woven from reeds that grew 6 feet high near today's West Richland. They roamed to the Cascades to hunt sheep, elk and deer, and to Ephrata to gather roots. They made canoes and fished the river for suckers, eels, salmon—both with nets and wooden hoops—and gathered fresh-water mussels.

They neither sought nor were given any reservation or treaty, and in 1942, quietly surrendered certain lands around White Bluff on the Columbia River for the Hanford Project, receiving protection for their ancient burial grounds. Under the wise leadership of Puck-Hyah-Toot, who learned ancient ways from Smohalla, the small group managed to live in two worlds successfully. Because of frequent marriage outside the tribe, only twelve full-blooded Wanapums remain today.

Early pioneers and cattlemen used a ford on the Columbia River near the Wanapums' lands. Most famous was Ben Snipes, who came to the area in 1854 to found a cattle kingdom that spread from The Dalles to the Yakima River. With the assistance of several Indians, friends more than mere employees, Snipes ran more than a hundred thousand cattle (and large herds of fine horses, cayuse mares bred to Hambletonian stallions) on the rolling Horse Heaven Hills and Yakima Valley.

Years later a magnificent palomino stallion dubbed the "Golden Ghost" (a descendant of Snipes' Hambletonian, no doubt) roamed the wild country with his band of mares, cleverly escaping horse hunters. When he finally was caught, his captor patiently but unsuccessfully tried to train him. Soon afterward the rancher died, and Clayton Speck of Sunnyside bought the stallion, trucked him to the wilderness and turned him loose to roam wild and free.

Snipes' initial stake was made by driving cattle herds to the hungry miners at Barkerville (Canada), crossing the Columbia River twice— once near Priest Rapids, once above today's Bridgeport. The crossings at Priest were aided by Wanapum Indians who formed an "alley" of canoes upstream and downstream to prevent cattle from bolting during the crossing. Unfortunately, Snipes lost his fortune during the Depression of 1893. His original crude cabin is in Sunnyside City Park, his grave in The Dalles.

Snipes was not alone, just the largest cattle rancher. Before wheat farms and Grand Coulee irrigation, the tangled bluffs and flats of the Columbia were more suited to ranching. A legendary cowboy was Ben Hutchinson, a giant 6 feet 6 inches tall, who raised horses east of Wanapum Dam. Neighbors said that as he approached on horseback, erect in a saddle with long tapaderos (leather decorations from the stirrups), it appeared that his legs touched the ground. When he became old and frail, he built a pulley on the barn roof to lift the heavy saddle onto his horse. He had chased the wild horses on the hills, mostly fugitives from ranches. Their trails through Crab Creek to watering holes on the Columbia River can still be detected.

The vast plains broke some men's minds. Rabbits ate every green thing. Occasionally the residents would get together and have a rabbit drive to thin their numbers. Neighbors were few, the wind blew dust to and fro, narrow trails often were blocked by drifting sand and tumbleweeds and the lonely yip-yip of coyotes sent prehensile shivers down one's spine.

An eccentric settler wallpapered his home with rattlesnake skins, decidedly smelly. A paid worker on the new Milwaukee Railroad had a conviction that he and God were building a railroad from Quincy to Smyrna. The man cleared brush as a right of way for some distance from his home, but got into trouble with the law when he tried to sell unlisted securities to raise capital. Worse off was a miner who saw a woman walking right through the wall into his house. She gave him specific directions as to the location of lost treasure on his farm. After unsuccessful digging, the man bought dynamite to blast. As he was tamping the first charge, the dynamite went off, sending the tamping stick upward through his jaw, coming out through his skull, the end of his aberrations forever.

With an eerie beauty of its own, dramatic near dusk and dawn and when a storm approaches, the land between Wenatchee and Richland has attracted sun-worshippers today. At least two extensive condominium resorts are active. Utilizing Columbia River irrigation water, growers have turned the easterly desert shores into vineyards and orchards. West of the river and beyond the large Yakima Firing Center (army) and the forbidding, deserted Rattlesnake Hills, the verdant Yakima River valley is rich with commercial produce gardens and fruit orchards, Yakima apples, in particular, known worldwide.

Sunset over the Columbia River.

Travel and Trivia
U.S. Border to Priest Rapids

Colville Chamber of Commerce, P.O. Box 267, Colville, WA 99114.

At the north end of **Northport** by the sawmill is the old smelter's smokestack, all that remains of a lively period. Adjacent to the mill is a grassy haven, a small city park and boat launch on the Columbia River. A few miles north on the Waneta highway is infamous **Deadman's Eddy**, still dangerous; can be seen from the road.

Ask locals at Northport where you could see the **Chinese ditches** from old mining days.

For a scenic drive take the road on the west side of the river southbound to Kettle Falls. "Chicken-track" gravel road for about ten miles, but maintained, then paved. Good views of **the dangerous Dalles**, although rocks were dynamited out of there.

Snag Cove Campground adjacent to Columbia River about six miles north of Kettle Falls on west side road, only a few spots.

Two miles below the **Kettle Falls bridge** over the Columbia, where the Rickey Rapids or Grand Rapids once were, there is a tiny marina tucked in behind a point. Good sailing in this part of **Lake Roosevelt** for miles and miles of broad river, lots of trees, scenic. A good NPS campground there, boat launch, marina with slips and buoys and houseboat rentals—**Kettle Falls Marina**, Kettle Falls, WA 99141. (509) 738-2120. You can rent canoes, patio boats, fishing skiffs and 52-foot houseboats entirely furnished which sleep twelve. Hundreds of miles of safe cruising and shoreside loafing. Two net pens there for trout. In Washington state 1-800-635-7585.

Recommended reading about Indians, heavily illustrated: *With One Sky Above Us*, by M. Gidley (New York: Putnam Sons, 1979). Also *Frank Matsura, Frontier Photographer* by JoAnn Roe (Seattle: Madrona Publishers, 1981) has many photos of Colville Tribes people. Several definitive histories of Indians by Robert Ruby and John Brown are in print.

On the east side of Columbia toward Kettle Falls is **St. Paul's Mission**, one of the oldest churches in Washington. It was the site for Indian fishing camps, burial grounds and below the bluff was Hudson's Bay Company Fort Colvile, now totally underwater, commemorated by a plaque. Father Anthony Ravalli, a Jesuit, encouraged the Indians to build St. Paul's.

By time of publication the new **Kettle Falls Interpretive Center** should be finished with pictures and displays emphasizing the importance of the site to the Indians, fishing, etc. Adjacent to the bridge.

Town and Country Days in Kettle Falls, first weekend in June. Grouch of the Year is chosen, too.

Lake Roosevelt Sailboat Regatta, July, ask Kettle Falls tourist information, Double H Motel (509) 738-6514.

Somewhat new are verdant **family-owned orchards** on the river bench from Kettle Falls southward. Many vie for your roadside or commercial purchases.

Historic St. Regis Mission, later a school for Indian children, is now **My Parents' Estate Bed and Breakfast Inn**. The old academy is lovingly restored and furnished beautifully. One mile east of Kettle Falls on Highway 395. (509) 738-6220.

Call Chuck Lacey about **tours of Kettle Falls Generating Station**, Washington Water Power Company (see text). (509) 738-2449. Also ask Boise Cascade, adjacent to Generating Station, if they can provide tours (509) 734-6421.

East Portal Interpretive Site along Highway 20, west of Kettle Falls, includes a half-mile Log Flume Trail. Learn something about logging history. Dine and mentally picture the old Hudson's Bay fort and Kettle Falls grumbling over rocks from **Barney's Cafe**, junction 395 and 20, Kettle Falls. Good standard food. Across the street **Hudson Bay Steak & Seafood** is proud of its "Murphy Steak," a 14-ounce tenderloin stuffed with garlic. Walls decorated with artifacts—snowshoes, saws, horse gear.

Eight miles east of Kettle Falls is **Colville**, a respectable community once less so as Pinkney City at the time of Ft. Colville, the military fort (see text). It's worth visiting **Stevens County Historical Museum** and **Keller House** (built in 1910, original wallpaper and glass), 700 North Wynne Street. Keller House hosts a holiday candlelight tour in December. Archives here for researchers. (509) 684-5968.

When you're hungry after visiting the museum, have sensational turtle pie at **D & P Restaurant**, 995 South Main, Colville. A huge selection of sinful pies.

Panorama Motel at south end of Colville is one of many good motels.

Colville PRCA Rodeo Father's Day weekend. Rendezvous Days first weekend of August.

Enjoy riverside scenes by taking Highway 25 south from Kettle Falls. Connects to Gifford-Inchelium Ferry westbound to the **Colville Indian Reservation**, or south through the interesting village of **Hunter's** (**Country Calico Gifts** there in an old church building), where there are net pens. See how grandma shopped at **Daisy Mae's General Store**, Hunter's.

Across the Spokane River near the junction with the Columbia is old **Fort Spokane**. Several buildings remain. A self-guided interpretive trail, National Park Service.

Near the infamous **Hellgate Rapids**, historic but defunct Lincoln, Fruitland and other disappeared towns, Win Self developed **Seven Bays Estates** on tortuous bluffs adjacent to the Columbia. Full marina service and boat rentals, an extensive RV park, store and—quite surprisingly in this remote location—a quality restaurant with fine cuisine, a concession of the **Colville Federated Tribes**. Near Seven Bays you can see where a big landslide blocked the Columbia River in 1906 (see text). No overnight facilities other than RV or camping. (509) 725-5794.

This area is the northerly edge of the barren Columbia Plain; the river veers west and north and steep bluffs force a motorist to drive south to **Creston** to proceed to Grand Coulee (Highway 2 and 174). The **Keller Ferry** from south of Wilbur toward Republic crosses Lake Roosevelt. No motels, River Rue RV Park near ferry.

At Keller Ferry is the chief marina for the Colville Federated Tribes' luxurious **Lake Roosevelt houseboat rentals**. Two net pens here. Main business offices for the houseboat rentals is **Roosevelt Recreational Enterprises**, Reservations Office, P. O. Box 587, Grand Coulee, WA 99133-0587. Outside Washington State (509) 633-0201, inside state 1-800-648-LAKE. More than 630 miles of shoreline to explore in a houseboat at least 46 feet in length with swim ladder, slide and all amenities. For midsummer rentals must reserve far ahead, even one year. September/October is equally good and reservations less tight. Rent small ski boats, too, at Keller Ferry Marina or Seven Bays.

Here's as good a place as any to **talk about fishing**. There are at least 25 species of fish in Roosevelt Lake, the most sought after being cutthroat and rainbow trout, mountain whitefish, northern squawfish, brook, brown and Dolly Varden trout, kokanee—a landlocked sockeye salmon. You can catch walleye, bullhead, perch, bass, ling cod, chinook salmon and gigantic sturgeon as large as 13 feet long weighing a half ton (you'll think you hooked onto a log). Trolling is the most popular method of fishing, but you can cast from shore with lures; waterdogs and crayfish are used for bass, some use worms or even whole kernel corn as bait. Fly fishermen would prefer some of the fast-flowing tributaries. Need Washington or Tribal fishing licenses. Ask a ranger station or contact **Coulee Dam National Recreational Area**, Superintendent, Box 37, Coulee Dam, WA 99116.

Grand Coulee Dam area:

Grand Coulee Dam Area **Chamber of Commerce**, P.O. Box 760, Grand Coulee, WA 99133. (509) 633-3074.

The manmade wonder of **Grand Coulee Dam** is enhanced by the nightly show, "Laser Lights," Memorial Day through September 30. Historical narration and laser art with the dam as a screen. Annual **Laser Light Festival** on Memorial Day weekend nominated as one of Top 100 Events in North America by American Bus Association. Good viewing from the deck of **Coulee House Motel** or free bleachers across the street. Over the Dam 5K and 10K run mid-August. Fantastic fireworks off the dam July 4. **Colorama Rodeo** second weekend of May.

The **Visitors Arrival Center** shows a film "Fountain of Life" as an introduction to tours. Photo exhibits and displays explain the massive project.

Pretend you are a dam worker by staying in **Four Winds Bed and Breakfast**, Grand Coulee, which used to be a dormitory for men. I am sure the rooms and splendiferous breakfasts were not a part of the original setup.

Colville Tribal Museum is in Coulee Dam, with interpretive displays of their cultures. Andy Joseph, historian, and others are very knowledgeable. 516 Birch Street.

The old **Wild Life Restaurant** on the main street of Grand Coulee is a *building* from B Street—but now is a respectable restaurant with good food, instead of a red light place.

The **Sky Deck Motel** on Banks Lake has big units, some housekeeping, adjacent to the water, quiet bay. Highway 155, Electric City, WA 99123. (509) 633-0290. Moped rentals nearby at Fun 'n Sun, Inc.

You can work the energy out of kids at **Coulee Playland Resort**, Highway 155, Electric City, a tree-lined park on Banks Lake with full RV hookups, boat rentals.

Absolutely drive Highway 155 south through the awesome **Grand Coulee**. There are one hundred RV hookups at **Steamboat Rock State Park**, plus tent camps and boat launch, right on the water in the Coulee. Continue on to **Dry Falls State Park**, a heritage site, to truly understand and marvel at the cataclysmic flood that carved out the coulees (see text). Interpretive center, Lake Lenore Caves, hiking, also **rattlesnakes galore** in barren areas—look and listen!

North of Grand Coulee Dam at **Nespelem** is the headquarters of the Colville Federated Tribes—offices, library, archives, etc. On July 4 each year Indians in full regalia gather from far and wide; as many as two thousand people camp out. A real experience. You must obtain permission from the **Tribal Office** to park overnight with a vehicle. Not far to motels in Grand Coulee area, but none whatsoever in Nespelem. In August at the **Omak Stampede**, forty miles west of Nespelem, Indians also set up a tepee encampment and have Indian dance competition. The Suicide Race attracts many Indian horseback competitors, also.

Just downriver from Grand Coulee, the **Chief Joseph Dam** has a visitor center.

At the confluence of the Okanogan River with the Columbia, there is an interpretive center about **Fort Okanogan**, the old Hudson's Bay post.

Nothing remains of the old riverboat docks at **Brewster** and **Bridgeport**. From the cove at the east end of Brewster, however, you can imagine the scene.

Lake Pateros Motor Inn is directly on a wide spot of the Columbia River; sleep 50 feet from the water. Cast your line from green lawns. A block or so south is a U-bolt used by riverboats to winch themselves up the Methow Rapids.

For a great side trip, drive up the **Methow Valley** from Pateros to restored western town of Winthrop, gateway to North Cascades Highway, spectacular mountain scenery. Try mountain-top **Sun Mountain Lodge**, horseback riding, rafting, etc. Office in downtown Winthrop.

A Winthrop artist, **Frederick W. Hubbard**, paints Northwest Indians, including arresting rendition of Chief Joseph, also Lincoln Rock on the Columbia River. Works are shown at **Hildabob's** and **The Woodsman Gallery** in Winthrop, or write Fred himself at P.O. Box 327, Winthrop, WA 98862. Works are often in four and five figures, but numbered prints of some available at modest prices.

At **Wells Dam** parking lot south of Pateros, a chunk of rock with Indian petroglyphs is exhibited. The Indians used ochre—iron ore pounded into dust and mixed with oil. Adjacent is a state fish hatchery.

Lake Chelan area:

Lake Chelan **Chamber of Commerce**, P.O. Box 216, Chelan, WA 98816. 1-800-4-CHELAN.

High above the Columbia River, its outlet plummeting through Chelan gorge and over Chelan Falls, is fifty-two-mile **Lake Chelan**, one of the state's most popular visitor destinations. Mountains rise straight up from the water in places on this 1,500-foot-deep lake. Boating, sailboarding, horseback riding, major resorts like Wapato Point, relatively warm water for swimming, good restaurants, night life ... it's all there.

Prime attraction is the **sightseeing trip on Lake Chelan** in either the *Lady Express* (fast) or the more leisurely *Lady of the Lake*, both big passenger boats with food aboard, like a mini-ocean cruise. Goes to unroaded wilderness at **Stehekin**, where one might stay overnight at a NPS concession lodge. Boat reservations a good idea. 1-800-4-CHELAN or (509) 682-2224.

River Walk, a walking park along the Chelan River at lake outlet. Chelan Falls and its gorge are below; **do not enter the gorge** as no one can predict water release from the dam. You can see the falls from the town of Chelan Falls.

Hang gliding national competition held at Chelan. One gets to tremendous heights because the lake is 1,200 feet above the river, causing thermal currents. Hang gliders have gone to 6,000-feet altitude and landed fifty miles away. Many sailing and other water-related regattas.

An interesting gallery is **Stage Stop Antiques**, junction of Highways 150 and 97A, 513 West Webster, Chelan. Rooms of antiques, collections of apple labels, postcards, old matted photos.

Columbia country influences the works of noted **artist Rod Weagant**, who also shows Rich Beyer sculptures by appointment. 1318 Washington Street, Manson, WA 98831. (509) 687-3959.

Allison Gallery specializes in gifts, arts, crafts of quality and home items, and shows work of artist Ron McGaughey (includes Columbia coulees). 71 Wapato Way, Manson, WA. (509) 687-3534.

Historical drama plus off-the-wall comedy prevails at **The Crockery**, downtown Chelan, Friday and Saturday nights, year-round. This dinner theater, very innovative and entertaining, is upstairs from the popular restaurant (where some people eat 20-ounce porterhouse steaks). Reservations advisable, limited seating. 114 Emerson. (509) 682-5925.

The most historic landmark in Chelan is **Campbell's Resort** on the lake at the foot of Woodin Avenue on eight acres. An Iowa farm boy and police magistrate, Judge Clinton C. Campbell purchased the hotel site for $400 in 1900, opening the Chelan Hotel (Campbell's) with a masquerade ball. There were 259 people for dinner on July 4, 1901, when horse races and a lively celebration crowded the town. By 1947, the successful Holden Mine up-lake further increased business. The resort today includes conference rooms for three hundred, plus the motel and top-notch restaurant. History has not been forgotten. Campbell's has its original hotel register, historic photos on walls and Judge

Campbell memorabilia. Box 278, 104 W. Woodin Avenue, Chelan WA 98816-0278. (509) 682-2561 or 1-800-553-8225.

Chelan, the Methow Valley and Wenatchee have become popular in winter for **cross-country skiing**. Snowmobiles available for rent at (509) 682-5125 or 663-0642, Chelan. **River House Bed and Breakfast** has a fine cross-country ski package, December through February. 307 Second, Chelan, WA 98816. (509) 682-5122.

In downtown Chelan at 142 E. Woodin Avenue, **Special Additions** has country gifts.

Bach Fest in late July, Chelan. Frequent sailing regattas and hang gliding events.

Wenatchee area:

Wenatchee Area **Visitors & Convention Bureau**, P.O. Box 850, Wenatchee, WA 98801. (509) 662-4774.

Mission Ridge Ski Area above Wenatchee boasts powder snow for downhill skiing from beginner to difficult, four chairs and rope tows. Nordic skiing, Winter Sunfest and major races. For information (509) 663-3200.

Between Brewster and Wenatchee (and beyond) the mighty Columbia still runs between dry, steep, rocky bluffs, a magnificent canyon that rivals those in Utah and Arizona. Near Entiat you can see where the 1872 earthquake jarred loose Ribbon Cliff; one good place from which to view it is **Daroga State Park**, one mile north and across the river from Entiat. The park on the Columbia River is delightfully green, RV hookups, tennis courts, very scenic. Lincoln Rock is approximately west of Rocky Reach Dam.

Steep, eroding sand hills on the eastern shore of the Columbia host Lombardy poplar trees, orchards and fields, like a scene from Switzerland. On the west shore cliffs rise up sheer and terrifying, bare of any vegetation.

Grand Coulee native, Clyde Pangborn, won the Asahi Shimbun prize for the first Pacific nonstop flight from Japan to Wenatchee in 1931. Plaque at **Pangborn Memorial Airport**.

At **Rocky Reach Dam's Visitor Center** near Wenatchee one may learn about the grain chutes that went from bluff to riverboat. "Gallery of the Columbia," photos of sternwheelers, river artifacts, pioneer displays, changing art exhibits.

See the striking Clovis fluted points and artifacts from the Richey Clovis Cache at **North Central Washington Regional Museum**, also regional history displays and a gift shop, including books about the area. Archives. 127 South Mission Street, Wenatchee, WA 98801-3030. (509) 664-5989.

Wenatchee Riverfront Park is an enlightened approach to river use.

Ohme Gardens three miles north of Wenatchee, above junction of Highways 2 and 97, April 15–October 16, seven days a week. 3327 Ohme Road, Wenatchee, WA 98801. (509) 662-5785. Overlooks Columbia River.

Washington State Apple Blossom Festival around May 1 each year. Plan ahead. Parade, queen, arts and crafts fair, relay races. (509) 662-3616.

Visit the **Washington Apple Commission Visitor Center** for film and displays about apple-growing. Gift shop for apple-related products. 2900 Euclid Avenue, Wenatchee, WA 98801. (509) 663-9600. A bit hard to find, going north toward Highways 2/97, turn toward river before freeway bridge.

At nearby **Cashmere** on Highway 2, tour **Aplets & Cotlets Candy Kitchen**. Samples, too, of confections made from apples, apricots, grapes and other fruits. Liberty Orchards Co., Inc., 117 Mission Street, P.O. Box C, Cashmere, WA 98815. (509) 782-2191.

Nearby is the **Pioneer Village and Chelan County Historical Museum**, Cashmere, unusually complete for a small museum.

Then dine in style at a charming old-fashioned restaurant with home-baked bread, fresh fruits when available, desserts from scratch and English afternoon tea. **The Pewter Pot**, 124-1/2 Cottage Avenue, Cashmere, WA 98815. (509) 782-2036.

Beyond Cashmere a few miles is an entire **Bavarian-style town** at the foot of towering mountain peaks. Devoted to tourism and special events—Autumn Leaf Festival, Christmas Lighting, Maifest, etc. Snow events in winter. Write Chamber of Commerce, P.O. Box 327, Leavenworth, WA 98826. (509) 548-5807.

Red-Tail Canyon Farm gives hayrides and chuckwagon barbecue for groups of 15 or more, and sleigh rides in winter for individuals with reservations. (509) 548-4512.

Greater Yakima Chamber of Commerce, P.O. Box 1490, Yakima, WA 98907. (509) 248-2021. Although it is not on the Columbia River, you should visit the **Yakima Nation Museum** at Toppenish, Washington and its restaurant, Heritage Inn. Excellent food and handsome decor. Indian chants as background to dining. Standard and Indian foods such as *Luk-a-meen*, little dumplings with flakes of salmon served with Indian fry bread.

U. S. Forest Service **Information Center for campgrounds** and activities: 428 West Woodin, Chelan, WA 98816. (509) 682-2576.

Wenatchee and **East Wenatchee**, an area of forty thousand, have numerous excellent motels, hotels and restaurants. Among them are

Chieftain Motel & Restaurant, 1005 North Wenatchee Avenue, Wenatchee, WA 98807. (509) 663-8141. In Washington 1-800-572-4456. Ski packages for Mission Ridge skiers. **West Coast Wenatchee Center Hotel** (also convention center, large capacity), 201 North Wenatchee Avenue, Wenatchee, WA 98801. (509) 662-1234 or 1-800-426-0670. **Rivers Inn and Rivers-Haven** Restaurant facing the river, 580 Valley Mall Parkway, East Wenatchee, WA 98802. (509) 884-1474. 1-800-922-3199 in Washington, 1-800-528-1234 elsewhere. **The Pink House**, bed and breakfast, 2504 #1 Canyon Road, Wenatchee, WA 98801. (509) 663-6031. **Prospector Pies**, a good all-around restaurant, 731 North Wenatchee Avenue, Wenatchee, WA 98801. (509) 662-1118. **Siraco's**, 17 South Mission Street, excellent and inexpensive Greek and American foods, including Rigatoni Greek Style, Pasteecho (stuffed grape leaves), chicken-fried steak, apricot cheesecake. (509) 663-7985. At **Murphy's Steakhouse** dance to a live band, 123 Easy Street, Wenatchee, WA 98801. (509) 663-6031.

State Parks along the Columbia River, Chief Joseph Dam to Vantage: **Chief Joseph State Park**, five miles northwest of Bridgeport on Lake Pateros, off State Route 173, Douglas County, boat launching, primitive camping. **Fort Okanogan State Park** on State Route 17, picnicking, interpretive center. **Daroga State Park**, eighteen miles north of East Wenatchee on Highway 97, east bank of Columbia, RV hookups, picnicking, boat moorage and launching, trails. **Lincoln Rock State Park**, north of East Wenatchee on Highway 97, east bank of Columbia, RV hookups, boat launching and moorage, amphitheater, guarded swimming beach. **Wenatchee Confluence State Park**, Olds Station Road, at confluence of Wenatchee River with Columbia. Close to city, RV hookups, swimming beach, boat launching, nature trails. **Gingko Petrified Forest Interpretive Center**, Interstate 90 and Columbia River, Vantage, picnicking, hiking trails in petrified wood area. **Gingko/Wanapum State Park** is south on west-bank road from Vantage, has hookups, boat launch, fishing (**Wanapum Dam Visitor Center** approached from east bank).

Grant County Visitor Information Center, P. O. Box 37, Ephrata, WA 98823. 1-800-992-6234. Ask about bird-watching, float trips, all types of boating, wildlife refuges along the lower coulees from Moses Lake south.

Vantage KOA and Motel, P. O. Box 135, Vantage, WA 98950. (509) 856-2230. Adequate and clean, it's the only one for miles around. Restaurant has good, general fare.

Gem and mineral shop adjacent to **Gingko Interpretive Center**. Petrified wood items for sale plus nonlocal gems and rocks, arrowheads.

Interested in **geology**? Write for list, "Publications of the Washington Division of Geology and Earth Resources," Mail Stop PY-12, Olympia, WA 98504.

Not that far away at **Ellensburg**, Washington, a major rodeo every Labor Day weekend, plus Kittitas County Fair.

An unforgettable experience—visually and musically—attend a **"Music in the Gorge"** concert in the open-air amphitheatre on a Columbia River bluff near **George**, Washington, east of Gingko Forest. Big name artists. Write 1123 Maple Avenue Southwest, Suite 100, Renton, WA 98055, or call (206) 226-7300 for summer schedule.

Desert Aire, restaurant, gift shop and real estate on the banks of the Columbia River between Wenatchee and Tri-Cities. Mattawa, WA 99344.

Stop at **Wanapum Dam**, visit museum in dam, books on area. Fish viewing area.

Crescent Bar Resort on the Columbia River has condominiums, campground, RV hookups, golf course, boat launch, tennis. 864 Crescent Bar Road, No. 29, Quincy, WA 98848. (509) 787-1511.

Suggested **reading about Yakima Indian Nation** and wars: *Ka-mi-akin* by A. J. Splawn (1917, see your library) and *Strangers on the Land* by Click Relander (Toppenish, WA: Yakima Indian Nation, 1962).

Tri-Cities and Down the River

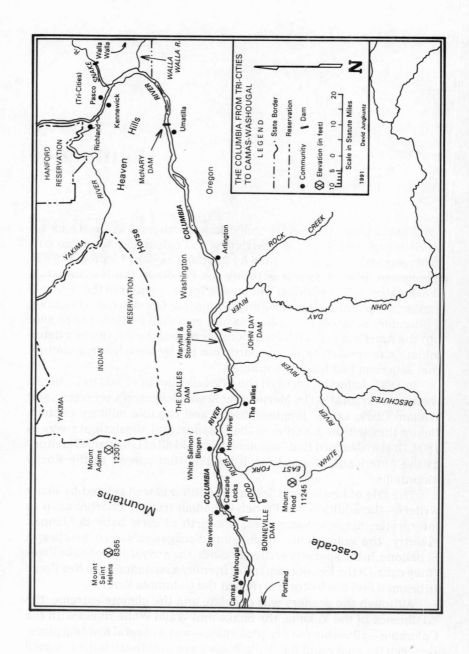

THE COLUMBIA FROM TRI-CITIES
TO CAMAS-WASHOUGAL

LEGEND

⚬ ⚬ ⚬ State Border
— · — · — Reservation
• Community ▸ Dam
⊗ Elevation (in feet)

Scale in Statute Miles
10 5 0 10 20

1991   David Jungkuntz

Confluence

As the eighteenth century ended, large sections of western America were unexplored. Especially intriguing to English and American governments was the news, verified by Captain Gray and Lieutenant W. R. Broughton, of a vast river entering the Pacific in the Northwest. In Washington, D.C., President Thomas Jefferson pondered the report of explorer Alexander Mackenzie suggesting that Great Britain should set a boundary south of the Columbia and establish settlements to shut out the Americans. British intentions increased the President's determination to send an exploring party into the western lands, a venture that Jefferson had long championed.

In 1803, Jefferson secured the princely sum of $2,500 to finance a westward exploration by Meriwether Lewis, Jefferson's secretary, and William Clark, Lewis' longtime friend and capable military captain. Before they left the junction of the Missouri and Mississippi rivers in 1804, the two learned that Napoleon had sold all of Louisiana Territory to the Americans, a vast French holding that spread to the Rocky Mountains.

The tale of Lewis and Clark's expedition is well related by many writers—the addition of a French-Canadian trapper Charbonneau as interpreter, his wife Sacagawea, the birth of their baby in Mandan country, the coincidence of meeting Sacagawea's own brother, a Shoshone, in the sparsely settled Rockies, the arrival at the Snake River (they called it the Kimooenim) after friendly assistance from Nez Perce tribesmen and the historic arrival at the Columbia River.

Although the scenery was desolate and the climate extreme, the confluence of the Yakima, the Snake and Walla Walla rivers with the Columbia—all within twenty-plus miles—was a natural meeting place. Between the Snake and the Walla Walla were traditional Indian council grounds, where Snake, Yakima, Cayuse and other bands pounded out uneasy alliances. In 1805, the Lewis and Clark expedition used the same grounds for a conference.

The journals of the expedition mention the arrival on October 16, 1805, at the confluence after the party successfully traversed several lively rapids on the Snake, probably where Ice Harbor Dam now is located.

> The Kimooenim empties itself into the Columbia. ... We halted above the point of junction on the Kimooenim to confer with the Indians, who had collected in great numbers to receive us. On landing we were met by our two chiefs ... and also the two Indians who had passed us a few days since on horseback; one of whom appeared to be a man of influence. ... After smoking with the Indians, we formed a camp at the point where the two rivers unite. ... A chief came from the Indian camp about a quarter of a mile up the Columbia, at the head of nearly two hundred men: they formed a regular procession, keeping time to the ... music of their drums, which they accompanied with their voices. (Meriwether Lewis, *Lewis and Clark Journals*, Vol. II [New York: J.B. Lippincott Company, 1961], 420.)

Much as it is today, the width of the Columbia below the junction was estimated at one to three miles. The junction marked a territorial division between Indian groups, with the Yakima Nation and their kindred on the west side, Nez Perce, Snake and Cayuse on the east and south of the Wallula bend. While the party rested, Captain Clark made a short side trip up the Columbia as far as the Yakima River, where he was greeted cordially by Yakima Indians. Clark commented that they were industrious and their civilization well established, but they suffered from eye disease and blindness, presumed to result from blowing sand and the glare from desert and river.

As the party made its way downriver through the numerous rapids (as many as one hundred existed prior to dams between the Snake and Portland), their encounters continued to be guardedly friendly. The Indians were reassured as to the expedition's peaceful intentions by Sacagawea's presence, for Indians never brought women on a war party. Intensely curious Indians clustered around at every stopping place and particularly delighted in the Americans' violin music and lively dancing of an evening. Of further wonder was York, Lewis's black helper.

Nearing the "Great Falls of the Columbia," or Celilo Falls, the men saw evidences of prior European or American visitors ... brass buttons, kettles, sailors' jackets, and talk of a trader Mr. Haley who lived down river.

Around Celilo Falls the Indians prepared fish to be traded to Indians of the Columbia Gorge, who then sold it to ships calling at the Columbia's mouth. The salmon was dried, then pulverized and placed in a basket of grass and reeds, lined with salmon skin, where it was pressed down firmly and covered with another salmon skin, laced tightly together. Several such baskets were stacked up and encased tightly in porous matting to make a ninety to one hundred pound bundle. The fish remained edible for years.

Below Celilo Falls, the expedition encountered still different Indian groups who skillfully manned high prowed canoes that were very seaworthy in rough water. They saw many sea otter from the Gorge to the ocean and ate well on fish and game. The main annoyance was a profusion of fleas. The Indians themselves moved their camps regularly to escape them. The narrator described the joyful end to their voyage on November 7, 1805:

> The river widens into a kind of bay crowded with low islands, subject to be overflowed occasionally by the tide. We had not gone far from this village [of Wahkiakums] when the fog cleared off, and we enjoyed the delightful prospect of ocean; that ocean, the object of all our labours, the reward of all our anxieties. This cheering view exhilarated the spirits of all the party, who were still more delighted on hearing the distant roar of the breakers. (*Ibid.*, 473.)

However, upon encamping, they became dangerously pinned down on a northside beach (Chinook), where the tide rose to inundate their camp, sweeping canoes away. Breakers were so high that they could not dream of crossing the broad estuary to shelter. Moving to a slightly better, but still exposed camp, the party was unable to cross the wild and mighty Columbia for almost three weeks.

Once on the more protected south side of the river, the weary and wet party members built cabins on the Lewis River, some distance from the windy Columbia, in a heavy woods where elk abounded. There they repaired clothing, traveled to the ocean to evaporate sea water for salt, traded what little goods they had with the Indians, and waited for spring and a return east.

When spring came, they were off upstream. Now they discovered the veiled entrance to the Willamette River and explored upstream past Portland's site. After further adventures, the party members were welcomed home by Jefferson. Their grueling but admirably executed trip was a key factor in securing the Columbia River country, the Oregon Territory, for the United States.

Then came the Astorians by sea to build a fort in 1810 near the mouth of the river, and David Thompson of Hudson's Bay was the next explorer to travel the Columbia River to the sea in 1811, as described earlier.

Among the Astorians was Alexander Ross, possibly the liveliest chronicler of that period, an adventurer who traveled with Thompson, Franchere, Cox and David Stuart. He was stationed at Fort Okanogan, Red River and elsewhere. Astor had sent a party to Astoria by ship and another overland under Wilson Price Hunt. The party was plagued by poor choice of a route, Indian troubles, dissension and deaths. The bedraggled survivors reached Astoria on February 15, 1812.

During their brief stay at Fort Astoria, the Astorians made two mistakes that had far-ranging negative repercussions. During an upriver trading trip, the Astorians had summarily hanged a man for taking a silver goblet from camp. Back at Fort Astoria, an officer sought to impress the Chinooks when he took an empty bottle, shook it and said it contained the smallpox disease—if they did not behave, he would release it. Thereafter, when Indians upriver got the disease by contact with whites, they thought the white man really did release smallpox on purpose.

In 1813 Pierre Dorion, an interpreter for Hunt, and eight other men under John Reed returned to Vale, Oregon, to set up a post. Because the Bannock Indians were so hostile, Reed built a second post on the Snake, where Marie Dorion happened to be on a fateful day. Hearing from a friendly Indian of a plot to kill the trappers, she and her two children rushed through the woods to warn them at the first post, encountering one survivor who told her of the attack, then died. At the post she found everyone dead, scalped and cut to pieces. Madame Dorion and her children spent two agonizing nights in the woods watching to see if Indians returned. It was winter and the youngsters were freezing, yet she was afraid to start a fire.

She told Alexander Ross later that, after dark, she went into the post and found fish scattered about. The provisions kept her and her children from starvation. Madame Dorion set out with her children packed in robes on her one horse, traveling through deep snow and over rocks for nine days. When she and the horse could no longer walk, she made a camp at an overhanging cliff, killed the horse for food and built a hut. After fifty-three lonely and fearful days, they trudged on. Madame Dorion became snow blind and stopped briefly, but fearing starvation had to continue. Finally she saw smoke. The camp was of friendly Walla Walla Indians. The plucky woman is remembered at Wallula with a plaque at Madame Dorion Memorial Park.

Alexander Ross had his own troubles with Indians in 1814. He traveled from his small outpost (Fort Okanogan) south to buy horses at the big summer encampment around Ellensburg. Ross boldly entered the camp with a few men and two women, one with a child, and sought to exchange trade goods for horses. Perhaps because they had lost relatives to smallpox, the Indians were sullen, jeering at the traders and running off their horses. Ross feigned indifference and went about trading for one horse at a time. Each time he made a purchase, hostiles drove the animal off.

Fearing the seizure of the women and child, Ross spirited them away by night and faced furious warriors the next morning. Matters further deteriorated when an Indian grabbed a sheath knife from the belt of a Canadian. The latter lunged at the thief. Suddenly hushed, the encampment waited. In a brilliant gesture Ross stepped into the fray, holding his own elaborately carved knife, hilt-first, to the Indian, saying that *here* was a knife for a chief. Suddenly the man smiled and waved the better knife, returning the other to its owner. The Indians then gave the Ross party food and returned all the horses.

Four years later, on the Columbia River north of the Walla Walla River, Alexander Ross and North West Company employees built a trading post, Fort Nez Perces. Ross described the treeless spot as "more like a lake than a river—with low green hills rising from its distant shore" [the Columbia River]—not very different from its appearance today. The local Indians' chief concern was that the traders would arm their mortal enemies, the Snakes. The strategically placed fort became known as the "Gibraltar of the Columbia," and, renamed Fort Walla Walla after the Hudson's Bay merger, operated until the closure of British-owned posts below the new Canadian-American border.

For the next three decades the fur traders used the river as a highway to supply trading posts thriving from Astoria to farthest British Columbia.

In 1824, Sir George Simpson, governor of Northern Operations for Hudson's Bay Company, arrived at Fort George (as Astoria had been renamed) with John McLoughlin on a survey of posts, after which McLoughlin was commissioned to move the Columbia River headquarters to Fort Vancouver across from today's Portland. The move would give the Hudson's Bay Company a fertile farming location in a better climate and escape from Chinook trade domination. Understandably Chief Comcomly viewed the move to Vancouver with dismay.

Under the leadership of Dr. John McLoughlin, impressive physically as well as mentally, Fort Vancouver became Hudson's Bay Company's anchor on the Columbia River. It rested on a pleasant shelf above the floods (where the city of Vancouver sprawls today), its pickets enclosing a fine factor's home, substantial dwellings for employees, warehouses, a school for employees' children, a trading post and other buildings. Outside the fence were well-tended gardens and orchards, calculated to gladden Sir George Simpson's heart, for he urged forts to become self-sustaining. A lively place, the fort gathered in furs from its district and dispatched supplies outbound as far as today's Kamloops and Prince George.

The post depended entirely on the Columbia River for transportation. Annually a supply ship came around the Horn from England, crossing the dangerous Columbia Bar and sailing upriver. Each spring a fast Express boat left for Hudson's Bay and Red River Settlement (Winnipeg), using the Columbia River as a highway to Boat Encampment, where the men transferred to horses. The return Express brought coveted mail, packets and light supplies, an occasion for fancy dinners at McLoughlin's home and grog for the voyageurs, those colorful fellows, largely of French or French-Indian ancestry, who manned the oars and knew every nuance of the treacherous Columbia River.

Who else but those voyageurs regularly ran the whole river, rapids and all, for years on end! Short, brawny men, the river navigators often sang cadences to give rhythm to their paddling, ate prodigiously and— off duty—drank the same. Their stories were spellbinding, enlivened by shading the truth a bit. Before arriving at a destination, they changed into their best clothing with colorful sashes, tied bright headbands around their locks, and delivered their Hudson's Bay Company official passengers with a flourish. By contrast, the latter, Scotsmen mostly, often arrived in broadcloth suits and hats.

A contingent of 175 farmers was sent by Hudson's Bay Company in 1841 from Red River Settlement down the Columbia River to work on farms at the Puget Sound Agricultural Company north of Fort Vancouver along the Cowlitz River. Unfortunately for Hudson's Bay Comapny, many farmers soon learned they could own land in Oregon's Willamette Valley and moved there.

The relationships between the Indians and Hudson's Bay Company were easy. Already the powerful Yakima tribe had vast herds of fine horses. Their Chief Kamiakin came to Fort Vancouver in 1840 to purchase the first cattle for ranching, buying more later from immigrants. The Yakima lands extended from the North Cascades Mountains to the Columbia-Snake confluence, including some of the Columbia Plateau and west of the Columbia to the Kittitas Valley (Ellensburg). Good ranchers on ideal grazing grounds, the Yakimas increased their herds dramatically. Indian women gathered camas and herbs in the mountains, and all joined in the fishing and trading at Celilo Falls on the Columbia. The Yakimas engaged in occasional skirmishes with rival Indian bands or raided them to carry off women. This was not uncommon, for Yakimas could marry relatives only beyond the eighth generation. Comparatively content, the Yakimas were north of the main path of westward expansion ... for now.

CHAPTER 15

The Immigrant Flood
Sparks War

It was well into the 1840s before the semifeudal Hudson's Bay Company was seriously challenged on the Columbia River—and then by simple American settlers and religious men, not merchants or soldiers. Despite the adverse political effects for Britain, the Hudson's Bay Company's kindly chief factor John McLoughlin helped American pilgrims get established in the Willamette Valley, often furnishing supplies on credit or free to destitute and weary families. His open-handed generosity and compassion would get him into difficulty with his penny-pinching boss, Governor George Simpson.

The settlers came in a trickle at first and then in a flood that did not diminish for more than a decade. Interest in "the Ory-gon" was sparked by the publication of explorers' journals and the speeches of mission-aries, all denominations, who came to save souls and returned east to gain financing to expand their efforts. Chief among the vocal mission-aries was Marcus Whitman. With his wife, Narcissa, a hardheaded business manager William Gray and a substantial party, Whitman founded a mission at Waiilatpu (Walla Walla) in 1836, ministering to the Cayuse Indians and others. On November 30, 1847, wrathful Cayuse parishioners murdered him, Narcissa Whitman and eleven men. The much-admired Hudson's Bay veteran, Peter Skene Ogden, came to negotiate for the release of forty-seven others taken prisoner.

This shocking event scarcely interrupted the tide of westward immigration along the Oregon Trail. Noted author David Lavender in his book, *Land of Giants*, wondered why the immigrants went that far. He pointed out that the majority of Oregon Trail migrants were "mostly family men, prosperous enough to buy substantial outfits." Such farmers could have purchased land in Iowa or Wisconsin at $1.25 an acre, instead of trekking two thousand difficult miles to unknown

Oregon. Lavender speculated that the restless urge to see what lay beyond was intriguing to the adventurous, and others thought moving west would stave off the claims of the British to the Northwest. Still others merely were land speculators.

Although smaller parties preceded them, the first major immigration to Oregon had begun with the thousand-person train that left Independence, Missouri, in the spring of 1843; along the way it dwindled and split, but most of the party arrived in Oregon.

Once at the Columbia River near Umatilla, some immigrants drifted safely downriver, portaging around Celilo Falls. Later parties sometimes trekked along the south shore to The Dalles, arriving weary and hungry, so near and yet so far from the fabled Willamette. The formidable Columbia Gorge with rapids and rain, hostile Indians and barely passable cattle trails awaited them. At The Dalles they dismantled their wagons, placing them on rafts. Appointed drovers followed with the cattle along a haphazard riverside trail on the south shore, laid out by Joel Palmer in 1846. The river travelers soon learned that they must put in to shore before the vicious rapids of the Cascades inexorably swept them away. The portage roads were quagmires, since immigrants usually arrived in fall. (They started from the Midwest in spring, in order to cross the mountains during summer, and arrived in Oregon at the rainy season.)

The six miles of Columbia Gorge Cascades seethed and foamed through an assortment of channels worn through basalt. At some point within the last thousand years a thunderous earthslide from Mount Hood blocked the Columbia and destroyed a natural bridge over the river. The resulting debris and rocks, plus the insistent rush of the river, created a mariner's nightmare of eddies, unpredictable currents and bars. The Cascades were in two main parts. At the Upper Cascades, the whole river was constricted to about 100 to 120 feet, which caused furious rapids to surge for about a 100 yards. Then the channel widened but was blocked (the Lower Cascades) for some distance by rocks and shallows, which caused great, dangerous whirlpools and eddies. On the north bank below the Cascades loomed Beacon Rock, 800 feet high, a volcanic remnant.

Since there were no actual falls, the rapids could be run by capable rivermen in stout boats, borne out by the express trips routinely made by Hudson's Bay voyageurs. But the crude rafts and makeshift boats plied by midwest farmers were almost unmanageable. The pioneers took to the land approximately where Bonneville Dam is now located. In chill, howling winds, lashed by rain and sometimes sleet, inadequately clad women and children struggled against fatal hypothermia, their menfolk warmer due to the exertion of carrying everything six miles on the portage road. What was all this about a balmy land where winter never came, as the orator back east had promised!

In 1847 pioneer woman Elizabeth Greer said of the portage road, "I carry my babe and lead, or rather carry, another through snow, mud and water, almost to my knees. ... I was so cold and numb that I could not tell by the feeling that I had any feet at all."

Since the Willamette River Valley was considerably south of the Columbia, some immigrants eyed the mountains around Mount Hood, wondering about an overland route. Among these was Samuel K. Barlow, who arrived at The Dalles in September 1845. After a cursory examination of the eastern foothills, Barlow and several other families pioneered a trail south of Mount Hood. By late October, it was obvious that snow would kill them if starvation didn't first. Barlow left two men to guard supplies southeast of Mount Hood, while the rest went ahead to the Willamette on foot and with pack horses.

The following year Barlow obtained a franchise to complete a toll road along that original trail and hacked out a barely passable wagon road. Earliest travelers believed him to be a confidence man, because they paid their toll at the eastern end, trekked happily on for four days and came to a wicked stretch of trail over big rocks and along frightening ledges (admittedly the scenery of Mount Hood was spectacular). Then, another day or so west, they encountered seemingly impassable Laurel Hill, where Barlow and his road were cursed roundly, but Barlow himself had gone through. Some immigrants attached trees to their wagons so they would not overrun the teams on the downward plunge; others tied ropes to trees and winched the wagons down. It scarcely seemed an improvement over the terrible Columbia Cascades. Later, a revised trail eased the descent.

Entrepreneurs began to improve the portage trails around rapids. Francis A. Chenoweth, a storekeeper at the upper landing, built a crude two-mile tram by July 1851, just a set of wooden rails and a wagonlike carrier pulled by a disconsolate mule. By 1856, Bradford & Company extended the wooden rails to the downriver end of the Middle Cascades, leaving yet two miles of portaging to the steamer landing below.

Whether despairing of gaining the Willamette or seizing the chance to serve river traffic, some pioneers settled there in the Columbia Gorge; at Hamilton and Bradford Islands; near Lower, Middle and Upper Cascades; and farther up river in the lovely Hood River Valley and the booming trade center, The Dalles.

Not all portions of the Oregon Trail were safe from Indians. On May 19, 1846, U.S. Congress approved $765,500 to staff ten sites with mounted riflemen. By September, a contingent under Brevet-Colonel William W. Loring reached The Dalles, where some troops were sent west along the Barlow Trail, others downriver in makeshift watercraft to set up Fort Vancouver, adjacent to the Hudson's Bay Company post.

Like the other Northwest tribes, except for the aberration at Waiilatpu, the Yakimas accepted (although with growing concern) the few traders, settlers and missionaries. They did not object when early cattleman Ben Snipes ran cattle on their lands. But they became alarmed at Lieutenant George B. McClellan's 1853 expedition to survey a route for the Northern Pacific Railroad through Yakima country.

The great Yakima Chief Kamiakin and Father C. M. Pandosy met McClellan at the Catholic Ahtanum Mission, where Kamiakin demanded to know his intentions. At Kamaikin's request, the Yakima Chief Owhi monitored McClellan's movements in the Wenatchi country and reported back to Kamiakin. Meanwhile, Isaac Stevens, newly appointed governor of Washington Territory, was surveying from East to West, making treaties with tribes as he went. Ominous news reached the Yakimas that the government was out to buy their land and remove them from it and that, if they refused to go, the soldiers would use force. Governor Stevens met with Chief Owhi in the summer of 1854 to set up a conference in 1855 about land purchase.

Kamiakin vowed the lands would not be surrendered and quietly sent high-level emissaries to all the tribes of eastern Washington and Oregon, and to some west of the mountains, urging a confederacy that would banish the white man forever. A great Indian council was held in 1854 at Grande Ronde Valley; for five days speeches were made and problems were aired. Most of the Indian chiefs were interested in starting a war, except for Hal-halt-los-sot (commonly dubbed Chief Lawyer for his negotiating abilities) of the Nez Perce and Stic-cas of the Cayuse, who wanted to hear Stevens' proposal first. Kamaikin dramatically stated his opinion: "We wish to be left alone in the lands of our forefathers ... but a pale-face stranger ... sends word to us that ... he wants it for the white man. Where can we go? ... Only a single mountain now separates us from the big salt water of the setting sun. ... Better to die like brave warriors on the battlefield than live among our vanquishers, despised." (A. J. Splawn, *Kamiakin* [Copyright by Mrs. A. J. Splawn, 1917], 24.)

An unusual union of tribes faced Governor Stevens at the council grounds of Walla Walla the following year, each group arriving in style, possibly four thousand Indians. While preliminary speeches and maneuvering went on, Chief Lawyer went to Governor Stevens and told him that the Cayuse intended to murder them all, that his Nez Perce would move into the Stevens camp to protect them. In so doing, he alienated many of his tribal friends. Conflicting stories spread as to the validity of the threat.

Stevens offered two reservations, one for the Nez Perce, another for Yakima, both with their related bands, and later added a third for the Walla Walla, Cayuse and Umatilla. Weary of conversation, Kamiakin and his chiefs made the mark of agreement, yielding twenty-nine thousand square miles of territory in exchange for a protected Yakima Indian Reservation of about 1.37 million acres (over two thousand square miles). The Nez Perce retained a large reservation, including the Wallowa valley for Chief Joseph's band; it was threatened removal of the latter that led to the 1877 Nez Perce war and the now-famous flight of Chief Joseph's people. The Umatilla Reserve was the same as that retained today. For such concessions the tribes received money, implements, and annuities. If the white men kept their promises, it did not appear too bad a deal, under the circumstances. If ... .

Before the ink was dry, and long before the treaties were ratified by the U.S. Senate (four years later), miners brazenly crossed lands from which they were legally banned. There were decent men among the military camps and the governmental officials who sent fruitless appeals to Washington, D.C., for permission to take action against the miners. The army built Fort Walla Walla near the old Whitman Mission as a precaution against war.

War drums began to inflame the tribes. The pretreaty confederacy was largely in place. Kamiakin, a leader respected by both sides, decided to fight. Miners enroute to Okanogan and Colville gold fields were warned not to pass. Qual-chan, Looking Glass, Peu-peu-mox-mox, Quil-ten-e-nock, even Leschi west of the mountains, were talking war. The killing began by disobedient miners, of Indians in retaliation and of the largely respected Yakima indian agent, A. J. Bolon (by three Indians) near The Dalles. The Yakimas turned in two of the three culprits to Captain J. J. Archer of the Ninth Infantry at Fort Simcoe, the third having committed suicide rather than be captured.

More lives were lost between 1855 and 1858. Recognizing that whoever controlled the gorge was master of the territory, the military from Fort Vancouver established a blockhouse (Fort Rains) at the Middle Cascades, just in time.

At 8:30 A.M., March 26, 1856, local Cascade Indians, Yakima warriors and Klickitats attacked the settlement at Upper Cascades, killing one man and wounding several in the first volley. Pandemonium reigned with forty men, women and children making for the stoutly built general store, some killed in the attempt. Late arrivals swam to the riverfront building. Inside, rifles were passed around, defenders shooting back from the store's second story. They watched the Indians loot and burn houses and warehouses. When Indians threw firebrands on the roof of the store, settlers doused the fire with cups of brine drawn from pork barrels.

Meanwhile, the steamer *Wasco* on the Oregon side of the river got away upstream. Just off the Columbia on Mill Creek, the steamer *Mary* managed to get steam going, but Indian bullets hit several crew members and others jumped overboard and drowned in the confusion.

By lying on the floor, Captain Hardin Chenowith steered the boat into the river and with a handful of fugitive settlers that clambered aboard, steamed off to The Dalles.

The Indians simultaneously assaulted Fort Rains, defended by nine troopers. Several nearby families ran to the blockhouse but a man was mortally wounded during the melee. One soldier was captured and cruelly tortured, his screams horrible to the helplessly listening blockhouse troopers. The contingent successfully defended the blockhouse, battering the enemy with their six-pounder cannon. Caught with no water supplies on hand, a man crept to a nearby saloon and raided the liquors to quench the defenders' thirst.

At the lower landing, Indians attacked, but an alarm had given time for everyone to flee in small boats downriver for Vancouver. Enroute they encountered young Lieutenant Phil Sheridan (only three years out of West Point) with forty soldiers aboard the steamer *Belle* and a Hudson's Bay bateau; Sheridan had been warned of the attack by a friendly Indian. No one was killed at the lower Cascades, but the Indians burned all nearby houses and looted or destroyed government stores. When the alarm reached Fort Dalles (which had been established during 1847 and 1850), two hundred men under George Wright and Edward Steptoe arrived on the *Mary*, the *Wasco* and a towed raft at the Upper Cascades on the third day of the battle.

Brevet Lieutenant Colonel Steptoe relieved soldiers and settlers at Fort Rains, and Sheridan's men pursued the Indians near Bradford Island, capturing several warriors and families. Confronted with defeat, the Cascade Indians placed all the blame on the Yakimas and their allies. Colonel Wright arrived shortly from the Upper Cascades, and his officers arrested thirteen men identified as leaders, bringing them to the upper landing. Nine were hanged, including Old Chenowith, the chief. Another was taken to jail in Vancouver, and three escaped to the Yakima camps. Short but vicious, this was the last Indian unrest in the gorge.

Hostilities moved into eastern Washington. In the long run, though, the Indians were outgunned by the army soldiers. The decisive victories led by Colonel George Wright largely quelled further disorders.

While sharply reduced from the territories once controlled, the huge Yakima Nation Reservation extends today roughly from Mount Adams in the North Cascades south to the Columbia River and is embraced by the Yakima River. The Yakimas have a well-organized tribal organization with leaders educated in modern economic ways but holding strongly to their heritage. Showcasing their heritage is the Yakima Tribal Museum in Toppenish, a splendid structure suggesting an Indian headdress. Adjacent to dioramas and archives is an attractive modern restaurant open to the public, serving all types of food. It is only one of the Yakima enterprises.

The Tri-Cities

With Indian resistance largely overcome, miners swarmed northward to Barkerville, Canada, to the international border and—in large numbers—to Idaho. The small community around the Hudson's Bay Company Fort Walla Walla at Wallula became a popular debarkation point for prospectors bound for Idaho after sternwheeler navigation began in 1859. The Chinese were content to sift through the Columbia River's sandbars north of the Tri-Cities.

Walla Walla already was a settlement of sorts, where a medical doctor, Dorsey Syng Baker, ran a store and raised cattle to sell to miners. He needed an outlet to the river at Wallula; so, with minimal capital, Baker and others built a narrow-gauge line using wooden rails strengthened with strap iron, although they used metal rails on curves and steep grades. Popular myth has it that Baker used rawhide instead of strap iron on some rail portions, and that coyotes chewed them off during lean times, causing locals to call it "Baker's Rawhide Railroad." Range cattle were a bigger problem, loafing on the tracks. Baker employed a tough farm dog to ride on the flatcars, jump off and scatter the cows before the train. According to passengers, the train was so slow that the dog had no problem.

Upriver the wind blew dust over the low-lying lands of today's Tri-Cities. It took a railroad, not a river, to spark settlement. In 1879 the Northern Pacific Railroad built a construction town named for J. C. Ainsworth, president of the Oregon Steam Navigation Company, which dominated Columbia River shipping. Ainsworth lay north of the Snake River, as wild and woolly a town as ever arose, inhabited by tough transients seeking transient solace in saloons and brothels. Fueled by drink, they continually fought each other. Ainsworth was not a fashionable address.

A Columbia River steamer, the *Spokane*, brought rails and supplies to a landing on the west bank to serve crews extending tracks westward through Yakima to the coast. A construction camp there, Huson (some called it Hades), soon became platted as Kennewick. The Indian name, "Kin-en-wack," meant "grassy place surrounded with water," an old wintering ground. It also was a tough place, and in 1902, vigilantes moved to expel thirty men considered "riff-raff."

About the same time Pasco was born (partly from buildings moved from Ainsworth). According to best sources, the name "Pasco" was given to the sere town by a Northern Pacific engineer, V. C. Bogue, who compared it to an equally uninviting Peruvian town, Cerro de Pasco, where he lived while building an Andean railroad. Until the bridge across the Snake was finished, Captain William P. Gray skippered the steamer *Frederick K. Billings* to haul freight across the river; the boat later hauled trains across the Columbia from Pasco to Kennewick.

Richland, the third of the Tri-Cities, was originally named Benton in 1905, but was forced to change its name due to postal confusion with Bentson. City fathers offered a town lot free as a prize for the name. When twelve people called it Richland, they drew lots, and the winner was Althea Rosencrance.

Well before Richland was formed, however, small towns along the Columbia River eased into being: Hanford (named for Judge C. H. Hanford of Seattle), White Bluffs, Ringgold. Hanford was a remount station of the United States Cavalry for change of horses enroute between Fort Simcoe and Fort Walla Walla.

The small towns were served by boats, the first of which was the *W. R. Todd*, then the *Mountain Gem* running for four years between Hanford and Pasco, the *Queen City Flyer*, and finally the *Hanford Flyer*, from Pasco and Kennewick until the advent of roads and automobiles.

Above these towns the Columbia was considered unnavigable. But the indomitable mariner, Captain W. P. Gray, challenged the power of Priest and Rock Island rapids in 1888, partly because he had filed a report in 1886 with the Oregon Steam Navigation Company that he felt the rapids could be surmounted. Commercial backers built two boats on the strength of the report, and in 1886, the two tested the waters—returning battered with frightened, defeated crews.

Business friends from Ellensburg then persuaded Gray to pilot a new boat, *The City of Ellensburgh*, upstream; feeling responsible for suggesting the original effort, he agreed. Carrying forty-five tons of freight and a handful of passengers, the 120-foot sternwheeler was lined up Priest Rapids without serious difficulty. At Rock Island Rapids the sturdy craft stood motionless against the swift current for about an hour. White-knuckled passengers were convinced they were doomed.

Amidst cheers from crew and shore spectators, Captain Gray permitted the craft to come dangerously close to large rocks to escape the main current and made it through the rapids. He completed his trip into the Okanogan River, and later made four additional trips on the route before low water.

Gray became deeply involved in Pasco's business life. Using kitchen equipment from the *Frederick P. Billings*, he rented a section house from the Northern Pacific and opened a restaurant. He also built a four-bedroom hotel, developed and sold lots as the Gray's Addition, continued as captain of the steamboat, raised hogs, and became land agent for the Northern Pacific. Together with promoter Louis C. Frey, Gray coined the still-used slogan "Keep Your Eye on Pasco," although many scoffed that there wasn't much there to keep an eye on. The feisty townsmen even made a bid for the State capital in 1890, losing to Olympia.

New settlements sprang up near the railroad. Twelve miles north of Pasco, when heavy rains knocked out a section of the Northern Pacific Railroad, a Cockney workman exclaimed, "There'll be 'ell to pay." A new town at the site arose as "Eltopay," changed to the more discreet "Eltopia" by later settlers. But why not? At Ainsworth there was a school named "I'll Be Damned School," a taxpayer's response when he was asked to pay his school tax.

Water from the Columbia made the Tri-Cities come to life. Verdant crops resulted from a myriad of irrigation plans. Land promoters distributed sensational literature, calling Kennewick "the California of the Northwest," and the sandbars of the Snake "The Italy of the Northwest." A pamphlet of 1912 claimed Kennewick was in a southern climate under northern skies. One settler remarked about the wonderful smell of virgin sagebrush soil after it was broken up by a plough and watered for the first time. It was true that, with water, farmers could raise soft fruits, grains, and vegetables; asparagus and potatoes became winners. In 1905, the parent company of Welch's Grape Juice was formed; it is still operating. The river served the farmers a second time by allowing barge traffic to call at Pasco, taking products to market.

Today new ways of marketing the area's products are appearing— products like pickled asparagus, gourmet vinegar (for all kinds of grapes grow well there), dried cherries encased in chocolate, fancy mustards. Three of the Northwest's finest wines, Columbia Crest, Quarry Lake and Preston, are produced nearby from grapes grown on site.

Early twentieth century farms were remote and life was hard. Rabbits damaged the crops. Dust storms rolled in like tornados, lasting for days. The settlers made their own fun. A pioneer, Otto Olds, told of the fears of children in the treeless desert that Santa could not find them, only to discover presents under a Christmas tree made of sagebrush limbs nailed to a piece of lumber. He recalled walking one day in a canyon with his grandchild, suddenly hearing music. Investigating, they observed Northern Pacific workmen of Italian descent, their train parked on a siding, dressed in their best Easter finery and celebrating the religious holiday with song and dance, accompanied by accordions.

The local Indians were very friendly around Hanford. Storekeepers sometimes "carried" Indian and white families through the winter; one remembered that an Indian man came in one spring to determine the amount he owed, saying, "OK, I go catch wild horses, sell 'em, and be back," and he did. Often in earlier days the Indians came to the river bottoms for wintering.

The river was everyone's lifeblood, not only for water, but for fun. The colorful riverboats *Umatilla* (more or less a workboat), *Twin Cities*, *Mountain Gem*, *Inland Empire*, *T. J. Peel* and the little *Hanford Flyer* were as much household words as Ford, Chris-Craft or Honda might be today. When the boats were free, they offered excursion trips, especially for special holidays or events. Memorably lively was the celebration at Wallula when the Celilo Canal downriver was opened in 1915, and a boatload of dignitaries came upriver.

One crossed the river on cable ferries where the Columbia was narrow, such as at White Bluffs, Hanford and Wallula. Ice in winter often interfered with their operations, piling up in dangerous floes. The river was too broad for a cable ferry between Kennewick and Pasco; so the pioneers perilously walked across the railway bridge over the Columbia, looking between the ties at the swift-flowing current. Farmers often built log rafts to transport their cattle and horses downriver.

One of the most curious cargos passing through on swift express trains was raw silk from Japan, so perishable and valuable that during fuel and water stops, guards emerged to surround the trains.

Some men acquired enough irrigated land to become wealthy. Pioneer Frank W. Schunemann came from California with six children and two wagons, about all they had, and later held splendid farmland through what is now downtown Pasco, two miles long and a mile wide. Schunemann sold most of his holding to investor James A. Moore of Seattle, who built a pretentious mansion adjacent to the river for his wife, who died before enjoying it. Sold to Thomas Carstens, the property became a cattle ranch and at one time had five miles of Columbia River frontage.

Times changed and the lands were broken up. The Moore mansion became a speakeasy during Prohibition, the best night club in the area and, beautifully restored, a fine restaurant today. The owners keep unraveling the place's history, including discovery of a secret compartment in an attic room, just large enough to hide someone or something.

There was an underground passage to the river for receiving illicit liquor, which made a handy septic tank.

Meanwhile, the very aspect that made the Tri-Cities so desolate became an asset—seemingly limitless open space. On April 6, 1926, Varney Air Lines, later a part of the new company called United Air Lines, initiated air mail service from Pasco to Elko, Nevada—somewhat inauspiciously when an incoming Varney airplane had engine failure over Wallula and was forced to land in the desert. However, an enthusiastic crowd watched a stagecoach arrive, symbolically carrying mail from Spokane to be sent to Elko. With much fanfare in 1976, the flight was commemorated in the same kind of airplane, a Swallow biplane.

After the Japanese attacked Pearl Harbor in December of 1941, the United States Navy purchased 2,285 acres north of Pasco for training navy aviators. During the next two years, eight hundred men went through primary flight training without a fatality. In December 1942, the first detachment of WAVES (female naval personnel) ever quartered on a naval station came to Pasco. On the Columbia River southeast of Pasco, the United States Army built a large Holding & Reconsignment Point operated by the Transportation Corps—a sort of way station for outgoing supplies, since seaports were overloaded with activity. Much of the material went to the Soviets as Lend-Lease.

That was only the beginning. Quietly in late 1942, mysterious government men asked strange questions and grimly looked over the half-deserted lands nearby. They were silent as to their objectives, even after February 23, 1943, when the U.S. government started proceedings under the War Powers Act to condemn 193,833 acres in Benton County for the Hanford Atomic Engineering Project. Included within the acreage were the towns of Hanford, White Bluffs and Richland. The following week the government leased an acreage of similar size and put a "hold" on new construction for still another 70,000 acres.

The site had abundant water, electricity from Grand Coulee and Bonneville dams, and remote lands—all required for the mysterious project. Four 6-foot diameter pipelines carried water thirteen miles from the Columbia to a "secret" building being constructed.

Uncommunicative, polite men came to each home, said the owners would receive "adequate compensation" and inventoried every bit of the contents right down to pencils. They went away, and still the residents did not know why they were being moved, only that they must go soon. They were told that, if they knew the reason, they would be proud to cooperate.

Some people called it "The Exodus." Twelve hundred uprooted residents moved, most of them philosophically. A few stunned homeowners received only thirty days of eviction notice, and after the government paid fair compensation for their properties, bulldozers came in and covered up most of the homes. The town of White Bluffs was almost leveled; only a couple of brick buildings and the old cable ferry ramp indicate that it ever existed.

Next came an influx of workers, engineers and scientists, about fifty-thousand of them, also close-mouthed. Across the sagebrush flats south of Saddle Mountain at old Hanford, an enormous camp of trailer houses was established, housing about thirteen thousand people. Newspapers were requested to keep to a minimum any news about the influx of people (the author indeed found the wartime newspapers extraordinarily uninformative).

Workers were forbidden to tell their relatives and acquaintances exactly where they were; they could be addressed only at a post office box in Yakima. Since workdays were long and days off limited, workers really could not go anywhere. The wind blew. The dust came. The wind blew. Some workers could not stand the secrecy, isolation and particularly the wind, which came to be known as the "termination wind," causing them to leave the project.

Surveyors canvassed Tri-Cities area residents to see if they could house "war workers." Restaurants in the Tri-Cities were overwhelmed and ran out of food; one of their biggest headaches was obtaining servers, and government authorities asked women if they could donate two or three hours a day "for the war effort." Pasco had an acute shortage of milk, indeed, a lively black market in milk, caused by a shortage of costly dairy-cattle feed and the appropriation of available milk for government use. Higher wages at the engineering project drew farm workers, and vegetables and fruit rotted in the field, even though the crops were designated for government workers' use.

At tiny Richland the government designed "The Village," with substantial homes and a shopping center, not exactly unattractive, but painted military gray and of forthright design. Before anyone would have believed it possible, people moved in.

The government offered to build one Protestant church and one Catholic church; other religions were on their own. People of various Protestant denominations worshipped together so harmoniously that, even today, they prefer to stay together as Central United Protestant Church.

But the gray buildings housing whatever they contained grew from the sand, and knowing people came and went from the buildings, saying nothing. Under an assumed name, the famed nuclear scientist Enrico Fermi spent time at the facility in consultation. Only after World War II was concluded with the startling explosions of the world's first atomic bombs did most of the workers know, and the Tri-Cities residents and world know what was being researched and produced there.

From 1944 until recent times the process leading to the manufacture of plutonium was performed at the Hanford site. There were two main steps in this process—the irradiation or bombardment of uranium metal in the reactors and the chemical separation processes necessary to recover useful plutonium from the irradiated fuel elements. Eight reactors were built quite close to the Columbia River for easy access to cooling water. Each heavy concrete building had its own cooling building, where the water was circulated, treated and eventually returned to the river. The reactors' end product, the irradiated uranium, was then transferred for chemical treatment. The chemical separation plants were deliberately located high on a plateau near the center of the Hanford site, far above the water table of the Columbia River, because there are admittedly some nasty chemical byproducts that must be carefully captured and controlled. No plutonium is being produced at this writing; the ninth and last production reactor was ordered shut down permanently in 1991.

The eight original reactors are deactivated, standing like artifacts from a bygone age, as indeed they are. Hanford Project workers used to call them "uranium piles," because the buildings look like a pile of concrete. Some say the first Hanford reactor should be declared a National Historic Site. The B Reactor, which produced the first plutonium for the atomic bomb tested at Trinity Site, New Mexico, was declared a National Historical Mechanical Engineering Landmark in 1976, a milestone in the U.S. Atomic Energy program.

For the next thirty years on this vast scientific reservation, the emphasis will be on thorough cleanup of old wastes, not carelessly handled at the time but placed in temporary storage tanks scheduled for more permanent disposal later. Authorities have designated specific soil areas according to the degree of contamination and fenced them off stoutly until they are cleared for use. The chemical separation wastes still containing radioactive material will be solidified in either a glass or thick grouting and left in the ground. Controversy rages on the subject, but the State of Washington and two federal agencies have agreed on a thirty-year "Tri-Party Agreement for Cleanup."

After World War II, much of the government's "hands-on" work at Hanford was assigned under contract to private corporations—Westinghouse Hanford Company, Battelle Memorial Institute, Kaiser Engineers Hanford Company, and the Hanford Environmental Health Foundation. Also having facilities on site are U. S. Ecology and the Washington Public Power Supply System (WPPSS).

During 1972, the WPPSS decided to build five reactors at Hanford to produce electrical power (20 percent of the nation's power now comes from nuclear plants). Hanford's ninth reactor had produced considerable electricity as a byproduct of plutonium manufacture from the 1960s until 1987. A combination of a recession, costly labor strife, and antagonistic public sentiment after the Three Mile Island nuclear accident caused WPPSS to fail financially in 1983, leaving bondholders unpaid, one of the worst public financial debacles in history. Washingtonians said WPPSS or "Whoops" was a suitable name.

In addition to working on costly but essential cleanup, the private firms at Hanford are researching exciting projects: a tiny nuclear reactor for power in space to serve the computers, communications equipment, and so on; better designs for nuclear-powered electrical generating plants; new alloys for longer fuel lifetime in future nuclear energy plants. At the Fast Flux Test Facility, materials testing is carried out, for example, to improve strengths of alloys, to produce isotopes for cancer treatment and to develop spinoff nuclear applications such as luggage inspection at airports.

Visitors would enjoy seeing the Hanford Science Center, the Fast Flux Test Facility and the WPPSS Visitor Center, all open to the public. Since authorities do not want strangers wandering around the Hanford lands—for their own good, as well as fearing terrorists—the grounds are patrolled by boat and helicopter and are off-limits to hunters and hikers.

The presence of such an enormous vacant landmass has attracted elk, several hundred mule deer, coyotes, raptors and waterfowl. Hanford authorities do not interfere with the animals but routinely monitor any dead birds or animals accidentally killed within the surrounding area. The Hanford Reach of the Columbia River, over 50 miles of free-flowing water, is home to blue heron, hatching geese and ducks, curlews, bald and golden eagles and hordes of small birds who favor the myriad deserted islets and marshes of this beautiful section of the Columbia. Water quality of the Columbia is tested frequently, and consistently receives top ratings, according to monitors. Boaters and fishermen enjoy the Hanford Reach.

Hanford is a National Environmental Research Park and has designated a 120-square-mile portion over the Rattlesnake Hills as an Arid Lands Ecology Reserve. Graduate students come from distant universities to study in this outdoor laboratory, still essentially as it was at Lewis and Clark's time. Students can view the natural regenerative processes after a grass fire, or see bobcats, badgers and coyotes having their young. North of Pasco the Columbia's Ringgold Hatchery enhances salmon production.

There is a widely based movement to have the Hanford Reach declared a Wild and Scenic River, prohibiting yet another dam proposed for that last open-river segment. It seems only fair that this one free-flowing, natural section should remain as an outdoor Columbia River Museum. The Reach also teems with spawning fall chinook salmon.

Because of historic floods and the backup of water from McNary Dam, the Corps of Engineers has confined the Columbia River through the Tri-Cities between levees up to 8 feet high. There is talk about persuading the Corps to lower the levees, so residents can have better access to the river—or even *see* it more easily, now that McNary Dam has largely eliminated flood concerns. To be sure, a handful of hotels and restaurants overlook the river, providing docks for patrons who come by boat of a summer evening. A cruise boat operates locally.

On the Kennewick side, about a quarter-mile-wide shelf of land stretches without levees for about five miles as Columbia Park. Buildings in the park were designed to cope with the probability that they would be inundated from time to time. Here, residents enjoy watching all manner of water events—the Columbia Cup for Unlimited Hydroplanes in July, the Christmas Lights Boat Parade, a big Salmon Derby in September, windsurfing and other spectator sports.

The slack water created behind McNary Dam, Lake Wallula, overran low areas upriver to form ideal wetlands for waterfowl; hundreds of varieties of birds are counted. On Clover Island, a natural island beyond the levees, the Port of Pasco and a few other businesses enjoy a parade of wildlife past their office windows—ducks and ducklings, mink, fish jumping, even a rare spotted sandpiper strolling across the lawn. An elk lives in downtown Kennewick, and deer meander through Pasco's port property, gazing unafraid at the proliferation of barges and tugs that come upriver from Astoria or Portland on the Columbia River.

Traffic on the
Marine Highway

Sternwheelers operated far upriver to the Snake as early as gold rush days. The shallow-draft, narrow-hulled sternwheeler was said to travel on "mists," her paddles hardly biting the water. Captains sometimes backed up narrow channels; they claimed that this made the boat more maneuverable in tight quarters. Sidewheelers required too much channel, and propeller-driven boats too much water.

The first paddlewheel steamer, the Hudson's Bay Company's *Beaver*, came to the Columbia River in 1836. However, Chief Factor John McLoughlin at Fort Vancouver, was disenchanted with using ships to supply northern posts; he ordered the *Beaver* north into Puget Sound to use Nisqually as a base.

In the mid-1850s a pioneer on the Willamette River, with more verve than grace, designed an odd paddlewheeler powered by six horses on a treadmill aboard ship. The next powered craft to enter the river was a screw-driven steamer, the *Massachusetts*, bringing army troops in May 1849, to staff the new military forts on the river. A year later the Pacific Mail Steamship Company sent the wooden twin-screw steamer *Carolina* to call at Astoria and Portland, more or less the beginning of regular mail service.

But it was the ungainly 90-foot sidewheel steamer *Columbia*, built of odds and ends at Astoria, that charmed Oregonians—for she was all theirs. The boat's shallow draft enabled her to navigate the shallow Willamette River and bring eagerly awaited mail from Astoria directly to Portland. She was the first of many passenger/freight steamers to work the river, followed by boats such as *Lot Whitcomb, Belle, Wallamet* and *Fashion* ("fashioned" from then-retired *Columbia*'s engines and parts of the *James P. Flint*).

By 1855, one could travel from Astoria to the Snake River, usually changing boats three times: at Portland, the Cascades and The Dalles.

There were also short portage roads between boats at the Cascades and The Dalles. From the Cascades to The Dalles, a partnership of Bradford & Company and L. W. Coe offered the *James P. Flint* and the *Mary* (which figured in the Indian war).

Bradford & Coe maintained a freight trail and then a railroad on the less precipitous north shore. On the south shore in October of 1855, army troops built a short portage trail around the Cascades. Soon entrepreneur W. R. Kilborn put teams on the road, in turn eclipsed by construction of the Oregon Portage Railroad by Joseph S. Ruckel and Harrison Olmstead. It had only wooden rails reinforced by iron, the cars pulled by mules. At The Dalles, Orlando Humason operated a fourteen-mile freight wagon portage service over the hills.

Meanwhile, under the leadership of riverboat captain J. C. Ainsworth, the Union Transportation Line was formed, a loose association of boat owners. They ordered a special locomotive to serve a portage railroad being built for The Dalles connection. Until completion of the railroad, the company lent the miniature locomotive to Ruckel for the Cascades. It was scarcely 6 feet tall with a 5-foot boiler and was dubbed the "Pony." On its initial run several formally clad dignitaries insisted on riding in the cab (which had no enclosure) and arrived scarcely recognizable from grime and soot.

Instead of fighting each other, the boat and portage road owners merged, forming a new firm named Oregon Steam Navigation Company (OSN) incorporated in 1860 by Ainsworth, Jacob Kamm (a fine mechanical engineer), D. F. Bradford, L. W. Coe and others. Into the common pot went the chief steamers on the routes and both portage railroads. When a real railroad was finished on the north shore, OSN discontinued Ruckel's railroad and moved the "Pony" to The Dalles.

For decades, the river was securely tied up in this giant monopoly. There were occasional competitors, but OSN either bankrupted them by short-rating for as long as necessary or bought them out. In 1862, for a whopping $10,000 annually, OSN bribed a rival to refrain from competing on the Columbia and ply only the Willamette River.

Columbia River shipping was instantly a profitable business, chiefly because of the gold strikes upriver and in Idaho. High but not outrageous rates were charged; however, a capacity load of five hundred passengers, each paying $23 for passage from Portland to the Walla Walla River port (Wallula), amounted to $11,500 per trip! Not to mention a whole deck full of freight. Later, when railroads came, a handsome hotel, the Umatilla House at The Dalles, housed travelers in style. It had two baths for 123 rooms plus a lavatory in the basement. Randall Mills in *Stern-Wheelers Up Columbia* said it was "... the best outside of Portland, in spite of its notoriously friendly fleas and occasionally chummy bedbugs and lice. Its fittings were elegant. ... [A guest] would get no single room—if he were lucky he only shared the room with three strangers." (Randall V. Mills, *Stern-Wheelers up Columbia* [Lincoln: University of Nebraska Press, 1947 and 1974], p. 45.)

For years the steamer *Colonel Wright*, built by R. R. Thompson and L. W. Coe in 1858, and initially captained by Leonard White, served the route from Celilo Falls to the Snake River. By 1866, there were other boats: *Nez Perce Chief, Yakima, Spray*, one of which left Celilo landing every second day at 4:30 A.M. and arrived at Lewiston two days later. Travelers bound for Salt Lake City and beyond got off at Umatilla, where four stage lines operated.

When the initial stockholders of OSN began to think about retirement, financier Henry Villard bought the whole conglomerate, renaming it Oregon Railway and Navigation Company to reflect the burgeoning railway construction era. Steam navigation would decline in direct proportion to the rise of railway travel in the Northwest.

By 1905 the Union Pacific chuffed along the Oregon side of the river, and in 1908 James J. Hill's Spokane, Portland & Seattle Railway ran along the north bank. Hill granted rights to the Great Northern and Northern Pacific to use his rails, then acquired the Portland-Astoria line. Determined to best archrival E. H. Harriman, financier of Southern Pacific and the Union Pacific, Hill proceeded to buy two ocean vessels and offer train service to San Francisco by placing the cars on the steamers.

The steamboats lasted far into the twentieth century. In their heyday the steamboats were as romantic as the Mississippi riverboats and faced far greater challenges on the treacherous Columbia River. As the nineteenth century wore on, the sternwheeler fleet became more sophisticated, adding vessels with carpets and shiny brassware, filigreed wood accents and polished balustrades. Meals were served on white linen cloths. One main salon boasted a grand piano, and many had gentlemen's salons where the smoke of the best Havanas swirled around the heads of natty businessmen, one foot on the rail as they enjoyed glasses of imported liquor.

Among the most splendid boats, primarily on the lower river between Portland and the Cascades or between Portland and Astoria, were the *Daisy Ainsworth, Wide West, Bailey Gatzert* and *T. J. Potter*, the latter sporting the largest plate glass mirror in the Northwest and a bird's-eye maple grand piano. In a spirit of fun the steamers loved to run impromptu races, the passengers cheering all the way, and no one ever bested the *Telephone* (1885 to 1918).

Sailings were not always smooth. Above the Cascades in 1858, the *Venture*, with forty passengers aboard, cast loose before getting up enough steam and shot through the Cascades rapids stern first, fetching up on a rock. The boat was undamaged, and no one was killed except a hysterical passenger who dove overboard. On the Willamette the *Gazelle*'s boiler blew up due to negligence of the attendants, sending cargo and passengers hurtling in all directions. Twenty-eight people died, thirty were injured. The famed *Telephone* caught fire nearing Astoria in 1887; her quick-thinking captain opened the throttle and rammed her at twenty miles per hour into a shallow bank. The passengers were thrown or jumped onto the mud flats to safety (only one man, drunk in his cabin, died), and the Astoria fire crews doused the blaze to save the craft.

The run from Celilo to Wallula was not for the faint-hearted. A succession of rapids challenged the power of sternwheelers. Captains respected the Umatilla Rapids, not the roughest but about three miles long with no relief. Winds then as now howled through the broad canyon of the Columbia, walled by 1,000-foot bluffs near Wallula, where the canyon narrowed to produce a venturi effect. The river could go from flat calm to 5-foot waves within minutes. Dust storms lowered visibility, as settlers plowed the deep silty soils on the bluffs above.

The U.S. Army Corps of Engineers, which had come to build forts and military roads at mid-century, assumed responsibility for maintaining navigation on the Columbia River. J. C. Ainsworth complained to Lieutenant W. H. Heuer of the Corps about the dangers to his boats on Umatilla, Homely and John Day rapids. Heuer responded by surveying the three, and concentrated on removing John Day Rock, completed by 1873, the first permanent change on the Columbia River. As a stage connection, Umatilla was as wild west as any Dodge City. Ranches were springing up in response to the nutritious Oregon bunch grass, cattle and horse operations, not dirt farms, and the cowboys liked to party. Major stock auctions drew crowds, the first operated by Frank Wink at The Dalles. Cattle and sheep were shipped by sternwheelers to market, too.

Arlington once was the largest wool-shipping port in the United States. Sheep trailed through the dusty streets to a sandbar on the river to be held in corrals and sheared, their wool bundled for direct shipment by boat. It also was a place to let off steam. Poker or billiards bets could be a thousand dollars per game.

By 1896 the Cascade Locks were completed at a cost of almost four million dollars to speed transportation. Two locks along a 3,000-foot canal raised the boats 42 feet, eliminating the perils of the Cascades. From the Port of Cascades Locks Marine Park today, one may see the shadowy remains of that busy canal and the locomotive "Pony."

Burgeoning livestock marketing and increasing tonnage of grain spawned the initiation of tug and barge services. By 1908 Shaver

Transportation Company used sternwheelers to shove rafts and escort ships; they were fast, tough and maneuverable.

The excursion sternwheeler *Columbia Gorge* operates each summer between Portland and Stevenson, going through the Bonneville Locks on some occasions, and the *Rose* operates on the Willamette. But the last *working* sternwheeler, the *Portland*, was retired in 1981. Her last captain was Gary Showalter. Former deckhand Kenneth Rea remembers nostalgically, "On a quiet night, moving up the Columbia, I just liked to hear the steam rushing through the stack and the soft whoosh of the paddles."

An ongoing obstacle to navigation was the wild water above The Dalles to Celilo Falls, conquered by installation of the Celilo Canal in 1915, eight and one-half miles long and about 8 to 9 feet deep, skirting the thundering falls frequented by Indian tribes for fishing since time immemorial. Four locks raised boats to the upper river. The canal made it possible to transport entire herds of cattle and sheep to market without the harrowing transfers from boat to boat.

Thus, construction of Bonneville Dam (and the later Dalles Dam) in the Columbia Gorge was not particularly related to a need for better lock-through than Celilo and Cascade Locks already provided. Rather it was in response to the growing need for electrical power, to stem repeatedly devastating floods when the Columbia rampaged, and to provide jobs for needy workers during the Depression. President Franklin D. Roosevelt was a believer in using the nation's rivers "to the utmost," and he was equally adamant about public versus private power.

Dry mesas and bluffs east of The Dalles.

In September 1933, Congress allocated $250,000 for surveys and $20 million for construction of Bonneville Dam. Since the location then was isolated, a residential village called Bonneville (Oregon) was built in 1934 for key employees involved in construction and later management of the hydroelectric facilities and fish ladders.

As in Grand Coulee, the general labor force was on its own; no facilities were provided except for a few tents with wooden floors. Eventually, a boarding house was built at Bonneville, but until then some workers slept in cars. A restaurant operator converted his three-sided woodshed into a bunkhouse, building four shelves to rent out to workers, three men and one woman. The woman said, "Oh mercy, it was cold! The first guy that got to his shelf was the one that got blankets because you stole them from everybody else. ... You wore your clothes, and shoes and boots."

There were very few women on the job, and homely or beautiful, they were sought after. Gambling was common, playing cards on a box or in a car. Poor conditions or not, workers were delighted to have a good-paying job. Some were residents unemployed since the sawmill closed in 1926. Workers would be covered with cement dust, dirty because sanitary facilities were scarce, but they ate well. They built simple homes with kerosene lights and outhouses, using water from the creek. Soon there were five restaurants and several taverns.

Although there are always rumors of men buried in concrete at dams, pouring techniques at Bonneville made this impossible. However, there were accidents from falling objects, and one summer, a repair barge was swept over a Bonneville spillway with three men killed. Reportedly, only nine men died in construction-related accidents. Concrete for the spillways was transported via buckets dangling from a highline across the river, so wide that sometimes the line disappeared into the fog. One brave man rode a bucket to watch operations as a spotter. To fend off cold in winter, he built a little steel stove on a platform in the bucket. Sparks flew all over in the wind.

Tour buses of people came to gawk at the progress of Bonneville Dam; then they would wind uphill to luxurious Cloud Cap Inn on the east face of Mount Hood.

All the time the dam was being built, a fish biologist was on hand to supervise the saving of salmon runs until fish ladders could be completed. A fish ladder is an ascending stairway with pools 16 feet by 40 feet, each 1 foot higher than the last, enabling migrating salmon to pass the dam. There are three ladders at Bonneville and others at all Columbia River dams up to Grand Coulee.

There was considerable controversy about the size of the locks and the wisdom of the construction of the dam, some people calling it a white elephant. Few could foresee the tremendous increase in demand for hydroelectric power, but during World War II the mushrooming industrial plants used all the power that Bonneville and Grand Coulee could put out. The two were and are on a grid that analyzes power needs, adjusting the amount of power generated. Franklin D. Roosevelt was there to dedicate Bonneville Dam's completion on September 28, 1937.

Low wheat prices during the Depression encouraged entrepreneurs to search for lower transportation rates. Veteran working sternwheel owner, Homer Shaver of Vancouver, and Lew Russell formed Shaver Forwarding Company to lease sternwheelers. They moved wheat out of the Horse Heaven Hills of Washington by truck to the river and downriver by barge.

Then the owner of a gasoline distributorship, Spokane businessman Kirk Thompson, sought cheaper delivery of petroleum. His brainchild, the *Mary Gail*, a sturdy 56-foot diesel twin-screw tug, came off the ways in November 1936 and went into service the following year. Under Thompson, Tidewater Barge Lines pioneered river shipping facilities. Elevators received grain at The Dalles, Arlington, Hogue-Warner (across from Paterson), Umatilla, Port Kelly (for Walla Walla) and Pasco. Ocean-going ships loaded from other elevators downriver at or near Portland.

Fierce competition reigned for several decades. The battle really was between the two tough rivermen, Lew Russell and Slim Lappaluoto, the latter a sinewy, lanky young man working on the *Mary Gail*. When Thompson offered Tidewater for sale, Russell outbid Lappaluoto and formed Tidewater-Shaver Barge Lines. Lappaluoto obtained financing and started the competitive Inland Navigation Company. He assisted a colleague, Carl Floten, in developing a dual-purpose barge that could safely transport petroleum upriver and convert to hauling grain downriver.

The two companies engaged in a Columbia River war, no holds barred, in rate-cutting, customer snatching and physical confrontation just short of mayhem. On one occasion a Lappaluoto barge got stuck on a rock above Celilo Falls. Unable to rock it loose, Lappaluoto filed an insurance claim for it. The insurance carrier put salvage up for bids and Lappaluoto put in a low bid, again outbid by Russell, who persuaded Grand Coulee Dam personnel to release three extra feet of water to float it. Russell's men waited below, and as the vessel careened crew-less through the rough Washington channel (the falls are in the middle, Celilo Canal on the Oregon side), they took it under control.

In a complex 1958 sale, Lappaluoto sold to his partners, part of Inland eventually going to Crowley Maritime Corporation, and went into Gulf of Mexico shipping in the 1960s. At meetings of old-time river people, the Sagebrush Sailors, the two old titans—Russell and Lappaluoto—trade good-natured insults.

Meanwhile, Tidewater remained a major force on the river. In 1983, the president and general manager of Tidewater, Ray Hickey, purchased the company from Lew Russell and family, then bought Columbia Marine Lines from Crowley. Today Tidewater Barge Lines holds a premier position on the river, eighteen tugs and one hundred barges operating from Lewiston to Astoria. Shaver Transportation Company and Brix Maritime (formerly Knappton) still run the river but have added powerful ocean tugs.

Until the addition of the McNary (1953), The Dalles (1957) and John Day (1968) dams, the Columbia River still showed its muscle. The tug captains welcomed the challenges; indeed, most of the old-timers moved on after the dams were built. It just was not exciting enough to work in slack water or ponds.

At mid-century over forty tugs worked between Portland and Lewiston. Loaded barges drew 6-1/2 to 7 feet of water, and many of the worst rapids were less than 6 feet deep; petroleum or freight had to be unloaded to reduce draft. Often, barges scraped bottom or hit rocks in the tortuous channels, even though the U.S. Army Corps of Engineers removed some of the worst channel obstacles. Until dams on the Snake River were built, most shipping stopped at Pasco.

Veteran Captain Keith Rodenbaugh says rapids were hard on engines. "We normally had 3,000 to 5,000 horsepower on the tugs and entered rapids at normal speed. If the load started getting away, we cranked in full power and frequently would blow a piston. We drifted back out and fixed the engine, tried again, and eventually got through."

Tug captains found the exit upstream from Celilo Canal always a thrill. Re-entry to the river was at a 45-degree angle to its flow and the 450-foot procession of tug and two or three barges could not turn until clear of the canal. Finally, with a powerful roar, the tug would man-handle the barges around, but the falls would be alarmingly close astern. "If we ever lost an engine ... ."

There were no thrusters then, the small boosters on modern supertugs that move the hull sideways, but tugs either had huge sweeps up to 8 feet long or three or four rudders across the tug's stern.

"On the tug *Winquatt* we had a big rudder in the middle and another on each side, like a barn door. To grasp the power of these tugs—there were three 1-1/4-inch cables attaching the tug to the barge, and in rapids, if you ever put the rudder hard-over, you would snap those cables like string," says Rodenbaugh.

The worst rapids included Hell Gate, just above Wishram or Celilo, where there were perpendicular bluffs (peppered with Indian drawings— spiders, scorpions, sun dials). There the tug/barge had to make a 180-degree swing. All the while, the entering Deschutes River ran across the

Columbia to bounce off the cliffs and roll back in a swirl. Other difficult spots were at the entrance of the rushing John Day River and the lengthy Umatilla Rapids. In the mid-1940s, a terrific storm arose suddenly with blizzard conditions, raising huge waves above Umatilla. Two boats and a barge were wrecked, but no one was hurt.

During spring high water, the Columbia's rampage frequently spread over lowlands and snatched chunks from the cliffs. The Celilo Canal would completely disappear, the masonry under water; so operations had to be suspended. The infamous flood of 1948 shut down shipping for days. Captain Rodenbaugh says the current was so swift the Columbia was crowning in the middle. The same flood completely inundated the town of Vanport. Upstream, south of Wenatchee, the river rose so high it neared the lower face of Rock Island Dam. The turbines ceased to operate, because there was insufficient fall of water to generate power.

Before the creation of pools or slack water by the dams, eastern Washington/Oregon weather was colder. The Columbia frequently froze over solid. In 1884, when snows buried the streets of The Dalles, an unpopular entrepreneur charged twenty-five cents to cross the streets through snow tunnels he had dug. In the 1940s powerful tugs like the *Viking* under Captain Cliff Light acted as icebreakers so The Dalles ferry could run and tugs with barges might move. In 1949, a freak cold snap struck, freezing the Columbia to a depth of 5 to 6 feet and the Celilo Canal totally. The tug *Winquatt* with Rodenbaugh in command was entrapped in ice for days near The Dalles. With the wind-chill factor, the temperature was -25° F.

Like a lion in chains, its waters smoothed by the dams, the Columbia River still storms and swirls. Professional fishing guide Christof Cook of Umatilla was recently swamped near dusk by a sudden fifty-mile-per-hour west wind. Before he gained shore in the darkness, he almost gave up swimming. He let his feet sink and touched bottom.

One sudden winter windstorm in the area clocked winds of 102 miles per hour, blowing huge trucks on their sides, and breaking brick walls and windows. Another odd phenomenon on the river is winter fog, dense curtains that lie only 5 or 6 feet deep over the river. Sitting in a boat, one is in fog; standing up, one's head may be in sunshine. For days or weeks the river may be a pleasure, but its moods can change suddenly and violently.

The still-wild shore between The Dalles and Wallula is broken only briefly by a few tiny settlements and the lush, irrigated vineyards of Columbia Crest Vineyards midway. Beaver, muskrat, and otter glide unafraid, and a part of the Pacific Flyway—the Umatilla Wildlife Refuge from Irrigon to Crow Butte—hosts flocks of birds. On the big Blalock Islands in the center of the refuge, the soft rush of wings and the lap of water mark the passage of white pelicans, egrets and sandhill cranes.

CHAPTER 18

Fishing and Logging

The rapid current of the Columbia, so formidable to mariners, was an attraction for salmon. Some people claimed that the Columbia was the world's richest fishing river. Certainly Northwest Indians along the Columbia River's twelve-hundred-mile length lived comfortably from its bounty. Possibly three-fourths of all the fish taken above Bonneville Dam came from Indian dip-net fishermen at Celilo, before it was stilled in 1957. An Indian not only fed his family but gained enough fish for bartering with other tribes. Latter-day biologists claim that the Indians harvested eighteen million tons of fish per year from the Columbia in the nineteenth century.

The wonderful salmon runs were utterly predictable, the different subgroups arriving at specific times. There were sockeye (called blueback by the Columbia fishermen), silversides, steelhead (a seagoing trout related to salmon), the Chinook (favored by canners) and until Grand Coulee Dam was completed, a splendid June run chinook, huge and prime. Rivermen called them channel fish or June hogs; others dubbed them royal chinook.

The last few hundred miles of the Columbia yield particularly prime salmon. It is early in the spawning run; their stomachs are empty, and their bodies are freed of sea lice by entering fresh water. By the time spawners approach their native streams far upriver, having gone without food for days, they are the "living dead"; indeed, early explorers unwittingly ate them at this stage and became violently ill. Upriver Indians dried such fish or made jerky out of them, which made them edible.

Hudson's Bay Company factors were the first to use salmon as a salable crop, salting them in barrels for export to England or Australia. The fish were reduced to oil, as well. The first American fish merchant did the Columbia no favors; Captain John Dominis of the brig *Owyhee* lightly pickled, salted and transported fifty-three barrels of salmon to Boston in 1830, pronounced almost inedible.

Boston ice merchant Nathaniel J. Wyeth organized the Columbia River Fishing and Trading Company and led two unsuccessful expeditions to the Portland area in 1832 and 1834. He landed on the pleasant island later called Sauvie and founded a farm he called Fort William, but by 1835, he was gone, his failure due to ill luck more than ineptness. The island was settled in 1838 by Laurent Sauvie, who operated a Hudson's Bay Company dairy farm.

Chinook Indians lived on the island, dug camas roots and wapato (which Indian women pried loose with bare toes from beneath the marsh waters), grew tobacco from seeds in wood ashes and fished for salmon. They used cedar bark nets nearly 200 feet long, weighted by rocks to hug the river bottom.

Shipping problems inhibited the fishing industry. The arrival in 1866 at Wahkiakum (north bank) of William and George Hume and Andrew S. Hapgood from California with their crude but effective canning methods initiated an incredible spiral of fishing frenzy, an intensive harvesting of salmon that lasted well into the 1900s. Only the depletion of the numbers of salmon slowed the industry.

By 1876, 450,000 cases (48 one-pound cans per case, totaling 21.6 million pounds) of canned salmon left Astoria or Portland annually for eastern America or foreign ports. This was largely the product of Hume canneries. By comparison, the average commercial catch during 1985 to 1989 was about nine million pounds annually.

Along the broad estuary, nets extended almost to mid-channel, a hard-cussing annoyance to ship captains. It was said the mighty Chinook salmon was dubbed the "channel fish" by upstream fishermen because it got through by following the ship channel.

Sea-hardened Scandinavians, particularly Finns, were attracted to the Columbia River, both for fishing and lumbering, an industry that soared to importance in the early 1900s. They fished in season, logged the balance of the time. With no particular regulation on fishing methods, the men trolled, manned gillnet boats, erected fish traps (particularly in Baker Bay) and set seine nets from shore. The traps collected sediment, too, contributing to the silting in of Baker's Bay.

On any fishing day a stranger arriving at Astoria by schooner was startled to see teams of horses far from shore, up to their bellies in water. On the shallow sand bars near the mouth of the Columbia, men buried a heavy log deep in the sand, attached one end of a seine net to it, then gave it to a waiting doryman. The rowers dragged the net in a large circle, returning to the beginning, where the net was quickly attached to horse teams and pulled swiftly out of the water. Or a team was used at each end of the net.

At The Dalles, where deep water extended to shore, dorymen laid a circle, and on shore, the land crew rushed to attach the lines to "the running team" that literally galloped up the bank to haul in the net before fish escaped. Fish companies had barns for the horses on shore there; at Astoria, they were often on barges. In the 1890s powerful purse-seine boats entered the scene but were soon ruled illegal. Later trollers operated offshore, intercepting the salmon before they could enter the river.

Fishermen considered fishing sites their property, and if anyone planned to drive new fish-trap pilings, he almost needed a marshal to guard him; the gillnetters would cast his boat loose or damage the pilings. Trollers carried barbed wire to throw into seine nets.

Territorial feelings ran high, leading to a "war" between Oregon gillnetters and Washington fish-trap men at Sand Island in Baker's Bay. Oregonians claimed their neighbors were taking an undue share of the salmon and, three hundred strong, stormed over to rip out nets. Sixty Washington National Guardsmen came to occupy and keep order at Sand Island, and two weeks later, federal soldiers from Fort Canby ousted the guard and replaced them on Sand Island to keep order. Washington guardsmen retreated to Ilwaco. Oregonians were outraged that federal troops had occupied Sand Island, a favorite fishing ground, and sent four hundred Oregon National Guardsmen to Astoria. On both shores, there was more social fervor than battle fever, with grand military balls and outings, parade drill and budding romances. It was the fishermen who were delighted to see the guardsmen leave, when their respective states said they were costing too much money. That the state line was in the middle of the river was reiterated, and neither state had authority beyond that point.

The original boundary at the middle of the channel proved impractical over the years. Sand Island has moved dramatically from currents and weather; earliest surveys showed it abreast of Point Adams, and by 1868, it was almost halfway across the Columbia's entrance. Today the original wide channel constituting that state border has narrowed to hug the Washington shore in the heavily silted-up Baker's Bay. Yet the state border runs through that same channel, just barely offshore from Washington—causing no end of jurisdictional problems. Furthermore, the main ship channel is much farther south today.

To obtain a fair price for their fish, fishermen formed the Fishermen's Protection Union at Astoria in May 1879; thereafter, officials negotiated a fixed price annually in advance of fishing season. Packers or canneries countered with cooperatives, such as the Columbia River Packers shortly after 1900. Before that, the Humes and Barby of Astoria and Seuferts at The Dalles dominated the industry.

Quite a few fishwheels operated at the Cascades, the first credited to Samuel Wilson in 1879, and the first patented wheel to Thornton Williams. Most Cascades fishermen sold to Warrendale Canneries (started about 1876), six miles west of Bradford Island, or to Rooster Rock Cannery, farther upriver. But few of the Cascades fishwheels were truly effective and some experimental; the swift and myriad channels of the rapids from The Dalles to Celilo Falls were more suitable for them. About twenty fishwheels operated there, either owned outright or controlled through purchase contracts by Seufert Canning Company. Operating from land (reefs or islands in the channel) or from barges, the fishwheel looked something like a waterwheel, only there were buckets instead of blades. The arms on the Seufert wheels usually were 20 feet long. They scooped up fish attracted to the narrow, swift channels and dumped them into fixed containers up to 50 feet deep. Adjustment for depth was critical to intercept the fish. Men had to operate silently lest they alarm the fish. Paint repelled them; so, the wheels remained natural. Most important to success was placement of the device, requiring an astute analysis of the salmon's path upriver—near this bank, by that reef. According to Francis Seufert: "What attracted the salmon to one place over another no one knew. ... These salmon followed definite paths in the river." (Francis Seufert, *Wheels of Fortune* [Oregon Historical Society, 1980], p. 25.)

When volume was low, fishwheel crews sent catches downriver by stringing them on a rope, then fastening the string to an empty barrel. They alerted the cannery downstream to watch for and pick up the catch. Fish pirates became wise to this method and snatched the fish or, in the dark of night, stole fish from operating wheels. Downstream pickup men for Warrendale's once found a naked dead man in the eddy, along with the barrel.

In 1907 Seufert's built cableways from receiving stations on shore to operating fishwheels for transporting caught salmon to the cannery; otherwise, scows with powerful motors picked up fish from the bins. They had to be strong. The vicious eddies that had drowned Hudson's Bay voyageurs still could swallow, stern or bow first, an entire boat that became caught in a vortex. Whirlpools as wide as 20 feet in diameter were common, and when the whirlpool broke, a huge boil arose, as much as 5 feet higher than the surrounding water. Worse yet, no one could thoroughly predict just where a whirlpool would open.

Celilo Indian fishermen sold most of their catch to Seufert's at the same rate as union fishermen. Some thirty or forty families lived near Celilo permanently, and migrants swelled the population to about one thousand people in fishing season. They built sturdy scaffolds of lashed logs that hung over the boiling cauldron of the river's many-channeled falls. They used no safety ropes (it was considered unmanly), and if they fell in, it was almost certain death. Some must have been relieved when the government required them to use a safety rope. Seufert's built cableways directly to prime sites to enable the Indian to ride out safely to his scaffold and send the fish back. By acquiring shorelands whenever offered for sale, Seufert's soon controlled that part of the river and denied access to fish-buyer competitors coming up from Astoria.

At The Dalles, single transient workers lived in bunkhouses and ate in mess houses. They were an orderly lot, heading to town on their day off for some carousing or conversation.

At Astoria, with more taverns and bawdy houses to choose from, the fishermen/loggers were a pretty raunchy group during their leisure time. Some wound up unwillingly far at sea. Working with unscrupulous tavern operators, ship owners shanghaied men—drugged them or grabbed those gloriously drunk, then took them aboard ships as crew. Authorities finally had to step in and sharply curb these practices. As decent women came to Astoria, a close-knit, religious family community of Finns grew up, still cohesive today.

Cannery workers at Astoria and The Dalles were almost always Chinese, because they worked for low wages and also had strong, nimble hands required in butchering and canning fish. The managers contracted with one person called the China Boss, telling him the numbers needed of each specialty, and the crew would materialize. The China Boss also managed the crew on-site. Most of these hard working, first-generation Americans planned to return to China but seldom did.

In 1926 the use of fishwheels was declared illegal in Oregon (and in 1934 in Washington) because they were too efficient, a contention severely attacked by Seufert family members. Gladys Seufert claims the problem was political, not actual, upriver versus downriver, resulting in the taking of more fish by gillnetters and seiners than fishwheels ever did.

Seufert's diversified by canning fruits and vegetables from the Hood River Valley until it ceased operations in 1954. After 1897, when an irrigation system was installed there, the famous Clark seedling strawberry, apples and pears dominated the area. Some defunct logging firms went into fruit production; today the valley produces over thirty percent of the winter pears in the United States.

The completion of The Dalles Dam in 1957 and subsequent flooding of Celilo Falls was the severe blow that ended Indian fishing. Yakima,

Umatilla, Warm Springs and Nez Perce Indians received $23.5 million for their ancestral fishing rights. As water rose behind The Dalles Dam, tearful Indians watched unbelieving as the falls quieted.

According to Gladys Seufert, a diver recently found that the infamous Columbia River silt has covered all but 20 feet of ancient Celilo Falls, formerly 50 feet high in normal water.

Both Seufert's and the Hume canneries processed sturgeon at times. Dwelling sluggishly near the river bottom, sturgeon attain several hundred pounds; indeed, giants of over a half ton have been taken, requiring teams of horses to drag them out. In earlier days eels were numerous around The Dalles, hanging from the banks and the spillways of the Celilo Canal; sturgeon especially bit on hooks baited with decaying eels.

As early as 1878, Astoria's cannery magnate Hume began agitating for salmon management or conservation. A fish commission established in 1891 by the Washington State Legislature urged Alfred E. Houchen and John McGowan to move their Bear River tideland private hatchery, ten years old, over to the Chinook River, where it became the first official state hatchery in 1895. The operation closed in 1935, but in 1969, using volunteers chiefly and especially led by Mel Leback, the hatchery reopened as Sea Resources.

Beginning as early as 1910, Oregon and Washington established a joint committee to work on fish policies. The problem always has been enormously complex, involving escapements (or lack thereof) upstream through dams, divisions between Indians, commercial and sports fishermen, divisions between Canada and the United States and so on. As late as January 1991, a major conference on the subject held at Kennewick, Washington, attempted to air the problems at least—if not the answers.

As mentioned previously, fishermen doubled as loggers. At first, the verdant forest covering both shores of the Columbia River, almost blotting out the sunlight, was considered a nuisance and an impediment to settlement. Portland was first known as "Stump Town," as the giant trees were sawed off with "misery whips" (two-man saws) a few feet off the ground. The stumps were whitewashed so that nighttime carriage travelers would not hit them.

The capital required of a logging firm tended to create large companies, but south of the Columbia in the Hood River Valley, Sterling Hanel founded a family enterprise in 1943, Hanel Lumber Company, that today has nearly three hundred employees, and is the only sawmill in the valley. Hanel's angle is to use small logs for creating dimensional lumber, and even smaller ones for chipping into wood chips to be shipped to market on Columbia River barges.

The pioneers burned forests to clear land, and natural droughts and breathtaking holocausts by Mother Nature destroyed vast areas. Notable was the Yacolt Burn of 1902, burning from the banks of the Columbia River halfway to Puget Sound. Historian Mark Parsons tells of three timbermen caught in the Yacolt Burn, taking refuge in a cave:

> Here they stayed while the night sky turned to screaming orange and reds. The big trees around them caught from the heat and exploded with deafening roars. Wild animals sought shelter with them in the corners of the cave, unaware of each other. ... On the third day they could come out of the cave but they could not walk the hot rocks. ... The countless stark sticks, that were three days ago giants of the woods, were now snags of the dead. (Mark E. Parsons, *Across Rushing Waters* [Camas, Washington: Mark E. Parsons, 1982], p. 56.)

Awesome was the devastation in 1933 of the Tillamook Burn, a super-fire that started accidentally near Glenwood, about twenty-five miles northwest of Portland, and exploded into an inferno that "crowned" (ran through the treetops), destroying 270,000 acres in twenty hours time, slowing somewhat but consuming another 40,000 acres before it was stopped, almost at the Pacific Ocean. Prime timber was reduced to firebrands propelled through the air by a self-generated wind or firestorm.

The flip side of the fire was that the forest was replanted with alacrity, one of the largest restoration projects ever tackled, and today the harvest of prime timber commences once more. Widespread destruction of forestlands came in May 1980, not from fire but from the concussion or blast from the Mount St. Helens eruption.

The earliest lumbering along the Columbia was to provide firewood for the sternwheelers' boilers, reportedly seventy-five cords per day in 1882 at Vancouver alone for boats plus meager settlers' needs. Willamette settler Ewing Young and Solomon Smith of the Wyeth party built a sawmill in 1836, Hudson's Bay Company at Vancouver had a sawmill, Michael T. Simmons and Jacobo Hansaker each owned a family mill. It took demand from California's gold-rush population (and later, the need for lumber to rebuild fire-torn San Francisco) to spur major investors into lumbering. Some of the world's finest fir trees, rivaling the California redwoods in height, grew in Washington and Oregon. When World War I came, the resilient, tough Sitka spruce was in demand for aircraft.

The *Portland Oregonian*, then owned by Henry L. Pittock, had a hand in the formation of the Columbia River Paper Company at Camas in 1883, because a mill at Oregon City was unable to produce sufficient newsprint for the newspaper. As James River Corporation today, the mill manufactures fine papers and tissue, no newsprint. A pioneer company operated until recently at Bridal Veil, across the river from Washougal, sending logs down a flume to the mill below. Large timber companies opened along the Columbia downriver from Portland.

Loggers from Maine or Minnesota forests soon learned to saw the big firs several feet off the ground; when cut nearer the ground, a tree would gush forth with as much as a barrel of pitch. Men worked with hand saws and horse teams, then with oxen on skid roads (smaller tree trunks placed side by side to form a rolling road). The handler or bullwhacker walked beside yokes of five to ten beasts, goading them on profanely. That master of Northwest stories and ex-lumberjack, Stewart Holbrook, said in his book, *Holy Old Mackinaw*, that, when the bullwhacker swore, the very bark of trees smoked, curled up and fell to the ground. If invective failed to get results, the man was known to walk the backs of the team with his calked boots.

Later came steam engines or donkeys that, attached to cables running over pulleys fixed to a high spar or tree, hoisted logs to the staging area well above the forest floor. At Sedro-Woolley, Washington, a small company, Skagit Steel, adapted a Fordson tractor as a gas-driven "donkey." The company laid down ordinary peeled logs end to end from woods to mill or river port, installed large back wheels on the tractor, and ran the tractor on the log "track" to pull logs out of the woods singly or on cars.

Logs must be moved to mills, and as cutting moved farther back into the hills from the river, timbermen built low dams on small Columbia tributaries, such as the Wind River. They stockpiled logs all summer and fall, and in spring when the river was at flood stage, destroyed the holding dam to send the logs careening down to the Columbia. Woe to the person who happened to be on shore when the torrent came down, but then there were few settlers in the woods. This practice was curtailed by law some years later.

Companies built logging railroads to bring out the logs. Some were of dubious quality, snaking through hills at grades no one would believe possible and creeping over untrustworthy trestles (although the author is not aware of any collapsing with trains).

Typically the loggers sought raucous living on their days off. Portland's August Erikson catered to them with "The Workingman's Club," a night spot as spacious as the mountain forests. It reputedly had the longest bar in the world (684 feet), pipe organ music and the famous free lunch—huge platters of sausages and soft bread, roast beef and the trimmings. The Workingman's Club still operated in 1970, outlasting others such as Fritz's, Blazier's (a family in the logging business), the House of All Nations and the legendary Nancy Boggs who operated a whorehouse on a barge—moving it to a different Columbia or Willamette river location if the police became too heavy-handed.

In addition to the giant logging company pioneers like Frederick Weyerhaeuser and A. B. Hammond, "gyppo" loggers invaded the forests—family operations where mom cooked, dad and the boys did the logging. The gyppo logger's wife tended to be the "go-fer," bumping over rutted roads to get groceries, spare parts for machines, arrange for funds and—all too often—find and drag back home a drunk logger from one of the taverns (the operator obligingly dumped the man into the back of her car).

But all the lumber and fish money was building Columbia River economy in big towns like Vancouver, Washington, and its counterpart, Portland, Oregon. With the wealth of the Willamette Valley's farms to market, the lumber from the flanks of Mount Hood and Mount St. Helens stacked awaiting shipment, and tinned and salted salmon piling up, Portland especially became a busy seaport. Huge lumber schooners of ocean draft could sail right up the Columbia into the Willamette, dredged deeper by the Port of Portland, totally protected from the elements, and connecting to local railroads.

Travel and Trivia
Tri-Cities and Down the River

Tri-Cities area:

Tri-Cities **Visitors & Convention Bureau**, 6951 West Grandridge Boulevard, Kennewick, WA 99336. At west end of Tri-Cities near Columbia Center, a little hard to find, follow signs off freeway. In state 1-800-835-0248, out of state (509) 735-8486.

Mid-Columbia Regional Library, 405 South Dayton, Kennewick; **Franklin County Historical Museum**, 305 North Fourth Avenue, Pasco; **East Benton County Historical Museum**, 205 Keewaydin Drive, Kennewick; **Columbia Basin College**, Pasco—all enlighten you about the rich history of the confluence of the rivers.

As many as 155 species of birds have been noted at **Potholes Reservoir** north of Pasco. Not far away is **Juniper Dunes Wilderness**, not a place you would expect in Washington.

Washington Dinner Train runs in summer between Prosser and Tri-Cities. Call Yakima WA 1-800-876-RAIL.

Letha's Fruit Room, P.O. Box 6376, Kennewick, WA 99336-0376. Ask for catalog of gourmet food products of area.

Ariel's, 617 The Parkway, Richland, WA 99352. (509) 946-3314. A great selection of local foods, vinegars, chocolate-covered cherries, gift packs in attractive setting.

Countryside Cottage, 5215 West Clearwater, Kennewick, WA 99336. (509) 783-9494. Also has local food packs and general gifts. When you're tired of shopping, good food and desserts one door away at **Village Deli**.

Metz Marina, Clover Island, Pasco, can put you on the Columbia River in a boat.

London Broiler, 1800 West Lewis, Pasco, WA 99301. (509) 545-1511. Very good pasta and Chinese buffet. Seafood fresh daily and steaks hand-cut. Yet all this is quite inexpensive.

To watch boats on the Columbia while dining: **Hanford House**, Richland; **Cedars** at Quality Inn on Clover Island, Pasco; **R. F. McDougall's** and The **Boulevard Bar & Grill**, both in Richland.

Moore Mansion, a must for history buffs and gourmet dining (see text). 200 Road 34, Pasco, WA 99301. Hard to find, approach via #395 to Sylvester, west to No. 34 Road, left to the river. Reservations (509) 547-8760.

Farmers' Market at 4th and Lewis, Pasco, is fun; all kinds of fresh vegetables, pickles, fruits, nuts.

Preston Premium Wines, 502 East Vineyard Drive, about five miles north, Pasco, WA 99301. (509) 545-1990. Balcony overlooking winery with furniture made from wine casks. Gifts include Christmas wreaths made from wine corks. Annual Christmas Lighting December 1— hundreds of lights and displays over the grounds. Kite Festival, May. "Catch the Crush," October.

Annual **International Wine Festival** held in October at the Red Lion Inn, Pasco, attracts about fifty-five major Northwest wineries, seminars for members, and a wine-tasting party open to public. Red Lion Inn is at 2525 North 20th at intersection of freeway and Highway 395.

Country Crafts at the **Appleseed Gallery**, 108 Vista Way, Kennewick, WA 99336. Eleven mini-shops, unusual items, paintings, children's stuff.

Two Rivers Park is a serene small park with bays off the Columbia River, ideal for small children's swimming. In fall transient Canadian geese, ducks. Drive southeasterly on Chemical Drive, turn left at Finley Road, Kennewick side of river.

Ask Visitor Information for **info on numerous festivals**. They include the big annual Sunfest, June; Cinco de Mayo (May 5) Festival (Hispanic); Christmas Lights Boat Parade, December; Salmon Derby, September; Budweiser Columbia Cup for Unlimited Hydroplanes and Tri-City Water Follies, July; Pasco Autumn Festival.

Columbia Park is the place to relax, walk, picnic, watch river events, on Kennewick side next to "Blue Bridge" over Columbia. Rowing shells, sailboats, paddle boats, fishing boats at Mac's Boatyard, west entry to park.

Viewing **Intercity Bridge**, the "other one," is worthwhile. The longest cable-stay bridge in North America with a span of 981 feet. In late sun or moonlight it looks like an ambitious spider put it up.

Ask a local bookstore or museum store for *See South-Central Washington, a Sunday Drive Guide*, by Jean Carol Davis. Good suggestions for short trips around Tri-Cities.

The vessel, *Sun Princess*, capacity forty-nine people, available for **charters on Columbia and Snake rivers**, cocktail cruises, catered meals. Sunshine Charters, Inc., Clover Island, Kennewick, WA 99336. (509) 547-0000 or 547-8625. (In season only.)

Your kids (and you, too) will love cooling off at **Oasis Waterworks**, 6321 West Canal, Kennewick, mid-May through Labor Day.

Sacajawea State Park, junction of Snake and Columbia, a quiet place to contemplate Lewis and Clark history in Interpretive Center and waterside park.

Visitor Center, **Fast Flux Test Facility**, north of Richland on Hanford Project. (509) 376-3026. Exhibits and a "must see" for science buffs. Close-up view of sodium-cooled nuclear reactor (modern one).

Hanford Science Center, downtown Richland, with historic exhibits and information.

WPPSS Plant 2 Visitor Center, close-up view of plant, video information. Maybe you can find out what went wrong (see text).

Tridec in Kennewick is a coordinated council for industrial development of the area, 901 North Colorado, Kennewick, WA 99336. (509) 735-1000. If business opportunities are your interest, see Tridec.

Brand **new book**, illustrated, covers background of Tri-Cities and several of its industries: *Tri-Cities* by Ted Van Arsdol. Available at bookstores.

Wallula Gap National Landmark south of Tri-Cities, where ancient Columbia River broke through the hills. Includes the Twin Sisters, two bold rock columns on east side of river. Picnicking, hiking or playing in sand, wildflowers in spring, interesting scenery.

Ice Harbor Dam on the Snake River above junction with Columbia, approach from south side, Highway 124.

Whitman Mission National Historic Site and Museum, 55 miles east at Walla Walla, museum and hill with sweeping view of the flat country.

Umatilla has a Labor Day weekend walleye derby, prizes for best fish.

Christof Cook, **Four Seasons Guide Service**, jet boat rentals, photographic trips, fishing, hunting. An experienced, enthusiastic young guide. (503) 922-5925, Umatilla.

Ranchers coming to **Olde Country Brand Restaurant** are given a block of wood on which to inscribe their brands, which are then displayed on the walls. Restaurant is a part of **Heather Inn**, a full resort with golf course near McNary Dam, 705 Willamette Avenue, Umatilla, OR 97882. (503) 922-5647. Heather Inn: 1-800-447-7529.

The town of **Echo**, south of I-84 a few miles, was on the Oregon Trail. Fort Henrietta was there. Each September hosts a big encampment of muzzle loaders.

A historic little town, **Umatilla** has at least two antique shops with fascinating memorabilia and *perhaps* some real treasures. (I am not knowledgeable about antiques.) Pendleton, Oregon, on I-84 36 miles south, is the home of the famous **Pendleton Rodeo**, held each September and of Pendleton Woolen Mills, known worldwide. Factory store.

Comfortable accommodations available at **Tillicum Motor Inn**, 1481 6th Street. (503) 922-3236.

At nearby **Hermiston** you can see big-league livestock auctions; sometimes several hundred horses sold. Oregon Trail pioneers, the local Bonney family (related to Billy the Kid) are among founders of such auctions.

There are no known boat rentals at Umatilla.

The vines of **Columbia Crest Winery** decorate the north side of the Columbia River west of Umatilla, worth stopping for a taste and a look. Highway 221, P.O. Box 231, Paterson, WA 99345. (509) 875-2061.

Looping northward, too, are the **Horse Heaven Hills**, treeless with lush grass, with a lonesome beauty of their own. Once home to wild horses, the hills are prime farmland.

The Dalles **Convention & Visitors Bureau**, 901 East Second, The Dalles, OR 97058. 1-800-255-3385.

The Dalles was historic at the time of Indian life, then Hudson's Bay travelers, Barlow Trail pioneers, and others. Two **self-guided walking tours** (get brochure from Visitors Bureau) cover historic homes and buildings, including The Dalles Art Center, the original Wasco County Courthouse from 1859, and Old St. Peter's Landmark, formerly a Catholic church. See Father Bronsgeest's little pipe organ, which he took on horseback to his far-flung parishes.

Fort Dalles Museum (only the Surgeon's Quarters remain) overlooks the river at West 15th Street (approach from Trevitt Street).

A new Columbia River **Interpretive Center** is in the wings near The Dalles; ask Visitors Bureau if it is open yet.

The **Shilo Inn**, The Dalles, overlooks the dam. From the dining room one sees bleak buildings of Indian Shaker Church from 1891. Wind Rock, believed to calm the Gorge winds, has been moved to this site from Rowena; some say that, since its move, it has lost its power and it has been windier since. From the original location in Umatilla House, the Shilo Inn O'Callahan's Bar now has the handcarved "Twin Virgins" back bar.

Board a train near the Shilo Inn for a **tour of The Dalles Dam**. Kids love it. A viewing room to see fish passing above the dam via fish ladders. Artifacts, petroglyphs and historical exhibits.

Oregon products, including salmon, "cherkins" (pickled cherries), whole grain wheat, Celilo seasoning, pressed wildflower note paper, gift packs, at **Cannon Packer**, 403 West 4th Street, The Dalles, OR 97058. (503) 296-3038.

Identify the profusion of **spring wildflowers** from the book, *Wildflowers of the Columbia Gorge*, by Russ Jolley (Portland: Oregon Historical Society Press, 1988).

Celilo Falls and its fisheries are gone but **Wilm's Hang-Ups** sells splendid prints of the falls for framing, 312-1/2 East 2nd Street, The Dalles, OR 97058. (503) 296-3226.

A wonderful book on **sternwheeler history** is *Blow for the Landing* by Fritz Timmen (Caldwell, ID: The Caxton Printers, 1973).

Artists depicting the Columbia River (Anthony Kiser) and Celilo Falls (Laura Ashbrenner) are exhibited at **The Oregon Trail Gallery**, formerly the Carnegie Library, at 4th and Washington, The Dalles. Local crafts, too.

An unusual boutique is **Columbia Clothing Company**, which teaches knitting and helps locals do custom sweaters for sale. Items made to order and lately added some commercial lines. 4th and Union. (503) 298-8882.

To understand the impact of **fishwheels on the Columbia**, read *Wheels of Fortune* by Francis Seufert edited by Thomas Vaughan. (Portland: The Oregon Historical Society, 1980). His family owned them.

Great view of The Dalles, the dams and the mountains from **The Inn at The Dalles**, Exit 87, up on a bench. (503) 296-1167.

In late July the **Fort Dalles Days** celebration includes a Mexican Rodeo with mariachi bands, rope tricks and a chili cookoff. The Mexican influence in the area comes originally from migrant workers to eastern Washington vineyards and fruit orchards. Many stayed to become substantial citizens. **Casa del Rio** in Cascade Square showcases authentic Mexican food.

Commanding a striking view of the Columbia River from the north side above The Dalles is **Maryhill Museum**, an unlikely location for a stunning collection of Auguste **Rodin sculpture**, Russian icons, traveling art exhibits, and Rumanian art (including **Queen Marie's gilt furniture**), plus an extensive **Native American Collection** pertinent to the river and its people. Maryhill was built by Samuel Hill, married to railroad magnate James J. Hill's daughter (no relation). After one look at the barren hills, she refused to live there. The mansion sits on 7,000 acres of Hill property. **Cafe at museum**. The intriguing history of Hill is contained in a book, *Sam Hill* by John E. Tuhy (Portland: Timber Press, 1983). **Special events** at this grand location all year. 35 Maryhill Museum Drive, Goldendale, WA 98620. (509) 773-3733. Open March 15 through November 15.

Nearby the wind whistles through the eerie columns of **Stonehenge**, a partial replica of the original on Salisbury Plains, England. Also built by Sam Hill as a memorial to veterans of World War I from Klickitat County.

About five miles east of Maryhill is **Wakemup Mound**, excavated first in 1924 and revealing more of the ten-thousand-year (or more) history of the Columbia River people.

The historic little town of **Arlington**, Oregon, where riverboats picked up wool from freshly shorn sheep, was moved from riverside to bluff to avoid being inundated by Lake Celilo. A waterside park there is a good place to muse on the changes.

Famous trumpeter "Doc" Severinsen was raised at the little town **Arlington**. The Belchers, managers of Village Inn Motel, can give you tips about Arlington's past.

Between The Dalles and Hood River, **Memaloose State Park** permits a poignant look at Memaloose Island, for centuries a burial island for local Indian people. The dead were wrapped tightly and stacked inside open log shelters, with their possessions. Part of the island was covered by rising waters behind the dam. Designated people respectfully removed Indian remains.

Travel a Barlow Road segment in **Mount Hood National Forest**. Call National Park Service (503) 963-7186 for information or write 19559 Southeast Division Street, Gresham, OR 97030.

At junction of highways 35 and 26 toward Mount Hood is the **Grave of a Pioneer Woman**, dedicated to all women of the Oregon Trail. The unidentified woman died there on the Barlow Trail.

Timberline Lodge at Mount Hood, a volcanic cone that looms above the south bank of the Columbia, was built during the Depression in 1937 as a shelter for skiers and hikers, today designated as a National Historic Landmark. Well worth a side trip. In winter Timberline teems with skiers. Use Highway 35 to Highway 26 from the Columbia Gorge, or from Portland all the way on Highway 26. Overnight facilities, dining, etc. Timberline Lodge, OR 97028. (503) 231-7979 in Portland for information.

Stonehenge replica built by Sam Hill as a memorial to Klickitat County World War I veterans.

Columbia River Gorge area:

The **Columbia River Gorge National Scenic Area** is an entity. **Waucoma Center**, extensive brochures, 902 Wasco Avenue, Hood River, OR 97031. (503) 386-2333.

Write for the **quarterly magazine**, "Columbia Gorge." About $3. Gorge Publishing, Inc., P.O. Box 918, Hood River, OR 97031. Contains updated data on dozens of visitor attractions.

Hood River **County Chamber of Commerce**, Port Marina Park, Hood River, OR 97031. (503) 386-2000 or 1-800-366-3530.

An unforeseen benefit of the frequent boisterous Columbia Gorge winds has been the soaring popularity of the waters for **sailboarding**. Even in chilly winter winds the colorful sailboards skim and dart across the water. The capital of it all is between Stevenson on the north shore and Hood River on the south, but The Dalles, Bingen, Cascade Locks share enthusiasts.

The Inn at Hood River is a few *feet* from the river, and has a close view of the lighted toll bridge to White Salmon, Washington, a pool, riverside grill and surrounding marketplace. Open-air, warm weather lounging while watching the sailboards and river barge traffic go by, or the moon over the river at night. 1108 East Marina Way, Hood River, OR 97031. 1-800-828-7873.

Bridge of the Gods in the Columbia Gorge.

Gorge sailboarding info also at **Skamania County Parks & Recreation** (509) 427-5141.

Hobie Cat Single-handed National Championships are in late August.

More than three hundred ambitious people **swim the 1.1 mile** Columbia River in earliest September for fun.

High Wind Classic, the Gorge's oldest **slalom sailboarding** event, in late June, and the world's largest slalom in July, Columbia Gorge Pro-Am.

Gorge Cities BlowOut, a race from Cascade Locks to Hood River in mid-July.

Spawned from the water-related activities, Luhr-Jensen & Sons, Inc., a small company, is now a prime **manufacturer of fishing lures**. The Columbia is one of the world's greatest fisheries. 400 Portway, Hood River, OR 97031. (503) 386-3811. **Tours**.

Intense interest in sailboarding and river sports has caused opening of factories for **specialized clothing** and equipment for these markets. Among them is Hood River Windsurfing downtown Hood River. Gorge Windsurfing, The Dalles, claims to be oldest on the river, neck and neck with Gorge Performance of Portland.

No small boat rentals in Hood River—too windy and dangerous for amateurs! **Rent a boat** WITH an operator, Mid-Columbia Water Sports, Dock Road. Personal motorized watercraft at Mid-Columbia Marina, Port Marine Park at the boat dock and at The Inn at Hood River. Houseboats at Gorge Pleasure Boats, P.O. Box 761, Hood River, OR 97031. (503) 386-1770

Sportsmen get thirsty, and **White Cap Brew Pub** aims to quench that with handcrafted ales, tastings and tours, too. Outdoor deck, music, view. Hood River Brewing Company, 506 Columbia, Hood River, OR 97031. (503) 386-2281.

A wonderfully rural feeling is captured at **Home Valley Bed and Breakfast**, north shore, with a splendid view of river activity, spacious and serene wooded grounds. Near entry of Wind River to Columbia. Boat launch nearby. Upper Lyons Road, Home Valley, WA 98648. (509) 427-7070.

The 83-year-old **Mount Hood Railroad** begins its season with a "Fruit Blossom Special" in mid-April, going from river to mountain through the orchard country. Reservations recommended, leaves from Hood River historic depot. (503) 386-3556.

At the **Hood River Historical Museum**, Port Marina Park, there is an American flag made in 1861 by six women, their families Union supporters. The flag was raised on July 4.

Historic Cloud Cap Inn on the north face of Mount Hood was finished in August 1889, and fell on mixed times during its hundred years. It is now a Historic Site in a National Historic District. The mind-boggling view is worth the trip. Ten miles of dirt road.

Some of the numerous **festivals in the Columbia Gorge** are Christmas on the Gorge, Fly the Wild Wind Fest, Bluegrass Fest, Sternwheeler Days. Ask any Gorge visitor center.

In late November motorists on I-84 marvel at the sight of the 65,000 Christmas lights on the grounds of **Columbia Gorge Hotel**. "Three-hour-type" brunches all year, groaning tables of food. Hotel was built in 1921 as home of Simon Benson, lumber magnate. **Wah-Gwin-Gwin Falls** tumbles 260 feet into the Columbia from the premises. 4000 Westcliff Drive (off I-84), Hood River, OR 97031. 1-800-345-1921.

The oldest hotel currently operating in the Gorge is **The Lyle Hotel** in Lyle, a ghost town on the north bank, on 7th Street off Highway 14, ten minutes east of Bingen. Foods like chinook salmon in a huckleberry sauce or Pier Pie. (509) 365-3010.

Horsebacking and rooms at **Fir Mountain Ranch**, 4051 Fir Mountain Road, Hood River, OR 97031. (503) 354-2753. South and east, about nine miles.

In the 1880s the Mt. Hood Hotel of Hood River was THE place to stay. Over the years it had a checkered history but is now graciously restored as **Hood River Hotel**, downtown, overlooking the Columbia. 102 Oak Street, Hood River, OR 97031. (503) 386-1900.

Near the hotel was the **Niguma Variety Store** of Taiki Kuma, built in 1905 by a Japanese immigrant. Japanese came to work in the Hood River orchard country and railroad.

In the Hood River Valley cherries, pears and vineyards have thrived since early times. Several **growers permit tours**. Ask the Visitors Center about Hood River Vineyards, Diamond Fruit Growers, Inc., Three Rivers Winery, River Bend Organic Farm and others. Also in that area tours available of Juanita's Tortilla Factory, a minority success story where tortillas were first manufactured for workers' needs, and demand for tortillas and chips has spread to distant markets.

Canned fruit gift packs are available at several gift stores.

When it snows, you can imagine yourself as a "Mountie" by taking a **dog-sled trip** out of Trout Lake. John Simonson (503) 761-7428. Or Phil's Guide Service gives you **a ride in Tucker Sno-Cats**, lunch in an Indian tepee and wonderful winter scenes. (503) 493-2641 or 395-2107.

Spring Creek National Fish Hatchery was opened in 1901 at Underwood on the north shore of the Columbia. Over seventeen million fingerlings are released each spring to travel to the ocean, returning 167 miles upstream at maturity to spawn at the hatchery. The hatchery helps to mitigate chinook salmon losses due to dam construction. Visitor Center open Monday through Friday. Environmental education tours arranged. Two miles west of Hood River/White Salmon bridge on Highway 14. (509) 493-1730.

For maps and information about **National Forest facilities for recreation**, ask U. S. Forest Service Information. Among several are Mt. Hood National Forest, 2955 Northwest Division Street, Gresham, OR 97030. (503) 667-0511. Gifford Pinchot National Forest, 500 West 12th Street, Vancouver, WA 98660. (206) 696-7500.

North of the river, east of Stevenson, **Carson Hot Springs** seemingly has never changed since 1900. In ancient facilities devotees come regularly to "take the baths" and receive massages. Some swear to miraculous regeneration. St. Martin's Hotel. (509) 427-8292.

Ape Caves on Road 83 west of Carson. The longest known lava tube (12,810 feet) has been developed for unguided use.

Take a side trip to **Wind River Arboretum** in Gifford Pinchot National Forest north of Carson, where the U. S. Forest Service has been testing suitability of trees for Northwest use since 1912. The nursery grows seedlings for reforestation and, upon specific order, for forests beyond the Northwest. It all got started to replace the devastation caused by forest fires, especially the disastrous Yacolt Burn of 1902. The Nursery ships eighteen to twenty million seedlings annually for replanting in the Northwest. At certain times seedlings are for sale to the public (in large quantities only).

One may approach **Mount St. Helens** from the Wind River area. The mountain literally exploded in May 1980 (see text). The view highway is not recommended for winter. Drive to the western portal off Interstate 5, exit 49, for an Interpretive Center open all year. Three lengths of narrated tours available. (206) 274-4038 or 274-6644.

The **Columbia River Scenic Highway**, originally from Portland to Hood River only, was dedicated in 1916, after herculean effort. It plays hide and seek with Interstate 84 on the south bank, accessing some of the Gorge's most wondrous scenery. Ask visitors bureaus for guide to **Mt. Hood Columbia Gorge Loop**. Included are Lewis and Clark State Park at the mouth of the Sandy River, many waterfalls, especially Multnomah Falls and Bridal Veil Falls, plus less-known ones like Upper and Lower Elowah Falls on McCord Creek east of Warrendale. You can drive on the Columbia River Highway 22 miles between Troutdale and Ainsworth State Park or 9 miles between Mosier and The Dalles. The latter was hacked out in Oregon Trail times as an alternative to floating downriver, but at Mosier pioneers could go no farther. **Vista House** on Crown Point, altitude 733 feet, on the scenic highway has a sweeping view of the Columbia.

Multnomah Falls, 620 feet high, is visible from I-84, also. Turn into parking lot. Snack or shop in the handsome stone Multnomah Falls Visitor Center at the foot of the falls and learn about Gorge geology and plants, too. Winter turns the falls into ice sculptures of "oohh" and "aahh" beauty. Watch for the infrequent below-freezing temperatures and go.

Beacon Rock on the north shore has been a landmark to Oregon Trail immigrants and mariners. A monolith second in size only to Gibraltar, it is 848 feet high. There is a 4,500-foot trail to the top, with handrails, not for the weary as there is a 15 percent grade. There are nonhookup campsites and a park at the Beacon Rock State Park.

A splendid **new lodge and convention center** is scheduled to open as early as spring 1992, near the Bridge of the Gods. A joint project of Skamania County and famed Salishan Lodge, with federal funding, too.

At Stevenson, the **Skamania County Historical Museum** has displays, artifacts, archives and the world's largest collection of rosaries. Interpretive center under construction already has nine-projector show on the Columbia River. Contributions welcomed. Downtown.

The Pink Coyote on main street of Stevenson sells local crafts and souvenirs.

Lots of **sailboard** instructors and rentals, Stevenson.

For a brief look at **the central Gorge**, embark on *Columbia Sightseer* out of Stevenson, late May through September, three cruises daily. (206) 427-8817.

The most beloved and **venerable river cruise** is on the sternwheeler, *Columbia Gorge*, operating between Portland and Cascade Locks. Special group cruises sometimes go through Bonneville locks. Food aboard. Reservations required. Theme trips such as "Valentine's Day," "Christmas Caroling Cruise," or "Pray for an Ice Storm Cruise." 606 Northwest Front Avenue, #A-1, Portland, OR 97201. (503) 223-3928. In summer (503) 374-8427. In early June the Port of Cascade Locks celebrates "Sternwheeler Days" to celebrate the return to the river of the *Columbia Gorge*. Salmon feed, street dance. (503) 374-8619.

The **Bridge of the Gods** spanning the Columbia River between a point near Stevenson and Cascade Locks is named for the Indian legend. It tells of a natural bridge at that point, destroyed during a battle between the gods of the mountains. Below the bridge the river is 200 feet deep at the foot of the old rapids.

Bonneville Dam, see both ends for interpretive material and displays, but main visitor center is on Oregon side.

From the riverside **Char-Burger**, a general restaurant and small bakery with luscious candy and coconut macaroons, one may watch ship traffic. Books on local history. Below Bridge of the Gods, 713 WaNaPa, Cascades Locks, OR.

The original portage railway locomotive "Pony" is exhibited in the **Port of Cascade Locks Marine Park**, a National Historic Site. An original toll building contains three floors of river displays. Outlines of the locks are still visible. Much of the rock work was performed by Italians, especially skilled in this art. The old sternwheeler depot is today's terminus for the sternwheeler *Columbia Gorge* with a gift shop.

Columbia River Collection, an **LP album of songs by Woodie Guthrie** (Cambridge: Rounder Records, 1987) made when he was an employee of Bonneville Power Administration. Available at Columbia Maritime Museum bookstore, Astoria and elsewhere.

Camas **Chamber of Commerce**. (206) 834-2472.

A branch of the famous **Pendleton Woolen Mills** is in Washougal, Washington, 217th Street, and offers tours of the fabric mill. See how they make the cloth before you buy the suit or shirt. (503) 226-4801.

Between Camas and Washougal on the north shore was **Parkersville**, one of the first incorporated settlements in Washington Territory. Only an old house, a sign and picnic grounds remain. However, next door is Parker House, one of the finest restaurants on the river.

Washougal has **Frontier Days**, the Friday-Sunday following July 4 at Cottonwood Beach (Columbia River). Sand castles contests, river-oriented events. Lt. Broughton came to this point on the river, anchoring across the Columbia at the Sandy River and rowing to the north shore.

The Leadbetter home on Lacamas Lake, Camas, is a Victorian mansion, a historic site, privately occupied. It was the summer home for the Oregonian Pittock and Leadbetter families.

Ask The James River Corporation in Camas about **tours of the paper mill**, originally Columbia River Paper Company, 1883.

Portland/Vancouver to the Sea

THE COLUMBIA FROM CAMAS-WASHOUGAL
TO THE PACIFIC OCEAN

LEGEND

● Community   ⊗ Elevation (in feet)

-·-·- State Border

Scale in Statute Miles

5   0   10   25

1991   David Jungkuntz

CHAPTER 20

Cities and Towns
Use the River

The lower Columbia River towns and cities were merchant cities born of the need to serve burgeoning businesses—especially fishing and logging, grains and cattle.

Portland, not centering on the Columbia River but always part of its economic area, started as a land claim filed in 1843 by Asa Lovejoy and William Overton. It was a mere clearing in the woods on the Willamette River, for upriver Oregon City, Champoeg and other towns dominated trade with Oregon Trail immigrants in the fertile Willamette Valley. To most immigrants, the Columbia River was more hazard than asset, a wild river to be endured for dangerous passages. But as the produce of the Willamette outstripped local consumption, ways of getting excesses to market became of paramount interest. Until the arrival of railroads in the 1880s, the choice was the Columbia River—either by coastal sailing ship or upriver by sternwheeler. The great falls of the Willamette near Oregon City effectively thwarted any direct access to valley farming communities.

Somewhat of a rover, Overton sold his half of the claim to Francis W. Pettygrove within a year. Both Lovejoy and Pettygrove were of New England merchant stock and recognized the potential of their claim as a future port. They platted a town on the west side of the river, while a handful of others settled east of the river, necessitating a ferry operation, and so it went.

Two key settlers gave impetus to growth—sea captain John H. Couch, filing a claim in 1846, and tanner Daniel Lownsdale, in 1845. Couch touted Portland as the gateway to the sea; Lownsdale laid out a road from Portland to today's Tualitin (Canyon Road) to bring in agricultural products. The road was made mud-proof by laying planks side by side, the Great Plank Road, six miles long. Consequently, instead of transshipping products via Oregon City and boats below the falls, pioneers could haul them directly to the seaport of Portland. The community was off and running. By 1850 the town had 821 people; in 1851 it was incorporated.

The Idaho gold rush gave further impetus to development. Hordes of prospectors clumped through town, transferring from sailing ships to riverboats, buying supplies. Sternwheelers transported cattle, sheep and grain downriver to the "big city" for export or processing. All this activity naturally created a great thirst; Henry Weinhard responded by moving his brewery from its Fort Vancouver location (founded in 1856) to Portland.

Portland became the mail boat's terminus in 1854, mail coming around the Horn on ships from the East Coast. The city developed a distinctly New England feeling as it grew. The ships' captains and mates, Eastern industrialists, and education-oriented settlers founded churches and built fine Victorian or Queen Anne-style homes facing the Willamette with a backdrop of Mount Hood. To show off its riches and beautiful site, citizens chipped in and staged the Lewis & Clark Exposition of 1905. There were statues of Lewis and Clark, photographs of a cigar raft 720 feet long, three hundred Curtis Indian prints, and fruit displays from twenty-four Oregon counties. The biggest hit was the Forestry Building, 100 feet by 200 feet, made of logs as long as 60 feet and 6 feet in diameter.

There was an underbelly to Portland, of course. "Respectable citizens" either closed their eyes or surreptitiously participated in the fun at roistering bars and cribs of the riverfront, traditionally belonging to sailors, loggers and railroad crews bent on spending all their hard-earned money.

When the California and Oregon Railroad (later, the Southern Pacific) was completed to Portland in 1869, and east/west service was assured through Oregon Railway & Navigation Company's Wallula connection to the Northern Pacific in 1883, Portland's preeminence as a commercial port was assured. By 1890 the city was a terminus for fifty-seven steamship lines. As a port, it incurred a disadvantage by being one hundred miles from the sea on a whimsical river of varying depth and current. Its advantage was being one hundred miles closer to landlocked markets. A century later, it boasted 430,000 largely satisfied residents who touted their city as The Rose City, for the flowers planted by Oregon Trail arrivals.

After the Civil War, shipping interests dredged the Willamette, since deeper-draft ships had to unload partially at St. Helens before proceeding to Portland. In 1891 the state created the Port of Portland to dredge and maintain a 25-foot channel from Portland to the ocean.

The city formed the Commission of Public Docks in 1910 to develop waterfront terminals, drydocks and other facilities, merging with the Port in 1970. Under the federal Rivers and Harbors Act of 1912, the Port has been required to keep the Willamette channel dredged to 30 feet, and to assist the U.S. Army Corps of Engineers in maintaining the shipping channel on the Columbia River to the ocean; in 1976 required depth was 40 feet, and further dredging is needed as ships become larger. In the 1920s the Port removed Post Office Bar near the confluence of the Willamette and Columbia, using the dredge materials to fill Swan Island and create Guilds Lake Industrial Park in northwest Portland. Swan Island became the site for Portland's first airport, dedicated by none other than Charles Lindbergh, flying in the Spirit of St. Louis only four months after his historic transoceanic flight.

Five generations of the Shaver Transportation Company family have been active on the Portland waterfront, starting with the sternwheeler captain George Shaver. His son, Captain J. W., served on the Port of Portland Commission, and his grandson, Captain George, on the Dock Commission. Fifth generation Mary operates a launch service. Another Columbia/Willamette pioneer dynasty was the Dant family, starting with the Dant and Russell Lumber Company and including the founding of States Line steamship line of thirty-two vessels.

Near the confluence of the two rivers, another scion of Portland, William Leadbetter, willed his 2,000 acres of duck-hunting lands to Willamette University. The Port purchased it in 1964 for multi-purpose use that includes two lakes, where ducklings still waddle behind their mothers every spring.

Across the mighty Columbia, perhaps two thousand Indians and mixed-race families of Hudson's Bay Company employees lived near Fort Vancouver. Americans settled nearby in Columbia City, the area becoming Vancouver in 1853, incorporated in 1857. Privately owned by the British Hudson's Bay Company, Fort Vancouver did not close until the 1860s (it burned down in 1866). Its kindly chief factor, Briton John McLoughlin, in disfavor with Hudson's Bay Company's Governor Simpson, founded the Imperial Mills after 1846, giving impetus to settlement of Oregon City. He became an American citizen in 1851.

More than agriculture, Vancouver's early growth was gleaned from its forests. Adjacent to the Columbia River, citizens cut wood for riverboats and hewed lumber for homes.

As already described, Indian unrest in eastern Washington and the Columbia Gorge led to the establishment of a small American military post on May 15, 1849—Columbia Barracks, then Fort Vancouver, later Vancouver Barracks, a sub-post to Fort Lewis. It has been home to portions of the Mounted Rifles; the First Artillery; the Fourth, Seventh and Fourteenth infantries; and finally the 104th Training Division of the Army Reserves. In 1917 to 1918, twenty-seven thousand enlisted men were sent to Vancouver Barracks, dispersed among lumber camps and mills to harvest spruce needed for airplanes. The Barracks includes a row of graceful officers' homes where splendid military parties have taken place, facing a broad, grassy parade ground.

Among the luminaries serving at this pleasant post were O. O. Howard and Nelson Miles (central figures in the skirmishes with the Nez Perce), Philip Sheridan of Civil War fame, William Harney (involved in Sioux Indian wars and the laughable "Pig War" at San Juan Island, Washington, when a British pig was shot by an American settler) George Marshall of World War II and Ulysses S. Grant, commander of the Union Army in the Civil War and later, president.

The young officer Grant turned to moonlighting to earn money for transporting his family west. With cohorts he shipped 100 tons of ice to California, but in adverse winds, the schooner took six weeks to make the trip, and Grant lost the cargo. He and a partner planted potatoes, but the Columbia River flooded and reclaimed the field. He even bought chickens and sent them to San Francisco; they died en route. Fortunately, he did better as an army general.

A sturdier version of revered Mother Teresa of the 1980s was Mother Joseph of the late 1800s, an industrious head of the Sisters of Charity of Providence in the Pacific Northwest. Arriving in Vancouver in 1856, Mother Joseph and four other nuns founded the first nonmilitary hospital, orphanage, shelter for the mentally disturbed and home for the aged in Washington Territory. She did the job often with her own two hands, as she was an accomplished carpenter and builder. Mother Joseph is one of two Washington State residents to be honored in the National Statuary Hall in Washington, D.C. The other is Marcus Whitman—illustrious company, indeed.

With a less-protected harbor than the Willamette affords Portland, and without the wealth from its valley, Vancouver never attained the population of Portland but remained a small city depending chiefly upon lumber-related industries. Today it offers anchorage for ten ships and dockside berthing for seven on the Columbia River itself. Around 1855, steamboats had to tie to an exposed river bank, but that year two floating wharves were installed—each with a saloon and store. Soon, permanent docks were built.

The only sandmold brick producer west of the Mississippi, the Hidden Brick Company has manufactured quality building brick in Vancouver from 1871 to the present. A dried prune industry has thrived since the 1880s, and Aluminum Company of America opened a big plant in September 1940. After January 1942, Vancouver was overwhelmed by the influx of workers at the new Kaiser Shipyards right on the Columbia River, a natural location for the industry. Portland also had received two Kaiser yards. Edgar Kaiser, son of magnate Henry Kaiser, managed the shipbuilding companies. He had gained business management experience on the Grand Coulee and Bonneville projects. The shipyards built Liberty ships, aircraft carriers, troop transports and floating drydocks—763 ships in all by war's end.

In December 1943, there were 98,300 employees in the three shipyards, and Kaiser bought 650 acres of land adjacent to the Columbia River in extreme north Portland, built a dike around the property, and established an entire temporary town to house his workers. Chiefly the town consisted of two-story apartment buildings, each containing fourteen apartments, over nine thousand units, making the town Vanport the second largest city in Oregon. The units were furnished and basic; however, residents found them extremely noisy. The mixture of total strangers thrust together led to sociological friction. Kaiser always intended that the buildings should be razed after the war. The Columbia River made the final decision.

Prior to Memorial Day 1948, heavy snows fell along the Columbia's Canadian and U.S. tributaries, followed by unusually warm temperatures and rain. The spring freshet turned into a torrent, causing uncontrollable damage along the entire river system. Grand Coulee and Bonneville Dams were unable to stem the waters. While several feet below the dike's summit, the river broke through a weak spot and poured into Vanport. The water rose swiftly, but with fifteen or twenty minutes time before it grew shoulder height, most residents escaped— the last of them forming a human chain. A few were trapped inside their dwellings or injured, unable to get out. The apartments had been built on supports, which acted like rafts when the water rose; entire buildings floated down river, crashing together and disintegrating; for a time they threatened to topple the Interstate Bridge. With new dams built since then, it is unlikely that the river can attain such monstrous flood levels again.

Kaiser's shipyards were closed when the need ceased, but Vancouver and Portland enjoyed some lasting industrial spin-offs. By the 1970s, Vancouver began to develop as a site for high-tech companies, among them Japanese firms, some introduced to the city by sister city relationships.

In 1980 small children found $5,800 in rotting $20 bills half-buried in the Columbia River sands about five miles northwest of Vancouver. The bills were traced to the loot received by hijacker D. B. Cooper nine years earlier at Seattle. He permitted passengers on Northwest Airlines flight 305 to get off, then demanded to be taken to Mexico. Somewhere over southern Washington, Cooper left the plane in a parachute, never to be seen again despite intensive searches. The town of Ariel, Washington, east of Kalama, still celebrates D. B. Cooper Days after Thanksgiving, cynically enjoying his unusual feat, but many believe he came down in the Columbia River.

Hudson's Bay Company employees often retired along the Columbia River—Tom McKay, stepson of Dr. McLoughlin, at Scappoose, and James Birnie at Cathlamet. The Chinook leader Casseno, son of Chief Comcomly, made his home near St. Helens. Near the confluence of the Willamette and Columbia in Oregon, St. Helens was founded by Captain H. M. Knighton in 1845 as Plymouth. Here the Charles R. McCormick Company bought a millsite in 1909, dealing in lumber and logging; they later built lumber schooners as St. Helens Shipbuilding Company.

McCormick's first steam schooner, with lines similar to sailing ships, was the *Multnomah*, launched on October 12, 1912, at a gala party. Following were the *Merced*, *Celilo*, *City of Portland* and others, the hulls towed to San Francisco for engines and fittings. After the 1930s the shipyard ceased operations, and the lumber site is operated by Boise Cascade. St. Helens is a quiet shadow of its former self, most of it preserved as a Historic Site. On the Willamette waterfront, dozens of small fixed houseboats or apartments rock gently in the wake of freighters passing by on the main navigation channel.

Before steam tugs took over around 1915, the giant lumber schooners around 200 feet long were dubbed the Scandinavian Fleet for their captains. Pope & Talbot Company clung to sailing ships even after most companies had tugs, and the Pacific lumber trade used schooners through World War I. The last wooden steam schooner built was the *Esther Johnson* at Portland in 1923, 208 feet long. The venerable wooden steam schooner *Wapama*, renamed *Tongass*, worked in Alaska until 1947, and in 1948 was purchased for the Maritime Museum on San Francisco's waterfront. She was lucky; some of them wound up hauling garbage or were scrapped.

One of the strangest Columbia Bar wrecks was that of the four-masted lumber schooner *North Bend*. She went solidly aground on Peacock Spit on January 5, 1928, and was abandoned after futile refloating attempts. Weeks later, lighthouse keepers swore the ship had moved. Sure enough, with shifting sand and tidal fluctuations, small pools of water formed and encouraged her progress. In his book *Windjammers of the Pacific Rim* (Seattle: Superior Publishing Company, 1968), Jim Gibbs described it as an "unexplained zeal for life ... as if some ghostly hand was guiding her." Thirteen months after she was wrecked, she worked her way clear through the spit and floated into Baker's Bay, her hull still intact.

A few miles above St. Helens, looming like a misplaced moonscape, is the steam-wreathed cooling tower (499 feet high) of the Trojan Nuclear Plant, where swallows incongruously nest around the rim. The power plant, operated by Portland General Electric Company, uses a small fraction of its 634-acre site, donating the rest for public use as picnic sites, hiking trails, a fish hatchery and a small fishing lake. The small plant provides more power than Bonneville Dam and produces about 20 percent of Oregon's electricity. It processes the cooling water to return it to the Columbia River at a temperature less than 1 percent hotter than at the intake point, and has operated for twenty-five years without mishap or any harmful discharges whatever.

As settlers moved onto Oregon shores, some of them fished, others grew peppermint (still do), but lumber fueled most of the growth. At Clatskanie, built then on stilts, pioneers like Simon Benson and James Flippin (an Oregon Trail herdsman for pioneer politician Jesse Applegate) logged the cedar and fir, sending them to the Clatskanie or Columbia River by flumes. Huge cigar rafts were assembled at the confluence of the rivers; the faint outlines of a cradle used to assemble them can be seen yet. The cigar raft had logs laid like a pair of parenthesis meeting at each end, then stacked neatly in between with other logs, and the whole thing lashed securely with chains. The pointed ends rode better than flat booms in the ocean swells, and most lumber was towed down the coast.

As steam power developed, tugs got bigger and stronger; one of the earliest was the 128-foot steel boat *Tatoosh*, operating first as a Columbia Bar tug in 1907. But ocean-capable tugs thereafter towed everything from lumber to barges with Alaska pipeline gear on them, moved ships into berths and wheat barges up and down the Columbia. Chief ocean-tug operators today include Crowley Maritime, Brix Maritime and Shaver Transportation.

In the woods, muscle was giving way to steam, too. At first loggers used ferocious-looking longhorn steers to pull logs. Then, steam tractors took over. One of the log companies painted all its equipment and structures red; even a dance hall facing the Columbia River was painted red. Excursion boats came to mingle with the loggers, and dances often lasted all night. In the camps or towns, boxing matches helped single men work off energy; the matches went on until one participant was knocked out—no TKO's there.

Today major lumber industries still headquarter from Rainier to Wauna—Stimson Lumber Company, James River Corporation and RSG Forest Products, which manufactures cedar fencing. Before modern refrigeration systems for boats, there were fish-buying stations all up and down this section of river shore so that fishermen did not lose time traveling to the canneries. There were horse seiners, too, on the lower Columbia River islands, just as there were on estuary sand bars. During World War II, an army ammunition depot was built at Mayger, present site of a Portland Gas and Electric Company plant.

On the last westerly bend of the Columbia River, the small towns of Kalama and Kelso were settled early—Kelso in 1884, while Kalama's first cabin was built in 1853 by pioneer Ezra Meeker. In 1871 Kalama became the Pacific Coast terminus of the Northern Pacific Railway Company. Population swelled to three or four thousand who thought Kalama would be the chief Columbia River port. The euphoria was temporary because when the railroad was extended to Tacoma in 1873, the headquarters were moved there. Kalama subsided to a whistle stop of perhaps twenty-five families. A bit larger today, its port tenaciously clings to wheat elevator and barge transportation businesses.

Kelso and Longview are virtually one city, but intense civic rivalry has marked their growth. At first, Kelso was the "metropolis," remaining the county seat of historic Cowlitz County, where Hudson's Bay Company tried so heroically to make Puget Sound Agricultural Colony pay. Like Portland, Kelso grew as a river port for farmers and loggers. One entrepreneur scorned traditional farming to take up ostrich raising around 1915 to 1920, giving it up partly because the birds were so hazardous—one good kick could kill a person.

The little town of Monticello predated Kelso, but situated precariously at the mouth of the Cowlitz River, it was decimated by floods. The settlement was founded in December 1849, by the Harry Darby Huntington immigrant party, arriving by canoe. Monticello's brief moment of glory came when, in 1852, a convention was held there by settlers north of the Columbia River to petition Congress for separate territorial status. Oregon Territory was vast, extending from California to Canada and east toward the Rockies. "Washingtonians" were tired of traveling to Oregon City for official business. The forty-four men met in rude summer camplike housing but got the job done. Washington Territory was formed March 3, 1853—"Washington" being second choice; it was almost named "Columbia" Territory.

Kelso was thirty-seven years old, well established, while upstart Longview's site was just a dense forest in 1921—a fateful year. The major lumber firm, Long-Bell Lumber Company, of Missouri and Weed, California, purchased a huge prime timber tract in Cowlitz County and planned a big lumber mill. A new town of Longview was planned—not just any town, either. Idealist as well as businessman, R. A. Long felt that here was an opportunity to build a beautiful, well-planned model city. In a foresighted zoning plan, the architects laid out commercial, industrial, residential and open areas. Landscaping was not overlooked. At first, the city looked a bit peculiar, for buildings were scattered over the large city tract in proper zones—allowing for the spaces to fill in gradually to serve a population estimated at 50,000 (which has never been attained).

With great expense and haste, Longview town sprang out of the forest—not a "Stumptown" as Portland had been, but a real town with a magnificent hotel, the Monticello, paved streets, and flowers. The largest lumber mill in the world opened in 1924, and the town was dedicated with feverish hoopla, including a lively speech by evangelist Billy Sunday and more staid presentations by the governor, senators and congressmen. Although there were alterations over the years to the master plan, Longview still ranks among the most attractive small cities of Washington.

Long-Bell Company is no more, but other lumber corporations thrive to make Longview and its overshadowed neighbor, Kelso, almost entirely lumber-supported towns.

Here on the Cowlitz and Columbia, where Washington Territory was born, an explosion shook the area to its core on May 18, 1980. Thirty-five miles east of Kelso/Longview, Mount St. Helens, pristinely majestic, erupted with such force that more than a thousand feet of its top disappeared, incinerated into a cloud of ash and dust. It sent a cloud 60,000 miles into the atmosphere, perceptibly sprinkling states and provinces far distant. The concussion flattened 250 square miles of mature, sturdy Douglas fir and hemlock, meticulously laying them in rows as orderly as the Great Plank Road. Following the contours of the mountains, the path of the killer wind could be traced easily. The eruptive cloud manufactured its own static electricity.

Ash falling across the Columbia River into eastern Washington was inches deep, plunging towns into darkness. Street lights came on. Cars moved slowly as if in a winter blizzard. Sixty-eight people died, most of them close to the mountain. In the superheated Toutle and Cowlitz rivers, thousands of fish died. On the Cowlitz the terror was not the minimal fallout of ash, but the maelstrom descending from the mountain's northwest side; debris and slurry from melted snow mixed with ground-up rock filled Spirit Lake and overflowed. A wall of destruction surged down the Toutle River, sweeping away bridges and houses, loose lumber and loosened trees, raging into the Cowlitz River and descending through Kelso and Longview to the Columbia. With little warning, residents fled the lowlands, but the river stayed a foot below flood stage at Longview/Kelso.

The following day a ship ran aground on a 20-foot mud bank off the Cowlitz River in the Columbia, a channel then 18 feet, normally 50 feet deep. Longview and Kelso fought to clear their water systems of silt. Twenty-two million cubic yards of silt wound up in the Columbia River.

About fifty ships were marooned upriver, most of them in Portland. Dozens of others milled around the lower river, waiting to get into port, or cancelled their calls. The Port of Portland and the Army Corps of Engineers threw every available dredge into service, deepening the Columbia channel so ships could escape. The deepest draft vessels could not leave the river for more than a month. The fine, easily shifting silt continues to plague the river.

Successive, less catastrophic eruptions left ash sifting onto the Columbia River towns, instead of eastern Washington. A homeowner in Astoria found the ash combining in drainpipes and downspouts to form a solid plug.

Marriage of River and Ocean

The lower Columbia River is a singular place—glassy smooth at times, dangerous yet mystically gripping in its beauty. The river is filled with islands, large and small, and ever-shifting sand bars. Except for dredging of a ship channel, the river runs wild and free, narrowing to a mile some places, widening to twelve midway through the estuary. At the infamous bar, the fury of unimaginable tons of fresh water meeting incoming ocean waves, intensified by frequent gale-force winds and towering swells, has been lessened only a little by the addition of jetties. Two thousand vessels have been lost within a fifteen-mile radius of the entrance, with losses of fifteen hundred lives in recorded history.

Yet, along the final hundred miles of the Columbia River, wended the commerce that made possible the prospering of Portland, Vancouver, and small towns and hamlets of romantic-sounding names— Kalama, Kelso, Longview, Cathlamet, Clatskanie, Ilwaco, Skamokawa. Ghostly remnants of others quietly make their claim on the river's history, all but forgotten except for rotting pilings, decayed cannery structures, homes with blackberry bushes growing through the walls.

Fishing and canneries first, lumbering second accounted for most of the defunct towns. They included Pillar Rock near the basalt landmark named by Lieutenant Broughton in 1792; Knappton, a sawmill run by Jim Vaughn and Samuel E. Barr; Altoona, a cannery town also called Hume's Station. Carlton Appelo, local historian, claims that it was named for Al, a popular fiddler to whom locals said, "Al, tune 'er up."

The steep terrain encouraged creativity. In 1910 the Olson Brothers Logging Company tunneled 650 feet through a hill near Deep River to get logs to water. An enterprising young Finnish immigrant, Helge Saari, delivered milk for twenty-one years, from 1921 to 1942, to river communities by rowboat, timing his arrival to coincide with the tides, for coves were bare at low tide. A Deep River grocery delivered supplies by railroad speeder car. Aging residents remember being isolated by spring freshets, when parts of buildings, uprooted trees and tumbleweeds from eastern Washington swept by to the sea.

Retired in Cathlamet, tugboat captain (Smith Tug & Barge, Rainier) Stanley Everman estimates that he has towed 5,600 log rafts with his 60-foot tug *Ajax*. Rafts typically were 750 feet by 55 feet. Logging companies stored logs in the sloughs among the myriad islands, particularly Carroll Channel, Rainierson Slough and Cathlamet Channel.

River men frequently were on the scene of wrecks. Everman rescued the crew of an Italian vessel, sunk to the superstructure on a dark and rainy night above Rainier. During the rare freezes of the river, tugs were used to break ice and bring supplies to small communities, encountering trouble themselves because ice would clog the water intake (cooling). Everman sees wildlife (including black bears, elk, deer) on the increase along the river, especially harbor seals and sea lions, which voraciously consume salmon.

On Tenasillihe Island there is a refuge for Columbia white-tailed deer, which, along with huge flocks of birds, inhabit the island and nearby Lewis and Clark Refuge, a group of islands partly under water at high tide. Kelso tug operator Michael Johnson has the unusual task of moving cattle to and from Tenasillihe Island to eat down the grass, for the deer prefer grass about two inches high.

A recreation of Fort Clatsop, the wintering place of Lewis and Clark. Near Astoria.

Storms and accidents are routine hazards of the river, but hardly "tidal waves," yet in January 1965, a big chunk of earth, formerly a viewpoint, slid thunderously into the Columbia west of Rainier, sending a giant wave onto nearby Puget Island. It wrenched loose a waterfront home, washed it 200 yards inland, and flung it over the dike, but the elderly occupant escaped unharmed. Another home was crushed along with its owner.

While Vancouver was the oldest Washington settlement, the grandfather of all in Oregon Territory was Astoria, beginning in 1811 as Fort Astoria, Astor's fur post. While the area was still under joint jurisdiction of Britain and the United States, Solomon Smith, a member of the Nathaniel Wyeth party, became the first to take up property at Clatsop Plains in 1840, marrying a daughter of Clatsop Chief Cobaway and opening a store. He was there to help the chilled survivors of the beautiful U.S. sloop of war, *Peacock*, when she struck the sands beneath frowning Cape Disappointment on July 18, 1841.

The *Peacock*'s captain, Lieutenant William Hudson, was under orders from surveyor Lieutenant Charles Wilkes to chart the Columbia River. Acting on notes given him by a Captain Spaulding, veteran of several Columbia River entries, Hudson attempted to enter the channel in low visibility. When he saw a breaking sea, he concluded he was too far south and turned away; instead, he was too far north and turned into the sands near Cape Disappointment. The ship broke up in high swells that slammed her repeatedly onto the spit, and the crew abandoned ship, their unfortunate adventure giving the name "Peacock Spit" to the sands around today's north jetty. The ship was neither the first nor the last to end her days near the treacherous Columbia entrance.

Despite its vagaries, the river was a creator. Carrying tons of silt and sand, the Columbia's current swirled northward to build Long Beach, the long spit embracing Willapa Bay. In fact, it continues to add to this, the longest continuous straight beach in the world. Cottages built on the shore in 1900 are a quarter-mile inland today. To compete with Oregon's Seaside and Cannon Beach, which attracted tourists from Portland, sternwheelers braved the turbulent estuary to transport beach-goers from rail's end at Astoria to Ilwaco on the Washington shore. One of the sturdier boats in 1865 was the *U. S. Grant*, under Clinton Kelley and later John H. D. Gray (relative of pioneer mariner W. P. Gray). At first, tourists were met at Baker's Bay by a horse-drawn stage driven by Louis Loomis, a rollicking ride for sure. With no roads on the spit, Loomis mostly drove the hard beach sands all the way to Nahcotta on Willapa Bay. Occasional waves swirled around the horses' feet, and a rogue breaker once briefly floated stage, horses and all.

In 1874, a wharf was built at Ilwaco, and the 110-foot *General Canby* furrowed through the broad reach from Astoria. To keep afloat, owners of Ilwaco Steam Navigation Company also hauled troops and supplies to army posts Fort Stevens (Oregon) and Fort Canby (Washington). Shortly afterward, the Oregon Railroad & Steam Navigation Company initiated a direct run from Portland to Ilwaco, but the swells overwhelmed its boat, and it had to be towed in. Thereafter, the federal government banned sternwheelers west of Smith's Point near Astoria.

The stages, though colorful and adventurous, were phased out in favor of a narrow-gauge railroad up Long Beach spit. Tracks were laid onto the wharf so that trains could back out close to the steamer. The first train left Ilwaco for Nahcotta on May 29, 1889, operating daily with canopied flatcars giving passengers splendid ocean views. Brisk freight traffic from Willapa Bay to Columbia River, chiefly oysters, helped finances.

The delightful, long-lasting little "Clamshell Railroad," stopped anywhere, taking several hours to travel the route. The versatile railway even hauled rescue crews to wreck sites, since ships frequently got into trouble near the Columbia Bar. During major storms train schedules were interrupted by huge breakers raging far inland!

The monopolistic river firm, Oregon Railway & Steam Navigation, acquired the railroad and Ilwaco's docks and buildings in 1900 and put on a direct Portland-Ilwaco steamer, the *T. J. Potter*. The firm added revenue by hauling logs from Willapa Bay to the Columbia, then laid tracks to Megler near Point Ellice (Washington end of Astoria Bridge) in protected, deep water, abandoning Ilwaco. Gradually automobiles replaced the charming Clamshell Railroad after 1930. A ferry ran between Megler and Astoria until 1966, when the trans-river Astoria Bridge was completed, 4.1 miles long with a shipping span 1,070 feet wide and almost 200 feet high. Ilwaco developed a charter-boat fishing industry; it is home to commercial fishermen and still is a gateway to Long Beach tourism.

Across the Columbia River, usually heaving with ocean swells, the camps of the Corps of Engineers, Upper Astoria, and the cannery workers' dwellings, Lower Astoria, became one. Entire fleets of small boats dotted the river, dubbed the "butterfly fleet" because the unique boat design has two sails on one mast. Once a year the sailor-fishermen competed in the Astoria Regatta. In 1915, almost three thousand gillnetters, three hundred trap owners and fifty seiners using horses were plying the lower river. Tuna fishing in the ocean began in 1938, the last tuna boats quitting about 1980. There was Uniontown, where most of the fishermen and logger Finns lived; a large Chinatown of cannery workers; Swill Town where those of questionable moral activity reigned;

and the scenic hillsides where ship captains, bar pilots, cannery owners and shopkeepers built modest and a few pretentious homes. Perhaps a third of Astoria's seven thousand residents were Chinese.

The 1900s concert hall—called The Louvre—built by August Erickson dominated the social life, not a rough place like his bar in Portland, but a gorgeous, three-story hall with rooms for games, concerts, two tasteful bars and no "monkey business."

Tourists came to Oregon beaches. In 1888 the Astoria and South Coast Railroad Company line to Seaside made travel faster, if not easier, as the passengers traveled on flatcars with "porch" rails and hard benches. D. K. Warren, for whom Warrenton on Clatsop Spit is named, was its president. Following the demise of bankrupt competitor companies, a group headed by A. B. Hammond completed the Astoria and Columbia River Railroad, building tracks from Astoria to Goble, leasing Northern Pacific's rails on into Portland. The first train left Astoria on May 16, 1898, to a din of whistles and bells from boats, churches and government buildings as it eased out over the Tongue Point trestle.

A broad highway to the interior, the Columbia River necessarily had to be fortified against potential enemies before the days of electronic detection. Cape Disappointment, the formidable headland north of the entrance, was a natural fortification, commanding a clear view of the Columbia River, the jetties and the Pacific Ocean for a score of miles. The government established a military reservation in 1852 on the site of Pacific City, moving away seventy buildings, most of them to Ilwaco, and built Fort Canby.

In 1856, the Cape Disappointment Lighthouse began beaming the way to the entrance, today the oldest lighthouse in use on the west coast. Its companion, North Head Lighthouse, was built in 1898. Fort Canby's fortifications and batteries were expanded and improved, and were manned until after World War II when new technology made them obsolete. The site became a state park that encompasses Peacock Spit, a beach below North Head whimsically called Waikiki Beach, and sandy camping areas.

At this striking location the Lewis and Clark Interpretive Center has opened with fine exhibits about the Expedition and also displays of lifesaving methods, shipwrecks and lighthouses.

On the storm-swept shore east of Ilwaco, where the Chinook Indians once made their home, the United States constructed Fort Columbia between 1896 and 1904. It was staffed by military services until after World War II. Fort Columbia's batteries never fired a shot in anger, and the facilities and grounds today are a state park.

On the Oregon shore at Clatsop Spit, Fort Stevens (built during the Civil War) guarded against incoming hostile ships. It became the largest of the forts by far, staffed by 2,500 troops during World War II. Soldiers from the fort mined the entrance to the Columbia River off and on from 1898 through World War II. Fort buildings were camouflaged with artificial trees, and a battery was installed on the ocean sands west of the fort.

A Japanese submarine actually fired on Fort Stevens on June 21, 1942, the shell landing 300 yards from Battery Russell, the only military installation in the continental United States fired upon by a foreign power later than the War of 1812. Japanese submarines also sank or fired on freighters and tankers off the mouth of the river and sent thousands of tiny incendiary devices floating over coastal Oregon, hoping to set devastating forest fires. In the rain, the efforts failed. Today Fort Stevens Military Museum, Interpretive Center, and grounds comprising 3,800 acres are open to the public. On the ocean beach the remains of the wreck *Peter Iredale* may be seen, and one can walk out a way on the jetty (although signs sternly warn of the dangers, since sneaker waves wash sightseers off the jetties almost every year).

With breaking swells visible almost continuously along the Columbia Bar, no wonder early explorers thought a solid beach existed there. However, jetties built by the Army Corps of Engineers tamed the entry so that wrecks of larger ships are infrequent today. The south jetty was finished in 1895, the north in 1917; secondary jetties inside the entry seek to control silting. To transport rock to the south jetty, engineers built a railroad in conjunction with the jetty as they went. One stormy night the four-masted schooner *Admiral* struck foul ground in a seventy-mile-per-hour wind and was hammered against the jetty, coming to rest on the rocks and rail trestle pilings. The fractured rails whipped like tentacles in the winds, helping to damage the ship. Five survivors managed to struggle up to the railway trestle, where alerted rescue crews cautiously crept through the night toward the wreck, the seas sending scud against the locomotive to create clouds of steam. They rescued the five. The Point Adams Life Crew saved seven others, using a breeches buoy. The ocean battered the *Admiral* to pieces, wreckage drifting across the bar, according to Jim Gibbs in his book *Pacific Graveyard*.

Astorians assumed their city would be *the* large maritime center, situated just inside the river entrance; however, lack of rail connections to interior markets until 1898 permitted Portland and Vancouver to upstage Astoria. In 1913 the Port of Astoria was incorporated, not recognizing defeat. Believing the town would be another San Francisco, the Port built three docks and 26 acres of warehouses (Astoria had only ten thousand residents), urging shipping companies to save the long haul upriver. But after World War I, the government dumped thousands of steamships on the market dirt cheap, and shipping companies steamed right on past Astoria, unconcerned about any small savings. Increased trucking also hurt the location.

The next blow was that, during the market crash of 1929, New York financiers defaulted on their bonds, leaving Astoria's port financially desperate. Instead of being a major port, Astoria remains a fishing port with three small pleasure-cruise companies calling, more than a hundred log ships annually, Canadian ships with newsprint for the Oregonian, and an occasional Russian ship—offshore cannery ships giving their sailors shore leave.

From the beginning, ships have depended on Astoria bar pilots to guide them safely through the meeting of Columbia River and Pacific Ocean, and upon the United States Coast Guardsmen from Ilwaco and Astoria to rescue them when they were in trouble.

Chinook Chief Comcomly is credited with being the first bar pilot, for seventeen years paid with trinkets to guide Hudson's Bay Company ships safely across the bar. Three ship captains, James Johnson, William Mouatt and James Scarborough, guided Hudson's Bay Company ships for a time after Comcomly's death in 1830. In August of 1846 a deserter from the *Peacock* (one James deSaule), who operated a trans-river canoe service, attempted his first and only pilotage; he brought the sloop-of-war *Shark* solidly aground on Clatsop Spit.

On December 16, 1848, the Oregon Territorial Legislature passed an act creating a State Pilot Board, authorizing it to employ a state bar pilot. Selah Reeves was the first. Unfortunately, he piled up his first two boats, too, the Hudson's Bay Company barque *Vancouver* and the whaler *Maine*, whereupon he was fired. The next pair, Geer and Alexander, used the boat to sell liquor to the Indians. Irate Clatsop tribal elders dragged them to the beach and repeatedly dunked them in the Columbia River, half-drowning them as a warning. Jackson Hustler was a capable pilot for a year or two, but not until the advent of George Flavel with his 64-foot schooner *California*, did the Columbia get a long-staying and reliable pilot.

Flavel was a tall, lean man with piercing blue eyes and a manner that earned him the nickname of "Hawk" behind his back. In his first two years on the bar, Captain Flavel also lost two ships. One must remember that a pilot is not the "lord," for the seas can overcome anyone. On January 29, 1852, Flavel was outbound aboard the small grain-loaded steamer *General Warren*, wallowing heavily in wind-whipped waves and snow. The creaky ship began to leak, and under orders from her captain, Flavel deliberately put the ship onto Clatsop Spit, where all night she was battered by foaming breakers. About 3:00 A.M. Flavel obtained nine volunteers and set off in the long boat under oars and managed to make Astoria harbor. Rescuers returned to the spit to find no one alive. The *General Warren* had disintegrated in the surf, and only bodies came ashore to be buried in a common grave.

The second accident involved the barque *Oriole*. At a crucial point when the *Oriole* was crossing the shallows, the wind stopped, leaving the barque at the mercy of currents. She, too, hit the Clatsop Spit, but all the crew members were saved.

Crucial to successful pilotage was obtaining a rugged boat to intercept ships outside the bar. Sometimes in the 1800s a pilot traveled with an outbound ship to San Francisco, where he picked up another scheduled for the Columbia River. Flavel's *California* proved equal to the tasks required, and his pilotage business grew, with four additional pilots hired to assist him. Rates for guiding vessels across the bar were from $10 to $12 a foot, and as commerce grew, so did Flavel's income. He branched out into partnership in a sawmill, operation of a trans-river ferry by sloop, a grocery, was county treasurer for a time, and in 1883, became president of the First National Bank of Astoria.

When marine engines became more reliable, the Oregon State Legislature of 1868 authorized subsidy of a steam tug of no less than 50 tons for a three-year period. Guess who was the first to get his name on the contract? Flavel, of course. He promptly ordered construction of the 101-foot tug *Astoria*, which was replaced by a new *Astoria* in 1887, the same year he finally retired from pilotage to his handsomely appointed home, now a museum, across from the county courthouse. He is credited with helping Astoria become a recognized seaport.

Today the bar pilots include a brave and extraordinarily capable cadre of about twenty-five men, many former ship captains or Coast Guardsmen with Master's Certificates. (*Customarily* but not necessarily there is only one bar pilot organization to a port.) The privately organized firm works under federal regulations, owning two boats— the *Columbia* for fair weather, the *Peacock* for foul—to transport the pilots to their rendezvous seventeen miles away.

The *Peacock* is of an unusual design: at the sharply defined stern is a sort of "way," where a smaller boat, called the daughter boat slides onto the larger one. This is launched when necessary to transport the pilot to or from a vessel. Imagine yourself poised at the brink of a tall wave, waiting for just the right moment to plummet forward and find the narrow niche of the mother boat! Piloting is not for the faint-hearted; indeed, these transfers outside the bar between two wildly rolling ships have taken the lives of bar pilots.

Despite the improvements made by the Army Corps of Engineers, the sands still shift, currents are unreliable depending on the river's height, and breakers always approach the bar from a new angle. A bar pilot undergoes at least two years of specific training, no matter how experienced he was in his prior commands.

The same is true of the river pilots, who take over from the bar pilots just off the Astoria docks. The River Pilots Association, also a private enterprise, is based in Portland. With the Columbia's ship channel monitored by the Corps of Engineers and thoroughly marked with navigation guides, ships still require local knowledge of shifting channels and changing currents. A pilot says he literally can feel the changes by the behavior of a ship; and to permit a ship to slide sidewise of the river could be a life-threatening disaster or initiate a collision. That is why a river pilot cannot be absent from the river more than sixty days, or he has to undergo a re-familiarization period with another pilot. He knows the minutest details of currents and depths around the different berths for docking, and learns to work with foreign ship crews with minimal language skills.

Serious weather is relatively rare during Pacific Northwest summers; for days at a time even the Columbia Bar can be almost flat, allowing pleasure and fishing boats easy transition. But when weather is bad, the bar is dangerous; winter weather is especially fickle. Here is where the U.S. Coast Guard comes in. Headquarters are at Astoria Airport, where especially equipped rescue helicopters are located. The Aids to Navigation Team at Tongue Point maintains buoys, lights, dayboards, etc. Tucked behind Cape Disappointment are two large Coast Guard cutters, plus several smaller but very special rescue boats—incredible craft that can roll entirely over in the surf and right themselves.

The Fort Canby Lifesaving Service was funded and established in 1877, with a nine-man rowboat and a beach wagon pulled by men or horses for rescues near shore. The men shot a line by cannon to the stricken vessel, then used a breeches buoy to get people off. In 1883 crews managed to get 175 passengers off the *Queen of the Pacific* when, in low visibility from forest fire smoke, she went on Clatsop Spit. The first lightship *Columbia* (No. 50) was stationed off the mouth of the river on April 11, 1892, and the last *Columbia* (No. 604) was replaced in 1979 by an electronic navigational buoy. During World War II, the Coast Guard patrolled beaches with dogs and horses.

Equipment continued to improve. In 1961 because of the enormous surf assailing the Columbia Bar, Cape Disappointment's lifesaving station was chosen to test a new 44-foot motorboat, a self-righting one. To train American and foreign personnel, the National Motor Lifeboat School was established there in 1968. Trainees must first hold grade E-3 or better in the Coast Guard and have six prior months of experience in motor lifeboat units. Training under actual bar conditions and on rescues is not for the timid; it takes steel nerves to choke down panic when the boat takes a 360-degree roll while you are head down in the water, strapped to the boat, for what seems like hours but is only seconds. A still more sophisticated and seaworthy 47-foot aluminum craft was introduced in 1991.

From Base Astoria, airborne patrols search for illicit activities, aided by the 200-foot cutter *Resolute*. In 1978 the Coast Guard captured a 167-foot freighter with 10 tons of marijuana aboard. Helicopter patrols check the Columbia River for oil spills, including marina checks for clandestine dumping by pleasure boats. The helicopter often removes people from a distressed vessel by basket on a lowered cable, or drops rescue swimmers to help people into the basket; if injured, they are placed on a litter first. Mostly in summer there are calls to rescue swimmers swept seaward by the strong undertow or swept off the jetties by high swells.

A Coast Guard officer says that the fishermen and crabbers working outside the bar seldom are careless; the ocean warrants too much respect for that. However, engines fail, rudders or controls break, and the radius offshore from the Columbia is no place to lose control.

A few years ago an Air National Guard F-4 airplane failed, and the pilot ejected forty miles offshore in bad weather and high seas. Using sophisticated communications, a CG helicopter located the pilot, put a rescue swimmer overboard and rescued the severely injured pilot. He was so dangerously hypothermic that one helicopter pilot crawled into the bag with the F-4 victim to add body warmth. The effort saved the man's life, even though he endured many surgical procedures afterward.

One of the worst disasters was on May 4, 1880, when the sea was flat and most of the fishing fleet was in the ocean. A freak wind over one hundred miles per hour arose suddenly, whipping the ocean into huge waves. In an article in *Western Boatman* (May/June 1984), Don Marshall debunks a popular, ever-expanding myth that 240 boats and 300 people were lost in that catastrophe. The toll was bad enough in *fact*, thirteen dead and a couple dozen capsized boats.

Shipwreck and rescue stories are endless on this dangerous coast of two thousand wrecks. One of the strangest and most riveting tales unfolded on January 12, 1991, while the author was on research in Astoria. To understand what happened that day, we must first review the dramatic events of January 12, 1961, thirty years earlier.

On that day, the Cape Disappointment Lifeboat Station received a distress call from the fishing craft *Mermaid* of Ilwaco, which had lost its rudder and was drifting into the surf near North Head. While the Coast Guard responded with a 36-foot self-righting boat and a standard 40-foot patrol boat, the weather—already terrible—worsened. In low visibility, the Coast Guard had difficulty finding the *Mermaid*. Dusk came.

Taking the boat in tow, the 40-foot Coast Guard boat under Petty Officer Darrell Murray labored into the swells toward the entrance, monitored by the 36-footer nearby. Murray asked the two fishermen aboard the *Mermaid* if they would transfer to the Coast Guard boat. When they refused, he radioed Point Adams for help from the 52-foot *Triumph*. In gale force winds now, the latter could not reach the other boats at Buoy 1 for two hours but then took the *Mermaid*'s tow from Murray.

In the following sea, the double-ender 36-footer rode reasonably well, but the 40-footer took a series of 25-foot and higher swells, slid down a huge wave and turned over. The crew of three surfaced and climbed aboard the hull. Meanwhile, the 36-footer sustained damage, too, and—knowing it could not negotiate the roiling bar—the coxswain Larry Edwards turned toward the lightship *Columbia* seven miles out to sea. As he turned, he saw Murray's boat upside down.

Edwards edged up to the hull and snatched the men off, but in the process severely smashed his own hull. With the stern awash, the engine room half-filled with water and minimal rudder control, Edwards made it to the lightship (escorted by the pilot boat *Peacock* which had responded to the disaster), but the Coast Guard boat sank after all were taken off. During the transfer one member of Edwards' crew was swept off the ladder, only to be plucked from a succeeding wave by the lightship's engineer.

Meanwhile, the big 52-foot Coast Guard *Triumph* was in trouble, too. The towline to the foundering fishing boat *Mermaid* broke in or near the breakers, and while the *Triumph* sought to retrieve the line, the Coast Guard craft rolled over. A crewman from the *Triumph* was picked up by the *Mermaid* somehow, but then it, too, was claimed by the sea. On the *Triumph*, Gordon Huggins emerged on deck from a watertight compartment fifteen minutes later when the boat righted itself to find the other five crewmen missing. The boat rolled again, throwing him into the sea; amazingly, he was cast up on shore.

The disaster was one of the worst tragedies played out on the bar— seven men and four boats lost, two survivors from the overturned boats (plus the plucky crew of the 36-foot boat that later sank).

Now, on this morning of January 12, 1991, exactly thirty years later, the survivors and participants of that terrible disaster gathered in Astoria to mourn, to remember and to be healed of their memories. On this anniversary day, an almost identical rescue attempt ended disastrously. Early that morning a 75-foot trawler, the *Sea King*, radioed that it had taken on dangerous amounts of water in the lazarette. The engine room then flooded, and the vessel was wallowing, with the pumps unable to cope.

The Coast Guard sent its 52-foot boat, the *Triumph* (namesake of the one lost thirty years earlier) to take the boat in tow. Off Peacock Spit and North Head once again, the drama continued. The Coast Guard helicopter came to lower men from the *Triumph* to assist with pumping on the *Sea King*. In the process of removing an injured man, a basket cable broke, spilling the man back on deck. The helicopter was in danger of winding the flapping cable in its rotor, and returned to base. Matters seemed stable enough to await flood tide, rather than attempting to tow against strong ebb currents. However, winds were heavy and the vessel unwieldy; when the tow commenced, the *Sea King* suddenly broached and slid below the surface, the *Triumph* crew cutting the tow line. Six men were pulled from the water, another was missing, and two died at the scene. One of them was a Coast Guardsman unable to escape the sinking boat.

Coast Guard mariners are required to respond to every distress call, no matter what the conditions. Their motto is, "You have to go out, you don't have to come back."

The Columbia, Scenic and Economic Treasure

So ends this river, Columbia's River, a fitting and defiant termination of a stream of multiple personality and mood. A river that gives life to the drylands of Washington and takes away the crumbling debris of earth from its eroding canyons and pulverized mountains. A freeway for ships and a highway for salmon. The thoroughfare on which man traveled to visit his neighbor and the killer that claimed his children in its swift rapids.

Along its tortuous 1,214 miles are diverse images. Bubbling water chattering across the gravel of its birth. The raucous cries of birds on the marshes of the birth valley. Snow and a stillness of the wild on Kinbasket Lake. Grizzly bears swinging their massive heads beside giant man-made dams. The reflections of bluff and forest on the lonely stretches of lake above Revelstoke. Happy cries of children swimming in the Arrow Lakes, and the splash of kokanee in distant coves. The growl of chain saws in the nearby forests and the puffs of steam from factories turning trees into paper for this book to be written on. Frightening giant whirlpools waiting to swallow up boats or people. Tiny fingerlings waiting to be loosed in the blue reaches of Lake Roosevelt that disappear into the distance.

The whine of turbines at Grand Coulee, Bonneville and lesser dams as they turn out electricity to light and heat our homes and run businesses, and the shrieks of seagulls as they wheel and dive to gobble up salmon trying to travel upstream. Cowboys silhouetted in still waters, their herds driven before them in scenes as old as America. The prehistoric cliffs looming above and reflected in the pools above Wenatchee. Arid lands that pant for water and reward one with greenery if they get it. Squat buildings seemingly from another land at Hanford, and the serene, reflective reaches beside them where the only sounds are bird calls and the soft plunk of jumping fish.

Straining to see across the glassy waters where Lewis and Clark delighted in their discovery of the River of the West at the Snake. A claustrophobic recognition of the danger of barren cliffs and rough waters below Wallula Gap. The echo of oxen and wagons lying ghostly and tangibly near Umatilla, where the Oregon Trail pioneers came to the river. Roaring Celilo Falls, now lying beneath still waters, but remembering the shouts of Indian fishermen and the slap of huge salmon.

The still awe-inspiring canyons and drowned rapids of the Columbia Gorge, with its snow-covered sentinels of Mount Hood and Mount St. Helens on either shore. Fleet sailboards skipping across the windswept river, challenging the swooping birds. Commerce and bustle of airplanes, automobiles and ships at Vancouver and Portland. The sky darkened with birds from refuges adjacent to urban centers, wildlife and people living amicably together. Losing oneself in the channels of the islands to imagine that no one else exists. Tramping the ragged shores teeming with reminders of rural past. Columbia's River, broad and swollen, spreading into bays and coves, then narrowing, gathering itself for its final thrust into the sea.

What lies ahead? The questions that are asked have complex answers. The questions include:

Under the Columbia Treaty, Americans' purchase of power from Canada expires thirty years after each project goes on line. The treaties will expire within a decade. How will this affect them?

How are salmon runs to be maintained without destroying our need for inexpensive power sources?

The shipping channels need dredging; where will the material be placed? Will land-use laws prevent filling river banks for industrial sites?

Can the life-taking Columbia Bar be yet improved to minimize its dangers? Should it be?

What is a just distribution of water rights among Indian people, ranchers, power makers, fishermen?

How can the Indian nations be assisted in making transitions to modern life? Practically, they cannot go back to a total salmon economy.

With management of wildlife, lopsided populations of sea lions, harbor seals, and birds are destroying more salmon than hatcheries can produce. What is an equitable solution?

How are recreational sports on the river and commercial shipping to coexist without harm to either?

Factories once seriously polluted the river, and individuals threw every kind of offal and garbage into it. Largely we have remedied these matters. How can we continue to clean up decades of neglect? What is the plan for dealing with an oil spill?

We think we have flooding under control, but what are the contingency plans for a flood of the magnitude of 1894 or 1948?

Northwest residents love their river dearly. Can we work together to create justice for all users?

The Willamette River (tributary) that runs through Portland.

CHAPTER 23

Travel and Trivia
Portland/Vancouver to the Sea

Portland area:

Portland/Oregon Visitors Association, 26 Southwest Salmon, Portland, OR 97204 (downtown next to Waterfront Park and fountain). (503) 222-2223.

Jantzen Beach/Oregon Welcome Center just south of I-5 interstate bridge, 12345 North Union, Hayden Island. (503) 285-1631.

A large cosmopolitan city, **Portland** boasts numerous sites of interest, an array of hotels, restaurants and museums and annual events too numerous to mention. Ask above sources for complete data—or buy *Portland* by Terence O'Donnell and Thomas Vaughan (Portland: Western Imprints, The Oregon Historical Society, 1984), a **guide and thumbnail history**. However, here are some special places pertinent to text.

To learn all about logging and lumbering, visit the **World Forestry Center**, 4033 Southwest Canyon Road, Portland, OR 97221. (503) 228-1367. Canyon Road is the route of the old Plank Road. See a large display of wood samples. The Center maintains a Magness Memorial Tree Farm south of Portland at Wilsonville, a demonstration forest, forestry classes, summer camps, etc. Privately funded, not part of the U. S. Forest Service.

In same complex as World Forestry Center are **Oregon Museum of Science and Industry** and **Metro Washington Park Zoo**, a great place for a family afternoon.

Along the Willamette River, **Tom McCall Waterfront Park** gives miles of walking paths, lawns, viewing of river traffic, plus fine restaurants and snack shops. Adjacent is the historic center of Portland—the good and the questionable areas of past days. Ask for **Powell's Walking Map of Downtown Portland**.

The **Oregon Historical Society** is one of the most active, well-organized groups of its kind in the nation. Its modern, several-story center at 1230 Southwest Park Avenue, Portland, houses displays, archives and library, a comprehensive book shop, places for special events. It publishes books, has a speakers bureau, and educational service department. Open every day. It was founded in 1873, moving to the present center in 1966.

The last *working* (commercial) stern or sidewheeler on the Columbia, the *Portland*, is being renovated. For now, **you can dine at the *River Queen***, anchored at 1300 Northwest Front Avenue, on the Willamette, for riverboat atmosphere. It was originally a ferry, then an excursion boat on the Columbia and Willamette during the Oregon Centennial. Good food and views of river activity. (503) 228-8633.

Lumber magnate Simon Benson built The Oregon Hotel, still magnificently operating as The **Benson Hotel** at 309 Southwest Broadway, Portland, OR 97205. (503) 228-2000, 1-800-426-0670. Benson also contributed water fountains to the city in hopes that his loggers off duty would drink water, not booze.

Afternoon tea at The Heathman Hotel, on the Register of Historic Places, Southwest Broadway at Salmon, Portland, is a worthwhile respite.

Take a trip to **Oregon City** and **Champoeg** (has historical pageant), where Oregon began. Dr. John McLoughlin's house, the National End of the Oregon Trail Interpretive Center, Clackamas County Historical Museum's "The Fifteen Windows to History," and other outstanding historical experiences. Ask Portland Visitors Association or Oregon Tri-City Chamber of Commerce, 718 McLoughlin Boulevard, Oregon City, OR 97045.

Tour **Blitz-Weinhard Brewery**, pioneer industry, every weekday afternoon. 1133 West Burnside, Portland, OR 97209. (503) 222-4351.

Mount Hood, the southerly sentinel over the Columbia Gorge, is a year-round playground. 1-800-452-1335 from Northwestern states. Also ask Visitors Association.

The new **Oregon Maritime Center and Museum** near Waterfront Park has ship models, photographs, archives. 113 Southwest Front Avenue.

Henry L. Pittock, at age twenty-four, took control of the then-weekly *Oregonian* on April 1, 1860. When he started work there seven years earlier, it is said he slept on a shelf below the counter and that it was so cold he poured boiling water on the composing stones to melt the ice. The *Oregonian* still is the voice of the area. Pittock's mansion, built when he was 79 years old, is at 3229 Northwest Pittock Drive.

You shouldn't leave Portland without seeing **Portland Center for the Performing Arts** for its architecture, and attend some cultural event.

The **Port of Portland** oversees maritime traffic, river traffic, real estate, aviation, grain elevators, dredging and who knows what else— all vital to the Columbia/Willamette residents. Exports and imports in 1989 totaled a whopping 14,452,162 short tons. Groups can ask for tours. Try Public Affairs (503) 231-5000.

C.E.S. Wood, a soldier quoted in this book for his description of an Indian encampment, became a painter and poet of Portland later. In 1888, he suggested holding an annual rose show. By 1907, Portland held its first **Rose Festival**. Each June, the major festival has events almost all month.

Schedule a cruise on the *M. V. Yorktown Clipper* from Portland to Seattle and Victoria each May and September. 1-800-325-0010.

40-Mile Loop is a **hiking and biking trail** system encircling Portland. Ask Portland Parks Bureau. (503) 796-5193.

Get information about or shop for state products at **Made in Oregon**, several locations. Call 1-800-828-9673 outside Oregon, 1-800-428-9673 inside Oregon.

To appreciate the Columbia River system from Astoria to Lewiston, Idaho, take the ***Executive Explorer* cruise boat** (three-deck catamaran, about fifty passengers) for five days, six nights. Comfort and style with narration about Lewis and Clark's journeys and Columbia River trivia. Side trips by bus to historic points. Spring and fall only. YachtShip CruiseLines, 523 Pine Street, Seattle, WA 98101. (206) 623-4245 or travel agent.

The three **Red Lion Inns** clustered near the I-5 bridge, Vancouver-Portland, all are on the Columbia River. The *Executive Explorer* and other boats leave from the Red Lion Jantzen Beach. **Jantzen Beach** once echoed to the delighted screams of visitors to its amusement park. Docks for private boats, convention facilities, excellent river views. Red Lion Columbia and Red Lion Jantzen Beach in Oregon, Red Lion at the Quay in Washington. Central reservations for Red Lion Inns 1-800-547-8010. In Oregon 1-800-452-0733.

Vancouver area:

Vancouver/Clark County Visitors & Convention Bureau, 404 East 15th Street, Suite 11, Vancouver, WA 98663. (206) 693-1313.

Practically under the Interstate Bridge over the river is **The Chart House**, once called The Bridge Tender. Historic Columbia River photos in the decor, including the steamer *Bailey Gatzert* and a Portland storefront in flood of 1894. Fine cuisine, terrace adjacent to the Columbia River. Complicated access: from I-5, take Camas exit. 101 East Columbia Way, Vancouver, WA 98661. (206) 693-9211.

Next door, also with a terrace, is a lively Mexican restaurant, **Who-Song & Larry's**, 111 East Columbia Way. Wide variety of food and

Washington apple dessert "chimi"—apples, Mexican fruit jam, walnuts, etc., fried in a tortilla. (206) 695-1198.

Find any waterfront restaurant to enjoy the delightful December **Christmas Parade of Boats** along the Willamette and Columbia rivers.

The oldest riverfront site is **Fort Vancouver National Historic Site**. The Hudson's Bay Company fort has been reconstructed in approximately the same location as the original; palings surround the fort buildings. One can almost hear the joyous songs of the voyageurs as they swept with flourish up to the docks of the fort to unload furs and supplies 150 years ago. Chief Factor McLoughlin's home. **Archives, book shop, film presentations**. Popular Brigade Encampment in late July gives a look backward. Known for the most spectacular **Fourth of July fireworks** in the West.

Adjacent to the British fort is Vancouver Barracks, the U.S. military post, still active. Officer's Row is a street of handsome homes. Self-guided tours from markers, and Marshall House is open for public tours.

Near the same complex is **Pearson Air Museum** at Pearson Air Park. The first aerial crossing of the Columbia River was a dirigible flight from Portland to **Vancouver Barracks** in 1905. The first crossing of the river by an airplane was in 1912 with Silas Christofferson flying from the barracks to a Portland country club. You can arrange for **scenic flights** over the river and Mount St. Helens at this field.

In 1937, three Soviet aviators who flew the first transpolar route landed at Vancouver after leaving Moscow enroute to San Francisco. The **Chkalov Monument** on Highway 14, one mile east of I-5.

Hand-cut your Christmas tree or just ride along on the Lewis & Clark Railway **Christmas Tree Trains**, traveling into the Clark County forests—a good chance to ride into history, too—Yacolt, center of the huge fire of 1902; Moulton Falls, site of a big sawmill; Yacolt Mountain Tunnel blasted from solid rock in 1902 to get logs out. Trains leave Battle Ground, Washington, not far northeast of Vancouver. Year-round trips ... the Saturday Evening Rib Train with old-fashioned dinner, etc. Lewis & Clark Railway Co., P.O. Box 604, Battle Ground, WA 98604. (206) 687-2626.

Also at Yacolt is the **Pomeroy Living History Farm**, an educational museum especially popular with children, showing farm life in the 1920s. June to October. Black Powder Muzzle Loaders there in June, hayrides, cider pressing other times. (206) 686-3537.

Northwest of Vancouver is the vast **Ridgefield National Wildlife Refuge**, 3,000 acres. Hike or fish and sneak up on wildlife with a camera. "Oaks to Wetlands Wildlife Trail." Ridgefield is across the Columbia River from the Sauvie Island Refuge. (206) 887-4106.

Hidden House, brick home of the early Vancouver magnate, Lowell Hidden, is now a restaurant. Original stained glass, door knobs, woodwork. 100 West 13th Street, Vancouver, WA 98661. Another "Hidden House" at 110 sells Victorian-era merchandise.

A monument commemorates the women who settled Oregon territory. **Pioneer Mother Statue**, Esther Short Park, 8th and Columbia, Vancouver.

Memorabilia about the Kaiser Shipyards days, pioneer women like Esther Short and Mother Joseph, other pioneers at **Clark County Historical Museum**, 16th and Main Street, Vancouver. Open Tuesday through Sunday.

North of Vancouver, 10 miles east of Woodland, a small community near the confluence of the Lewis River with the Columbia, the **Cedar Creek Grist Mill** was built in 1876. It is the only operating 19th century grist mill in Washington and is completely restored, including an operating log flume. Off County Road 16 on Grist Mill Rd.

To the Estuary:

Nathaniel Wyeth may have failed, but he recognized pleasant country when he founded Fort William. See **Sauvie Island** accessed only from a bridge off U. S. Highway 30. A **wildlife refuge** at the north end provides superb bird-watching, hiking and fishing. From **Reeder Beach** on the Multnomah Channel you can almost touch passing ships. Reeder has campsites and RV hookups, salmon fishing off the beach. This once was a riverboat stop. The western channel is preferred by pleasure boats and also has many houseboat dwellers.

Trojan Nuclear Plant has a visitor center with educational displays about energy. The surrounding grounds are open to the public and heavily used. Trojan, 71760 Columbia River Highway (Highway 30), Rainier, OR 97048. (503) 464-7200.

Just south on the Willamette is **Goble Landing**, neat RV camp and boat launching site onto quiet channel. (503) 556-6510.

St. Helens might be called a living ghost town, not deserted but not the burgeoning metropolis it once was. Old shipbuilding and loggers' center next to the water is entirely preserved, houses wander up and down over the hills, a wonderful museum building. Part of **St. Helens Hotel Restaurant's** building is the original hotel, later St. Helens City Hall. Its cozy Klondike Tavern was moved there and attached. The 28-foot bar and 1906 National Cash Register are original. Complimentary salted peanuts; if you don't throw the shells on the floor, you have to buy drinks for all. 71 Cowlitz Street, St. Helens, OR 97051. (503) 397-4297.

Historic Days late May in St. Helens, tours of historic homes, parades, etc.

En route between Portland and Astoria, **Hump's** at Clatskanie gives you fresh sandwiches and delightful dining adjacent to the **Clatskanie River**; watch ducks while you eat. Small boats come up the river from the Columbia River to dock and dine. Hump's started as a candy shop and still sells yummy home-made candy. Try shrimp cooked in the shell. Center of Clatskanie on Highway 30.

Logger Simon Benson once built a home here (not open), and Tom Flippin, sawmill owner, built a pretentious mansion known as **"The Castle,"** open to the public. Phone (503) 728-3608.

Jones Beach on the Columbia west of Clatskanie is fast becoming another prime windsurfing spot. Not many facilities.

Nearby is **King Salmon Lodge** at Westport, half ghost town, a few feet from a live creek with ducks. It once was a dormitory. Nice period rooms, bed and breakfast, plus Sunday brunch open to all. P.O. Box 5111, Westport, OR 97016. (503) 455-2400.

River Ranch, a 48-lot subdivision in Clatsop County east of Wauna faces the main ship channel on the Columbia, only a thousand yards away from homes. If ship-watching rings your bell, you might want to investigate.

To mark the **200th anniversary of Captain Gray's entry** into the Columbia River, the Oregon Historical Society and the Columbia River Heritage Association are developing and marking a wildlife and canoe touring route through the estuary islands of the lower river, to be called **Columbia River Heritage Canoe Trail**. It will begin near Clatskanie and meander to a termination at the John Day River east of Astoria. Part of the 45-mile trail goes through the shallow waters of Lewis & Clark National Wildlife Refuge, part follows Lewis and Clark expedition's route as gleaned from their diaries.

Also being developed is the **Heritage Trail**, a 325-mile-long Oregon-Washington Columbia River scenic route.

Regional **Tourism Information** Program of Southwest Washington, P.O. Box 876, Longview, WA 98632. (206) 425-1211.

Kalama has a **twenty-two-unit RV park and marina** on docks adjacent to the Columbia River. Boat launch. Port of Kalama, P.O. Box 70, Kalama, WA 98625. (206) 673-2325.

Monticello Hotel was the historic center of social life at R. A. Long's planned city of Longview (see text). Stately old hotel with four quite grand suites (conventional motel next door has regular rooms). The restaurant is noted for its prime rib and chateaubriand. 1405 17th Avenue, Longview, WA 98632. (206) 423-9900.

High on the imposing lobby walls of the Monticello Hotel are forty-six **oil portraits** by Joe Knowles. These particularly pertain to Columbia River history, including works about Robert Gray, John J. Astor,

Chief Joseph, Wreck of the ship *Peacock*, and so on. Knowles is considered a fine painter, not too well known and somewhat eccentric. He once went stark naked into the woods for several weeks to prove that man still could survive in nature.

The **Saturday Farmers Market** in Longview showcases Cowlitz County produce and products.

Kelso Volcano and Tourist Information Center just off I-5 includes pictorial and scientific exhibits about St. Helens' eruption in 1980, classified as a museum. The local airports offer scenic flights, and five miles west of Castle Rock, north on I-5, is the chief **interpretive center for Mount St. Helens**.

The temperate river climate contributes to the success of the **Hulda Klager Gardens**, where a pioneer woman developed new varieties of lilacs. Now fifty varieties shown. Just off I-5 at Woodland, see and smell in the spring.

Cowlitz County Museum includes exhibits on early settlement, the Hudson's Bay Company involvement and such. Downtown Kelso. 405 Allen Street, Kelso, WA 98626. (206) 577-3119.

Washington State Historical Society has displays, artifacts and archival information. 315 North Stadium Way, Tacoma, WA 98403. (206) 593-2830. Also the **Washington State Library**, AJ-11, Olympia, WA 98504. (206) 753-4024.

Lower Columbia **Economic Development Council**, P.O. Box 98, Skamokawa, WA 98647. (206) 795-3996.

Combining rural forest and riverside boat-watching is **Gallery Bed and Breakfast**. Columbia River art gallery, too. On State Road 4 east of Cathlamet. 4 Little Cape Horn, Cathlamet, WA 98612. (206) 425-7395.

Country Keepers Bed and Breakfast Inn commands a view of the town and glimpses of the river. Right downtown in the old town. 61 Main Street, P.O. Box 35, Cathlamet, WA 98612. (206) 795-3030.

You can eat well, Cajun emphasis and general, at **Birnie's Retreat** (original name of Cathlamet) which has a chef who wins awards in food competitions. Main Street, Cathlamet.

The **Wahkiakum Courthouse** was built in 1921, still in use at Cathlamet, and the town was home to Congresswoman Julia Butler Hansen. Check out her book, *Singing Paddles*.

On nearby Puget Island, home to horse seiners and farmers of early days, you can watch ships on the Columbia River from **Our Place Bed and Breakfast**, 305 North Welcome Slough Road (on Puget Island), Cathlamet, WA 98612. (206) 849-4328. Approach from north shore by bridge, from Oregon shore by small ferry at Rainier. One unit is a fisherman's net house, with its own fireplace and kitchen.

To gain an insight into **fishing** in highly readable fashion, look for

Fish and Ships by R.W. Andrews and A.K. Larssen (Seattle: Superior Publishing Company, 1959).

West of Cathlamet in picturesque **Skamokawa**, named for an upstanding Indian chief, is Redmen Hall, a restored pioneer schoolhouse. This extremely rural Washington shore of the river, its winding roads, houses on pilings, dilapidated canneries (see text), etc., is not unlike sections of the New England coast.

Boat owners like **Elochoman Marina**, 3rd Street, Cathlamet. It is totally protected and modern, two hundred slips, boat launching, entrance to the river.

Enjoy a day or a week beside the river at **Skamokawa Vista Park**, Skamokawa town. Campsites, picnicking. (206) 795-8605.

Bald Eagle Days celebrates the selection of the eagle as our national bird. July in Cathlamet.

For in-depth **history of the small north-shore towns**, ask locally for Carlton Appelo's books.

Gray's River Covered Bridge is in excellent repair, just off Highway 4 west of Cathlamet.

For information on the large, interesting **wildlife refuges** in or near the lower river: Julia Butler Hansen National Wildlife Refuge, P.O. Box 566, Cathlamet WA 98612. (206) 795-3915. Lewis & Clark National Wildlife Refuge, c/o Willapa National Wildlife Refuge, Ilwaco, WA 98624. (206) 484-3482.

For basic RV camping, but a few feet from the river, try **Mauch's Sundown RV Park**, west of Astoria bridge on Highway 101.

Long Beach Peninsula area:

Long Beach Peninsula Visitors Bureau. P.O. Box 562, Long Beach, WA 98631. 1-800-451-2542 inside WA, 1-800-451-2540 Northwest states; (206) 642-2400. Ilwaco is gateway to Long Beach, a playground more than 25 miles long.

Fort Columbia (see text) includes an interpretive center and museum. A youth hostel there. Well-kept residence barracks and old batteries. Adjacent to Highway 101. Fort Columbia State Park, P.O. Box 236, Chinook, WA 98614. (206) 777-8221.

Sea Resources on Highway 101, Chinook, is a salmon hatchery. See text.

A plaque near Highway 101 between the bridge and Chinook commemorates **Lewis and Clark's camp**, then a miserable one awash in storm-driven tidewaters. The beach then was back against the cliff.

Lewis and Clark would have loved it. You can dine at a 1900-era church near their old camp. **Sanctuary Restaurant**, Highway 101 and Hazel Street, Chinook, WA (206) 777-8380.

At Cape Disappointment above Ilwaco, **Fort Canby State Park** was fortified for decades (see text). Batteries and buildings remain. At the same site is **Lewis & Clark Interpretive Center** with fine exhibits about the expedition, shipwrecks and lifesaving at the Columbia Bar, too. The park includes the north jetty, Peacock Spit, numerous camping spaces. **Walk the Coastal Trail** among giant Sitka spruce trees; ask for "Common Wildflowers" brochure. Fort Canby State Park, P.O. Box 488, Ilwaco, WA 98624.

Also within this complex are the **Cape Disappointment Lighthouse**, oldest working one on West Coast, and **North Head Lighthouse**.

The **National Motor Lifeboat School** and **Coast Guard Station** are tucked in behind Cape Disappointment. Some areas open to public. Bring identification. (206) 642-2382.

WARNING: THE PARKS AND TOWNS POST WARNINGS. BE SURE TO HEED THEM. EACH YEAR PEOPLE ARE SWEPT OUT TO SEA FROM JETTIES OR BEACHES. "Rogue" waves occur here, breakers far higher than the average ones.

There are lively **stories about shipwrecks** in Don Marshall's book, *Oregon Shipwrecks.* It includes material on Columbia River and tributaries.

Be sure to visit **Ilwaco Heritage Museum**. Includes gallery of maps and navigational instruments used in early explorations, Chinook Indian lore, an overlay map showing changes in the Columbia River entrance, etc. Books for sale. Downtown.

Ilwaco has a reputation for **excellent charter boat catches**. Many reliable boats operate from Ilwaco, among them (according to locals): **Ilwaco Charter Service**, Inc. (206) 642-3232; **Hobo Charters** (206) 642-2300; **Tidewind Charters** (206) 642-2111; **Pacific Salmon Charters** (206) 642-3466. Pacific Salmon also has **scenic excursion boats** twice daily in season and acceptable weather. Includes a trip to the point where the wreck *Isabella* is emerging from the sand after decades.

To celebrate Washington's Centennial in 1989, sixteen artists painted **murals throughout the Long Beach Peninsula**. Watch for them on buildings.

Bed and Breakfast houses and inns abound on the peninsula. Two notable ones are: **Shelburne Country Inn**, Seaview, built in 1896, has antique-appointed rooms, and an acclaimed **Shoalwater Restaurant** (206) 642-2442. Coast Watch, Ocean Park, adjacent to dunes (206) 665-6774. Overlooking the harbor at Ilwaco is **KOLA House**, 211 Pearl Avenue. (206) 642-2819.

Drive your car on Long Beach's **hard sands**, the same beach that Loomis Stage once traveled.

Numerous festivals are staged on the Peninsula. Exceptional is the **International Kite Festival** in late August that includes competitive events. Participants and spectators from many countries. In 1987, 20,009 kites were in the air at one time. There are **two jazz festivals**: Dixieland in late April, Jazz and Oysters at Oysterville in August. **Ilwaco Cranberry Festival** in October celebrates the harvest of 500 acres of cranberries.

Although not on the Columbia River, nearby **Willapa Bay** has a vast shellfish industry. Also you can see a pristine 274-acre cedar grove, some trees 11 feet in diameter, at **Willapa National Wildlife Refuge**.

Crossing the 4.1 mile **Astoria Bridge** is an experience. The ship channel portion, 1,070 feet wide, rises 200 feet above the water at the highway level, the supporting structure much higher. You get the impression, especially in the frequent fog, of an impossible angle of rise going south, but it is only an illusion. The bridge opened in 1966, replacing a ferry. You can run across the bridge on a day in mid-October, the **Great Columbia Crossing Bridge Run**.

Astoria area:

Astoria Area **Chamber of Commerce**, 111 West Marine Drive, P.O. Box 176, Astoria, OR 97103. (503) 325-6311.

There are **many Astoria overnight facilities**. Beside the river facing a working commercial and pleasure boat marina is another **Red Lion Inn**, 400 Industry Street, almost under the bridge. 1-800-547-8010 or (503) 325-7373. The **Shilo Inn**, quite new, is centrally located among visitor attractions east of Young's Bay on Highway 101, Warrenton. (503) 861-2181. K. C.'s **Mansion by the Sea** is an outstanding bed and breakfast house with a view of the river. It's the historic Benjamin Young home built in 1888. 3652 Duane Street, Astoria, OR 97103. (503) 325-6172. **Kampers West Kampground** has almost two hundred spaces adjacent to the Columbia River. 1140 North Warrenton Drive, Warrenton, OR 97146. (503) 861-1814.

To get oriented in this historical Columbia River city, **visit the following museums first**.

Fort Clatsop, about five miles out of Astoria, is where Lewis and Clark spent the winter. Recreated low buildings and living history activities, including occasional muzzle loader firing, give you a vivid picture of life there. 101 South over Young's Bay, watch for signs. Fort Clatsop National Memorial, Route 3, Box 604-FC, Astoria, OR 97103. (503) 861-2471.

You can learn about regional history, see artifacts from the wreck of *Peter Iredale*, and gain insight into maritime figures at **The Heritage Center Museum**, 16th and Exchange, plus **Flavel House** (see text), 8th and Duane.

The **Columbia River Maritime Museum** may be one of the world's greatest. Exhibits, galleries, and archives deal with the fur trade and exploration period, fishing, sailing and steam vessels, and river history. The "butterfly fleet" boats are exhibited (see text) and other vessels and artifacts. In the river outside is the lightship *Columbia*; **you can go aboard**. From a patio you can watch big ships passing by, the channel being very close in. Foot of 17th Street at the river. 1792 Marine Drive, Astoria, OR 97103. (503) 325-2323.

The **Astor Public Library**, 450 10th Street has unusually complete historical collections. At 15th and Exchange Streets is a bastion representing **old Fort Astoria**. Nearby, too, is a monument inscribed in Japanese and English to honor **Ranald MacDonald**, grandson of Chief Comcomly, son of a Hudson's Bay trader, who was the first teacher of English to interpreters in Japan, before Commodore Perry.

John Jacob Astor's descendants and the Northern Pacific Railway constructed a 123-foot column atop **Coxcomb Hill** in 1926, honoring early history with fourteen pictorial friezes. You can climb the 166 steps for a sweeping view.

From a **tower at the foot of H Street** (same as 6th Street) passing ships and boats on the Columbia River seem to be within arm's length.

On Clatsop Spit at **Fort Stevens State Park** relive **military history at the Museum**, the batteries, and the residence/office areas. Samples of mines taken from the Columbia River entrance after wars. Details of Japanese submarine attack give you a shudder. The 3800-acre park includes **large numbers of campsites**, including 213 RV sites with hookups. You can walk miles of beach, see the old trestle for a train that brought rock to build the jetty. There is a viewing tower for the north jetty. The bare bones of the wreck *Peter Iredale* are on Clatsop's ocean beach. Again **be careful on beach areas**.

Author Jim Gibbs writes **about sea and coast**. Among his books are *Oregon's Salty Coast* (Seattle: Superior Publishing Company, 1978) and *West Coast Windjammers* (Seattle: Superior Publishing Company, 1968).

Take a sunrise and croissant or sunset and champagne **cruise on the Columbia**. Other special or regular fishing charters, too. Astoria Cruise & Charters, 352 Industry, Astoria, OR 97103. (503) 325-0990.

This **fishing charter** company accepts large and small groups: **Columbia Pacific Charters**. (503) 861-1527 in summer, 861-3303 in winter.

Another fishing charter firm is **Warrenton Deep Sea Fishing**. (503) 861-1233.

(Note: **Charter boats abound**. The above are considered reliable but there are numerous other good companies.)

The canneries have almost disappeared from Astoria, but three generations of Josephsons have lived there—gillnetters, horse seiners, and now **smoked salmon processors**. Buy traditional cold smoked salmon or hot smoked salmon, other fish-related or Oregon-produced products, or order by mail. Josephson's Smokehouse, 106 Marine Drive, P. O. Box 412 Astoria, OR 97103. 1-800-772-3474.

A freight dock atmosphere permeates a **riverside building of small shops**, a deli, and **Pier 11 Feedstore**, really a view restaurant with superb prime rib, fresh sea food, peanut butter pie. 77 11th Street, Astoria. (503) 325-0279.

Shallon Winery, Astoria, has a colorful "old winemaker" experimenting with fruit and whey wines, including Lemon Meringue Wine, Spiced Apple, Cran du Lait. Worth a visit. 1598 Duane Street.

Tiny hole-in-the-wall **Kim's Kitchen** offers authentic Korean dishes, pies and soups, a change of cuisine. 225 14th Street, Astoria. (503) 325-1047.

Finnish and Scandinavian lore is remembered at **Cafe Uniontown** in a 1907 building at 218 West Marine Drive, Astoria (503) 325-8708. (See text.)

In good weather a wonderful way to see the complex islands, Columbia Bar and ocean beaches is a scenic flight. **Astoria Flight Center**, Astoria Airport. (503) 861-1222.

Art works and prints, plus Northwest crafts, should be seen at **Ricciardi Gallery**, which holds an invitational showing in early August, the "River Show," all materials pertaining to the Columbia River. Artists featured in the gallery include Steven McLeod, son of a fisherman; Eric Wiegardt who does watercolors of fishing boats; Howard Rosenfeld with drypoint engravings of sailing ships. 108 Tenth Street, Astoria, OR 97103. (503) 325-5450.

A good place to look for eagles is at **Twilight Eagle Sanctuary Viewing Platform**, east of Astoria on Highway 30, turn left at Burnside just past mile marker 88. Go half a mile.

The flavor of Astoria's past is celebrated at the **Scandinavian Midsummer Festival** in late June. Stuff yourself with special foods, too.

The historic **Astoria Regatta** is in mid-August. Once the gillnetters from the "butterfly fleet" competed for the Java Cup, but today most are conventional sailboats. There are home tours and visiting ships.

/

Selected
Bibliography

The complete bibliography has been filed with the Columbia Gorge Interpretive Center in Stevenson, Washington, where it is available for perusal. Of approximately two hundred books and manuscripts consulted, the following were particularly useful:

"A Salute to Timber," special section, *White Salmon Enterprise*, *The Dalles Weekly Reminder*, and *Hood River News*, November 7-9, 1989.

Cross, Francis E., and Parkin, Charles M., Jr. *Sea Venture*. St. Petersburg, FL: Valkyrie Publishing House, Inc., 1981.

Dark, Russell. "History of Bar Pilots," unpublished manuscript in Astor Public Library, Astoria, OR.

Downs, Art. *Paddlewheels on the Frontier*. Sidney, BC: Gray's Publishing Ltd., 1972.

Feagans, Raymond J. *The Railroad that Ran By the Tide*. Berkeley, CA; Howell-NorthBooks, 1972.

Freeman, Lewis R. *Down the Columbia*. New York: Dodd, Mead and Company, 1921.

From Pioneers to Power. Grand Coulee, WA: Bicentennial Association Committee, 1965.

Gibbs, Jim. *Windjammers of the Pacific Rim*. Seattle: Superior Publishing Company, 1968.

Golden Memories. Golden, BC: Golden and District Historical Society, 1982.

Gray, W. H. *A History of Oregon*. Portland, OR: W. H. Gray, 1870.

Green, William Spotswood. *Among the Selkirk Glaciers*. London and New York: Macmillan and Co., 1890.

History of Skamania County. Stevenson, WA: Skamania Historical Society, 1958 [?].

Holbrook, Stewart. *Holy Old Mackinaw*. New York: The Macmillan Company, 1956.

Howay, Frederick W. *Voyages of the "Columbia."* Boston: The Massachusetts Historical Society, 1941.

Kerr, Charles C. "The World of the World," anthology of newspaper articles 1905-80, *Wenatchee Daily World*.

Kosachova, N. G. "The Doukhobors," in *Russian Canadians*. Ottawa: Borealis Press, 1983.

Lawrence, M. J. *The Columbia Unveiled*. Los Angeles: The Times-Mirror Press.

_____. *Lewis and Clark's Journals*. New York: A. S. Barnes and Company, 1904.

Lewis, Meriwether. Introduction by Archibald Hanna. *Lewis and Clark Expedition*, 3 vols. Philadelphia and New York: J. B. Lippincott, 1961.

Lockley, Fred. *History of the Columbia River Valley*. Chicago: The S. J. Clarke Publishing Company, 1928.

Lyman, William Denison. *The Columbia River*. New York and London: G.P. Putnam's Sons, 1917.

McClelland, John M., Jr. *Longview*. Portland, OR: Binfords & Mort, 1949.

Maben, Manly. *Vanport*. Portland, OR: Oregon Historical Society Press, 1987.

Marshall, Don. *Oregon Shipwrecks*. Portland, OR: Binfords & Mort, 1984.

Miller, Emma Gene. *Clatsop County Oregon*. Portland, OR: Binfords & Mort, 1958.

Purdy, Ruby Fay. *The Rose City of the World*. Portland, OR: Binfords & Mort, 1947.

The Quarterdeck, selected editions. Columbia Maritime Museum, Astoria, OR.

"Rainshadow," historial pamphlet prepared by Royal City High School (WA) Social Studies Class. Wanapum Dam Visitors Center.

Raufer, Sister Maria. O. P. *Black Robes and Indians*. Milwaukee: The Bruce Publishing Company, 1966.

Ross, Alexander, edited by Thwaites, Reuben Gold. *Adventures of the First Settlers on the Oregon or Columbia River*. Cleveland: The Arthur H. Clark Company, 1904.

Ruby, Robert H., and Brown, John A. *Half-Sun on the Columbia*. Norman: University of Oklahoma Press, 1965.

_____. *The Spokane Indians*. Norman: University of Oklahoma Press, 1970.

Seufert, Francis. *Wheels of Fortune*. Edited by Thomas Vaughan. Portland, OR: Oregon Historical Society, 1980.

Splawn, A. J. *Ka-mi-akin*. Mrs. A. J. Splawn, 1917. [Bellingham Public Library, Washington.]

"The Story of the Columbia Basin Project." Washington, D.C.: U.S. Government Printing Office.

Turner, Robert D. *Sternwheelers and Steam Tugs*. Victoria, BC: Sono Nis Press, 1984.

Tyrrell, J.B., editor. *David Thompson's Narrative*. Toronto: The Champlain Society, 1916.

Van Arsdol, Ted. *Vancouver*. Northridge, CA: Windsor Publications, 1986.

Wheeler, A. O. *The Selkirk Range*. Ottawa: Government Printing Bureau, 1905.

White, Derryll. *Fort Steele*. Surrey, BC: Heritage House Publishing Company Ltd., 1988.

Index